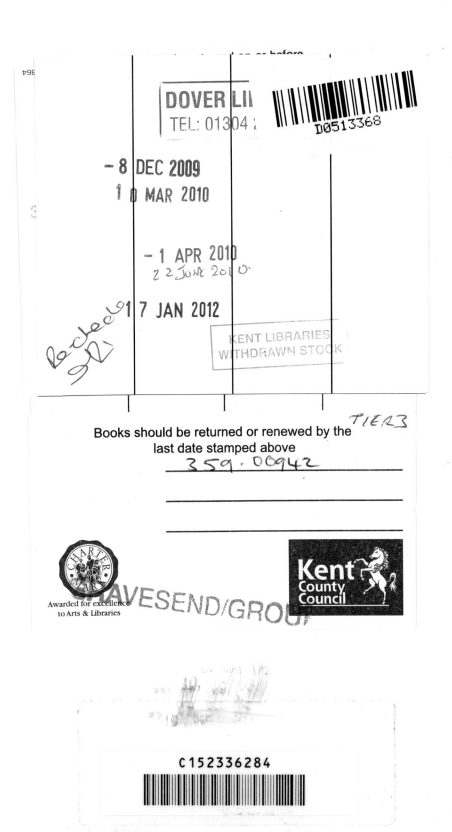

AFT THROUGH THE HAWSEPIPE

Aft Through
The Hawsepipe

by

BRYAN SMALLEY

The Memoir Club

© Bryan Smalley 2004

First published in 2004 by
The Memoir Club
Stanhope Old Hall
Stanhope
Weardale
County Durham

British Library Cataloguing in
Publication Data.
A catalogue record for this book
is available from the
British Library.

ISBN: 1 84104 096 7

Typeset by George Wishart & Associates, Whitley Bay.
Printed by CPI, Bath.

*To my wife Gilly, our sons David and Ian,
Ian's wife Nikki and our grandsons Jack
and Sam, and to all those Boy Seamen and
Submariners who shared the load with me.*

Foreword

by
Lady Fieldhouse
Widow of Admiral of the Fleet the Lord Fieldhouse of Gosport GCB GBE

I FIRST MET Bryan Smalley in HM Submarine *Acheron* when my husband John Fieldhouse had been appointed to his first command. Bryan joined the boat in June 1956, as the navigator, and thus qualified for a pitifully small amount of extra pay (I think it was about £1.1s.0d. a day – old money) known as 'hard lying money'.

The submarine base at that time was in Rothesay, Isle of Bute, which was not exactly a paradise for social entertainment, and the submarines were hard worked. Nevertheless, good times and fun were had by all.

Bryan went on to gain more experience in the brand new submarine HMS *Porpoise* and HMS *Tabard* and then to command HMS *Aurochs*, the latter after he had passed the dreaded 'perisher' as the submarine commanding officers' qualifying course was known and which was the Waterloo of quite a few would be COs.

What I found exciting about the book was that becoming a Naval officer, having joined as a boy seaman and Naval rating, he viewed some aspects of the service in a slightly different way to that of the thirteen year old Dartmouth cadets or public school boy entries. He was in the service during a time of enormous change both in the country and in the Royal Navy, and his ability to take these changes in his stride and to work with them was remarkable. He was a breath of fresh air in many respects, to many people.

My husband, as his CO, had the highest regard for him and I think this book will be a fascinating reminder of a time gone by for a wide audience, but especially for submariners of that time.

I wish the book every success.

Acknowledgements

I would like to thank a number of people and organisations whose staff have helped me in the writing of this book. Jeff Tall, Margaret Bidmead, Debbie Corner, Colin Way and the staff of the RN Submarine Museum, Gosport; the staff at the Public Record Office, Kew; the staff of the Imperial War Museum; John Grove and Mike Collis for clarifying some of the stories about *Porpoise*; ex Boy Seamen Tom Robson, John McCarron and Maurice Blyth of the HMS *Bruce* Association; Sue Bradman and the staff of the Crail Museum; Tina Pittuck and the staff of The Parachute Regiment Museum; Kaye Thompson and Lynn Davidson of The Memoir Club and Meg Ross my editor. Additionally, I wish to thank Suzanne Kyrle Pope for her encouragement and Lady Fieldhouse for writing a foreword. I am grateful to everyone for their help and support. Finally I would like to thank my wife, Gilly, for all her help and tolerance and assistance in proof reading several times over. Thank you all.

Contents

Illustrations

CHAPTER 1

From Civilian Boy to
Boy Seaman RN 1947-48

I HAVE INTENDED writing this book since I retired from the Navy in 1970 but there has always been something of a higher priority which has prevented me. On reaching my 70th birthday I decided that it must take first priority.

Superficially, I did little of outstanding importance throughout my Naval service, but when one looks more deeply, I was involved in a number of significant changes which could be said to have changed the world and the way we live in it. When I joined in 1947 the country was still suffering from the after-effects of the war. The Navy's ships were either old and needed replacement, or they had been constructed in such a hurry that their life expectancy was limited. A massive re-design and building programme was therefore necessary. To emphasise the changes it should be noted that when I joined the Service there were a number of ships with coal-fired boilers and my last ship was nuclear powered. On joining, much of the equipment could best be described as 'agricultural' but on retirement much of the equipment was operated electrically and even that was beginning to benefit from miniaturisation and moving on towards electronics. By 1970 we were living in a different world.

Another aspect of my service was that I passed from the lower deck to officer status: a process known as 'going aft through the hawsepipe'. I stress that my advancement resulted because of excellent Naval training and selection procedures and not because of my ability.

Finally, my service in submarines was during a period of enormously significant change. When I joined the Submarine Service the entire submarine fleet was of World War II vintage. I saw the introduction of the snort mast; the building and demise of HTP fuelled submarines and torpedoes; the introduction of wire guided and homing torpedoes; and the debut of nuclear power and rocket propelled missiles. That in itself is significant.

At the time I joined the Navy most British people were relaxing after the rigours of the war without realising what was happening on the world scene. It was less than two years since the American B25 superfortress *Enola Gay* had dropped an atomic bomb on Hiroshima. This cataclysmic event might have put aside thought of all future wars but instead it prompted Stalin to order his scientists to start work immediately on providing the Russians with a nuclear capability. As the Communist threat unfolded Churchill was moved to use the phrase 'the Iron Curtain'.

I was brought up the youngest of a family of four children all of whom were girls except myself. On my father's side, my grandfather was a coal merchant with a business in Mexborough, Yorkshire. My father had served in the Army during the 1914-18 war as a driver and had then started a number of businesses. During most of my early years he was a poultry farmer. If one needed a single word to describe him, the best would be 'reprobate'. He was a womaniser and irresponsible with money. He spent several periods in gaol, mainly for unpaid debts, particularly to the Inland Revenue. My memories of him at times when he did come home were of taking him his early morning glass of Andrews' Liver Salts and letting the bubbles tickle my nose. I also watched my mother going through his pockets looking for incriminating evidence whilst he was sleeping off the excesses of the night before. The most enjoyable memory is that of the smell of a cigar on Christmas Day. At all other times he only smoked cigarettes.

The best word to describe my mother would be 'puritanical'. Her father was a coal miner. He had strong views and preached every Sunday in the local chapel. My mother could play both the violin and the organ. She was a complete mismatch for my father, but one has to remember that many men had been killed during the First World War and choice was limited.

My mother left my father when I was 10 after he had beaten one of my sisters. She was then left in the position of earning a wage to support us. My mother's strong Christian beliefs and her acute sense of right and wrong gave her the foundations on which to build a united and loving family. This was only achieved by making many personal sacrifices on her part. I was something of an oddity, being the only male in the household. I was always referred to as 'Boy' until the day I joined the Navy. I attended Hampton Hill Primary School within the Middlesex Education Authority. The headmaster, Mr Alford, was allowed to award one scholarship each year to Hampton Grammar School which in those days was fee paying although still administered by the Middlesex Education Authority. Mr Alford awarded me the scholarship, I suspect more out of sympathy rather than for my educational aptitude. At Hampton, the Headmaster went under the name of 'Bossy' Mason, not without justification. He ran a 'Live' system whereby all attendances at extra-curricular activities were credited with points, and if pupils obtained sufficient points they were declared 'Live' at the end of term which was recorded in the parents' termly report with a large red letter 'L'. According to the headmaster I was very 'Dead'. This was because he refused to recognise my attendances at the local Sea Scout troop as it was outside the school's sphere of influence. My mother had also encouraged me to apply for a position as a chorister at the Chapel Royal, Hampton Court Palace which I was lucky enough to obtain. This was a further activity which earned me no credit at the school. As the family income was low, I received free school meals and was excused wearing school uniform. This incited a certain amount of bullying from some of the less understanding boys.

Doubtless my scouting activities helped develop my interest in the sea but I believe that the feeling for the sea was inherent long before my scouting days. One boy in our class at Hampton tried for 'Dartmouth' at the age of thirteen but failed. Another boy, who came from a Shaftesbury Home which looked after orphaned children, joined as a Boy Seaman before me. This opened my mind to the possibilities of a career in that direction. I recall assessing the benefits of earning one's own living independent of family support; having free accommodation provided, and particularly, after researching the matter, discovering that if I worked hard I could retire on a pension at the age of forty. So the answer to the question frequently asked: 'Why did you join the Navy?' would be that it was a mixture of motives and ambitions. I was breaking away from a family of women; escaping from a school that I didn't particularly like; taking a job where, from the very beginning, I would be supporting myself; and having the opportunity of seeing the world. In short, I was running away to sea to join the Royal Navy in its most junior rank.

Young boys had served in the Royal Navy for many years. They were first officially recognised by an Act of Parliament in 1847.

I had just turned fifteen when I decided to join the Navy much to my headmaster's anger and my mother's sorrow. There were strict regulations regarding academic ability, behaviour and physical fitness.

I applied to join as soon as I had reached the minimum joining age of 15. I was duly called to the recruiting centre in Acton (West London) for tests and interviews to see if I met the requirements listed above. The centre was run by retired service personnel and was under the charge of a Royal Marine sergeant. There were about twelve candidates in the group. We were all just past our fifteenth birthdays and most had come straight from school. The sergeant was pristine in his uniform, compared with us, a motley collection of gangling, pimply-faced adolescents. The day started with much repetitive form filling followed by academic tests. I felt that these were relatively easy. Then the sergeant held a group interview and briefing. He followed the prescribed list of questions regardless of their relevance. One of the first questions was whether we were married. There was much jocularity which annoyed the sergeant. The next question was whether we had any children. More hilarity, at which the sergeant blew his top. We then realised that this was serious business.

Having obtained all the information he required, the sergeant explained that we had to undergo a medical examination. He told us that this would be undertaken by a retired Naval Surgeon Captain. He emphasised that during the colour blindness test the Surgeon Captain would show us a number of different coloured lights one of which would be 'purple'. When we saw this we were to say that it was 'magenta'. If we said 'purple' the Captain would fail us. When I entered the examination room I was faced by a man who was obviously fond of the bottle. He was dressed in a white overall to create an air of authority. He peered at me through small sunken watery eyes set above large purple cheeks, or perhaps I should say 'magenta'. However I managed to get through the test without upsetting him. I avoided calling purple – purple and later discovered that I had passed with a Grade A1.

Having passed the preliminary interview a letter finally arrived calling me for a final interview on 10 June 1947. I recall that this letter addressed me as 'Dear Sir', noticeably for the first time. Until then I had been 'Master Smalley', and it seemed to me that overnight I had reached manhood. I was to report to the recruiting officer at Acton at 10.00 a.m. for further tests, and if successful I would travel that night to HMS *Bruce*, the Boys' Training Establishment at Crail, Fife by the overnight train from King's Cross. I left school two days before I was due to leave home so that my mother and I could have a day out together. As it was a lovely day we decided to go for a walk and took a bus to Teddington Lock, then crossing to the other side of the River Thames we were able to walk to Twickenham where we could cross the river again by the 'penny ferry' and take a bus home. We chatted about nothing in particular but it was obvious to me that there was something on my mother's mind which she was unable to bring out. We had completed the round trip and were walking home from the bus stop. I was conscious that my mother was bringing herself to speak. Finally, as we were walking in through the gate she turned quickly to me and said: 'You won't go with those women, will you?' I wasn't naive enough to misunderstand her, but reassured her. It occurred to me that it was the only discussion I ever had with my mother on the perils (or joys) of sexual experience.

The next day it was necessary to make an early start. The packing was done. New soap-bag, toothpaste and brush, face cloth and other necessities had been carefully purchased and my mother gave careful instructions how I was to tidy myself up before arriving at Crail, because 'First impressions count, you know, Boy'. Eventually I was off to a new life, leaving my mother at the gate in tears.

After we had all passed the final tests we were taken to a local café for lunch and we hung about until it was time to move over to King's Cross to await the night train to Edinburgh. Before this we were given 'the King's shilling' plus one and ninepence subsistence money to last us until we got to Crail.

After a long wait we boarded the train which eventually pulled out of the station and the long night journey started. The trip was memorable because the mother of one boy had supplied him with a package of raw onion sandwiches.

At Edinburgh we disembarked leaving the authorities to fumigate the compartment whilst we were grateful to breathe fresh air at last. We were met by a Petty Officer who put us on the slow train to Crail on the East Neuk of Fife. The railway took us across the Forth Bridge from which some of the boys threw their King's shilling in order to bring them luck. I had never owned a shilling before and decided to keep mine safely in my pocket. The journey followed a wonderful scenic route which meandered along the north bank of the Forth estuary passing places with idyllic sounding names such as Burntisland and Pittenweem.

At last we arrived at Crail where a lorry was waiting to take us to *Bruce*. With it came Petty Officer Scott who told us that he was to be one of our instructors and Divisional Petty Officer. He was short and stocky and shouted rather than spoke, in order to impress his authority on us. He subsequently became known to us as 'Scotty', but not within his hearing. After stopping and checking in at the main gate we re-boarded the lorry and were taken to our accommodation. We ascended a gentle gradient until we reached the huts which comprised the accommodation. One of these was the 'New Entry Block'. We were told that we would spend the next six weeks here preparing for the proper course of instruction. We discovered that New Entries were referred to as 'nozzers'. The remaining part of the day was fairly gentle with explanations of the layout of the establishment, and we were taken to the galley and dining hall for our first meal. We were then issued with our bedding and kit. As soon as we had been issued with our kit we were told to parcel up all our belongings and post them home. That put an end to my mother's hope that I would make a good impression with the underclothes and toilet gear which she had purchased at great sacrifice.

As I settled into my bed that night I felt proud that I was now a Boy Seaman 2nd Class and part of a Navy which, even if not the biggest, was certainly the best. The Royal Navy in 1947 comprised: 6 battleships, 2 monitors, 22 aircraft

Boy 2nd Class Bryan Smalley.

carriers, 30 cruisers, 3 cruiser-minelayers, 118 destroyers, 68 submarines, 190 frigates and trawlers, minesweepers, coastal forces craft and many other miscellaneous vessels.

On our first morning we were woken at 5.30 a.m. which we learnt was the normal time. This was 'Reveille', the first bugle call of the day, also known as 'Charlie Charlie' which rhymed with the opening notes. We were told that the first part of the day would be spent cleaning our accommodation block, then after breakfast we would continue with our joining routine. We were very soon given the regulation haircut. Then began a bewildering series of talks and classes to teach us the ways of the Navy. It seemed that everything was different to civilian life and that uniformity was of paramount importance.

We spent much time on the parade ground learning how to march and salute. We only marched on ceremonial occasions, at other times we 'doubled', that is, marching on the run. In time we learned to double using the minimum effort, a practice known as the 'Crail Crawl'.

One of the first things instilled into us was the complete acceptance of all orders. We were told to obey all orders and complain afterwards if we felt we had received an unjust one. As so many people were ordering us about, we were likely to obtain conflicting orders. The rule was that we should 'always obey the last order'.

In due course we were able to give the outward appearance of a disciplined body of men.

It didn't take us long to discover that although the instructors were first class at their job they didn't always have a wide ranging vocabulary. For their convenience they repeatedly used a number of well tried, and well worn, phrases. When they wanted us to fall into a group with three ranks the standard order would be: 'Get fell in three deep. That's one behind the other, twice!' Instructors keen to instil in us a need be on parade early would say: 'Them wot's keen gets fell in previous.'

Even our uniforms were steeped in tradition. Our bell bottomed trousers made of blue serge had to be turned inside out for ironing. Each leg was then folded in a concertina fashion to give seven horizontal creases representing the seven seas. It made them particularly easy to stow. Our upper gear consisted of a blue knitted woollen jersey. Above that we wore a blue serge jumper with a deep 'V' neck. Fitted over this was a dark blue collar with three thin white stripes around its edge representing Nelson's three famous battles, Copenhagen, the Nile and Trafalgar. Running down from the collar was a folded black silk scarf which was secured at the waist with a length of blue tape tied in a bow. In our best uniforms we also wore a white lanyard running under the collar and looped in a curl round the blue tape. We had to mark all our kit with our name, mainly to avoid theft.

A kit inspection was to become a fairly regular occurrence. Where possible, all items of clothing had to be rolled neatly to the length of the Seamanship Manual. They were then held in the rolled up position with two stops of sailmakers' seaming twine set the width of a Seamanship Manual apart. These items were laid at either side of the large kit bag which was placed to show our name at the base. The 'ditty box' at the front was accompanied by our boots on each side. Boots were highly polished with laces neatly showing. Shoe brushes scrubbed clean were formed around the ditty box and caps stacked neatly one above the other.

The routine in the dining hall was equally important. We sat at tables of eight with four each side. Each day we would move up one space. A boy at one end of the table had to collect the food from the serving hatch. He had a wire rack which held eight plates. As each plate was passed up the table its contents would diminish, but the recipient would get his own back when he took his turn at duty.

We were also taught how the Divisional system worked in the Navy. Its purpose was to break down the ship's company into manageable groups. Its principal benefit was that the officers and petty officers knew the men for whom they were responsible and the men knew who to go to when they had a problem.

We were also allocated to watches, Port and Starboard. These could be divided again into first and second part of Starboard and Port respectively. Each watch took turns at duty out of working hours and was required to attend fire drill and to clean up for evening rounds. When leave was granted at the weekend it would be to a specific watch. We were issued with a 'station card' which was known as a 'breathing licence' to identify which watch we belonged to.

We also learnt something of the history of the establishment. It was already obvious that we were on the site of an old Naval airfield. It had been built in 1918 by Laings but was taken over during World War II to train Navy pilots to drop torpedoes and to learn the art of aircraft carrier deck landings. It was named HMS *Jackdaw*. Initially it accommodated 778 Squadron and later 780 Squadron. The Fleet Air Arm gave it up in March 1947 when it underwent some refurbishing before commissioning as HMS *Bruce* for boys' training about six weeks before we arrived. We were the second intake of boys.

It soon became apparent to us that the officers and senior ratings were all specially selected before appointment to *Bruce*. Many of them had served with distinction during the war.

Our Captain was T.W. 'Tiger' Marsh DSO. He had joined the Navy as a boy seaman and was constantly held up as an example of what a boy could achieve if he worked sufficiently hard. 'Tiger' Marsh didn't get his nickname by chance, although he was always extremely fair.

The First Lieutenant was Lt. Cdr. N.L.A. Jewell MBE DSC Legion of Merit (USA), who had come to fame by floating a body ashore off the coast of Spain from the submarine *Seraph* with false papers about the expected invasion of Europe. This was explained in the book *The Man Who Never Was*. Later he took the French General Giraud off the Axis occupied North African coast. The general refused to embark in a British submarine so *Seraph* pretended to be American. This incident was also recorded in *The Ship With Two Captains*.

Pay in the Navy was calculated on a daily basis. At this time the pay scales were as follows: Admiral of the Fleet £9 a day = £3,285 per annum, Captain Marsh was paid £3.14s. a day = £1,350 p.a., Petty Officer Scott 9 shillings a day = £164 p.a. Boy Seamen Second Class were theoretically paid 1s.6d. a day = £27 per annum, but most of that was kept back to pay for any items of kit that we lost or items that we might damage, and payment for any other items that the authorities might deem to be our responsibility. We received 5 shillings every fortnight as spending money.

As our six weeks' training as nozzers drew to an end, we prepared to move on to the next stage. Some of the boys volunteered to become communication ratings. There were two categories, signalmen 'bunting tossers' and telegraphists 'sparkers'. I decided to remain as a seaman.

Before we moved from the nozzers' block there was also some academic streaming. After a short examination we were divided into AC (Advanced Class) or GC (General Class). The AC boys became Class 117, and the GCs Class 28. I was to join Class 117.

Bruce was divided into four Divisions, each named after a famous admiral: Anson, Benbow, Collingwood and Drake. We were allocated to Drake Division. But before we moved into our new Divisions we were due for our summer leave.

Although we had only been in the Navy a few weeks we had discovered that the way we were being made to dress was not the way any self respecting 'tiddly' Jack Tar would appear when back in his home town. First a bow-wave was needed in the front of the cap which would be worn 'flat a back' on the head. Then the regulation bow in the cap ribbon over the left ear had to be dispensed with. This meant acquiring a new cap ribbon so that it could be tied in a saucy manner over the left eye. The jumper had to have a wide 'U' shaped opening at the front and the bell bottoms had to be as flared as possible. Many other refinements were necessary including the bleaching of the blue collar to a light blue giving a false impression of having spent a long time in the 'Andrew'.

Even in the short six weeks that I'd been away from home I had grown to such an extent that none of my civilian clothes fitted me.

On our return from leave we moved into Drake block. Our Divisional Officer was Lieutenant 'Geordie' Leslie MBE. His MBE was always a point of interest and we heard many tales from our Petty Officers and class instructors why it was awarded. We never knew which tale to believe and so we settled for the story of how he had deprived a mad cook of a meat cleaver as he stormed the bridge of a destroyer with the intention of murdering the captain. I learned the true story later. In December 1944, he was the first lieutenant of HMS

Cassandra when she was torpedoed 190 miles north of Murmansk on her way back from Russia. The captain was killed and Lt. Leslie became acting commanding officer.

Lt. Leslie was assisted by the Divisional Instructor, Chief Petty Officer Robinson. 'Scotty' became responsible for seamanship instruction and PO Thompson ('Tommo') was the gunnery instructor.

We discovered that we didn't really understand the formidable discipline which had been inflicted on us by joining the Navy until we came back from our first long leave. Those boys who decided that they didn't like serving in the Navy and didn't bother to come back, soon found a posse of Leading Patrolmen (the Navy's policemen) on their doorstep. We discovered that there is a fine distinction between being classified as 'being absent without leave' and 'desertion'. A deserter is someone who has shown no intention of returning to his ship. Some of the miscreants were charged with desertion. A crime of this magnitude could not be punished by the Captain. Instead he had to obtain approval from his superior to award the punishment that he recommended. The approval came back to the ship in the form of a Warrant.

The scales of punishment were laid out in the Articles of War.

Article of War No. 1 ordered the Commanding Officer to hold public worship in his ship.

Article 2 listed eleven offences which could lead to the death penalty which included desertion in the face of the enemy. Punishment for desertion in other circumstances had a maximum penalty of penal servitude.

When the Captain received the Warrant allowing him to punish the *Bruce* deserters we were all mustered on the parade ground. The offenders were then marched to a position facing us all. They were flanked by burly Leading Patrolmen, and then the warrant was read. We were awestruck to hear the officer start by reading out the appropriate Article of War before pronouncing sentence. It was with relief that the offenders were only sent to detention for a period of several days.

Birching had been temporarily suspended six years before and luckily it was never reintroduced. But caning of boys up to a maximum of twelve strokes was permitted and we soon learnt that it was frequently administered and was a painful experience.

Boys caught swearing were given a piece of soap to chew and then swallow.

For some of us, all the punishments meted out only strengthened our resolve that the system wouldn't beat us. Occasionally a boy would strike back and he found to his cost that the system was bigger and more powerful than any one individual. The other lesser punishments were 'Number Elevens' and

'Number Eights'. Yes, even the punishments were categorized by numbers! They comprised getting up early and extra work and drill.

It was at this time that we learnt of an interesting custom regarding deserters' kit which was auctioned to the other ratings. The proceeds went to the 'pusser' (the Navy), and we were advised to keep our bids low. On the other hand when a rating died, his kit was auctioned in the same way, but the proceeds went to his next-of-kin which led to remarkably generous bids.

In our new environment in Drake Division we settled into a more rigorous routine. We rose each morning at 5.30. We washed and dressed and went over to the dining hall for cocoa ('Ki') and biscuits followed by PT. We then cleaned our living quarters and provided working parties to help clean the galley, skirmish the parade ground and roadways for litter, and perform other domestic chores. We stopped in time to have breakfast and be ready to fall in on the parade ground at 0800 in the summer, and 0900 in the winter for Divisions and Colours. We received formal instruction in the morning and played sport in the afternoon. We mustered again at 1700 for 'evening quarters' in 'night clothing' and had instruction again until 1930, stopping in time for supper. Then we cleaned up the messes and bathrooms for rounds, ready for bed again at 2100. On Wednesday evening we went to the cinema within the camp, and on Sundays we had compulsory church service.

Our day was fully utilised from the moment we rose at Reveille until we had to 'Pipe Down'. The formal instruction comprised about half academic studies with the remaining half split into seamanship and gunnery. Our schoolmaster was Instructor Sub-Lieutenant 'Taff' Jones, an ex-RAF Sergeant Pilot.

It was only when we went down to the hangars for our training in seamanship and gunnery that we discovered that the hill from the training area to the accommodation was known as 'Heartbreak Hill'. It got its name through the activities of the Chief Gunnery Instructor (CGI) Harry 'Sparrow' Hoskins. The hill was a steady incline of about half a mile leading up to the living quarters and galley. We were to get to know every inch of tar macadam before long because 'Sparrow' Hoskins had the habit of standing at the top twice a day when we doubled up for our dinner and supper. Any class caught talking, or not holding their forearms at the prescribed horizontal position, or dragging their feet, were turned about and doubled back to the bottom, and if there was no defaulting class Sparrow picked on one at random just for good measure. Initially, Scotty would double along behind us, taking advantage of the fact that he could see us but we couldn't see him. Privately he was scared to death. If 'Sparrow' Hoskins saw 'this lot' before they could be sorted out, Scotty knew he'd 'have his guts for garters'.

In due course one boy was selected as the class leader and given the rate of Petty Boy Officer. 'Ginger' Boyd, a tall lanky Geordie who had the gift of the gab, was chosen from our class.

In addition to the academic, seamanship and gunnery training we also had to learn to climb the mast. This was situated at the side of the Parade Ground. It was 135 feet high and comprised three sections. From ground level, the ratlines ran at an angle of 60° to the first platform 60 feet above the ground. As the ratlines came under the platform another set ran out to the edge of the platform. These formed 'the devil's elbow'. As you climbed this it was a sheer drop but fortunately a safety net was provided. The second stage was another climb up ratlines and then a straight climb to the top known as the 'button'. When important visitors came we manned the mast. One boy was selected to stand on the button and was known as the 'Button Boy'. It was customary for the visiting dignitary to give him a shilling.

The nearest swimming bath was at HMS *Caledonia* in Rosyth. We were taken there by bus to do our provisional swimming test. We did this wearing a 'duck suit'. It was made of white coarse linen which had been the standard working dress of the British matelot until the beginning of the war.

Apart from these occasional visits outside the gates we were only allowed leave on Saturday from 1300 to 1600 provided we weren't in the duty watch. On Sunday we 'escaped' from *Bruce* by attending the Church of Scotland padre's youth club in Pittenweem.

Boys above sixteen were allowed to smoke, and cigarettes were a valuable commodity especially just before our fortnightly pay was due. To extract the maximum output of a cigarette it was smoked by holding the head of a pin which had been inserted into the cigarette's extreme end.

We did all our gun drill on 4" guns which were the largest guns using fixed ammunition, that is, with the cartridge case and shell in one piece. They were hand loaded as opposed to a tray and rammer. For many of the boys the ammunition must have been heavier than they were and it was a favourite punishment of the POs and particularly Sparrow Hoskins to make us double round with the ammunition over our shoulders or to stand holding it above our heads.

We had a number of whalers and cutters at Anstruther and we were taken out of the harbour by Scotty as seamanship was his responsibility. Authority was maintained by the use of a 'stonnicky', a short piece of rope with a 'standing Turk's head' knot at one end.

Occasionally Lt. Leslie would take us out sailing. He would often take us to the Isle of May about six miles offshore. We took newspapers for the

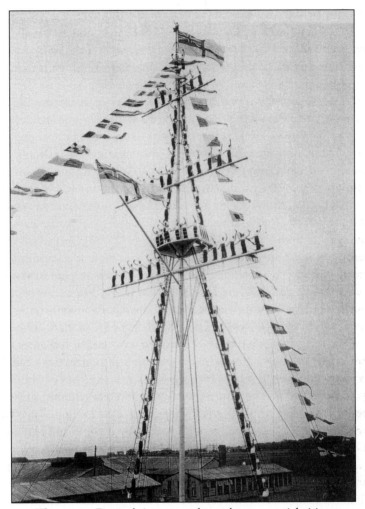

The mast at Bruce *being manned to welcome a special visitor.*

lighthouse-keeper and we enjoyed a 'banyan' (picnic) from our 'bag meal' on an otherwise deserted island.

During the 18th week of our course we sat examinations in education, seamanship and gunnery. As a result everyone in our class was promoted to Boy First Class on 22 November 1947. This entitled us to wear a small red star on our left arm, but on our best uniforms it was gold. We wore it with great pride. Our nominal pay went up to 2 shillings a day (£36 per annum). We actually received 6 shillings a fortnight, with the rest being retained as 'credits'.

The only books we were allowed were the Bible and the seamanship manual. We had no radio or newspapers and there was no television service at that time.

Chocolate in the Navy is called 'nutty'. As it was rationed many of us would save it to take home on leave.

Even at the time that I joined the Navy it had a great understanding of man management. At the beginning of each year or whenever a commanding officer changed, ratings were entitled to inspect a part of their service documents. Two particular points were shown to the rating, his 'character' assessment and his 'efficiency'. Character could be assessed as VG, Good, Fair, Indifferent or Bad. The assessment was clearly categorized relating to the amount of punishment a rating had been awarded during the previous year. Efficiency was marked as Superior, Satisfactory, Moderate or Inferior. There were other parts of the assessment which weren't shown to the rating. At one point when Geordie Leslie was preparing the reports for our inspection there was great excitement amongst the boys as he had left his office unlocked with the papers on the desk. When none of the petty officers were about we sneaked in one by one to look at the confidential part of the report. Mine only had two words on it: 'Needs watching.' This could have two meanings. Either my DO didn't trust me, or he felt I was destined for higher things. I assumed it meant the former as I hadn't been selected as a class leader or given any other responsibility. I was rather hurt as I was one of the few boys who did his best to keep out of trouble.

On one occasion I had committed some now forgotten offence and was told to lay out my kit by 'Scotty'. It was to be inspected by Lt. Leslie when he did the night rounds at 2100. I laid my kit out as best I could and feeling that I couldn't improve on it, I sat down to write home. Scotty caught me and told me to carry on getting my kit laid out. When Lt. Leslie did his rounds he checked each item of clothing and made me undo all the stops on the rolled items. He then said that it wasn't satisfactory and he would re-inspect it after I had laid it out again. It was obvious to me that Scotty had pre-warned him and told him to fail me on the inspection, but I avoided the usual punishment handed out to boys who had a bad kit or who were dirty. They had to wear a red tin hat until their kit or cleanliness was up to scratch. This was not the only use for a tin hat. Boys under punishment had to wear green tin hats. Regardless of colour, all the tin hats had their leather lining removed to make them particularly uncomfortable.

When life is spent with every minute of the day accounted for, time quickly passes, and so our first year in the Navy soon came to an end. We were examined on all subjects including religious knowledge and we were told that we were to be examined on the book of Luke. We had a particularly unpleasant boy in our class called Phillips; in fact he was the class bully. He boasted that he was determined to win at least one prize and said that he intended winning the prize for religious knowledge. I determined that he shouldn't, and read Luke through so many times that I almost knew it by heart. When the results were announced I learnt that I had won the prizes for Seamanship and Academic Subjects. I also won the prize for Religious Knowledge. I don't think that such a prize has been won before with such un-Christian motives.

My service papers recorded that I completed my course at *Bruce* with a first class pass on 14 June.

CHAPTER 2

…and so to sea! 1948

AFTER A FORTNIGHT'S leave we returned to *Bruce* and prepared to move on. Most of us left *Bruce* with regret and although our instructors had given us a rough time we were sorry to leave them behind. Our first year's training ashore was now meant to be consolidated by three months' sea experience. The bus journey soon had us and our kit alongside our first ships at Rosyth. Mine was to be *Wakeful* which I joined on 11 July 1948. *Wakeful* had been completed in February 1944 as one of the seven Wager class destroyers. She displaced 1,700 tons and was armed with 4 x 4.7" guns, 4 x 20mm anti aircraft guns and 4 depth charge racks as well as torpedoes.

Our group was called the training squadron which comprised *Whirlwind*, *Wrangler*, *Wizard* and *Wakeful*. *Wakeful* was the senior ship and was commanded by a Post Captain (i.e. four stripes). He was in command of the whole squadron and was referred to as Captain (D) for 'Destroyers'. The second in command of the Squadron was a Commander who also had his own ship. The remaining COs were Lieutenant Commanders. The Captain (D)'s ship was recognised by a large black band painted round the top part of the funnel. The next senior ship was referred to as a 'half leader' and had a thinner black line round the funnel.

Our Captain was Royston Wright but it was the Petty Officers who remain memorable. They weren't specially chosen as instructors as our previous POs had been.

Our PO made a point of collecting our mail as soon as it was ready for distribution. He would take it into his mess and keep it whilst we waited anxiously for our letters. On one occasion one of the boys had the temerity to knock on the door of the POs' mess to ask if we could have it. He took a severe beating for his impudence. I did my best to keep well clear of this unpleasant character. I knew he had it in for me as he called me 'the boy who speaks like a five pound note'.

My most vivid memory of sleeping in a ship for the first time is of the constant noise. Initially the hum of the generators and fans, and if you slept forward, the clinking of the anchor cable would prevent sleep. On my first night on board I found the noise quite upsetting but after a time I dropped off to sleep. I awoke to a great shemozzle with people clustered round my hammock and faces of officers peering in. As one does when waking in the middle of a deep sleep I had no idea where I was. It seems that someone had looked into my hammock and seeing me lying there asleep but with my eyes wide open assumed that I was dead. He had rushed off to tell the duty PO, who had then gone to the Officer of the Day who had called the doctor and hence the shemozzle. Eventually I got used to the noise and slept more normally and in due course I found that I couldn't sleep unless familiar noises were in the background indicating that all was well.

Whilst we were at sea we would learn of all the duties which we would be expected to undertake as qualified seamen. These comprised: lookout which we did with binoculars whilst standing in the wings of the bridge; lifebuoy sentry whose post was on the quarterdeck ready to drop a lifebuoy over the side if anyone fell overboard; and boat's crew when we waited by the whaler ready to lower it in the water and man it if required. Occasionally we would act as boatswain's mate and be allowed to take a turn at steering the ship.

Conditions on the messdeck were sparse by today's standards. Messes were barely furnished. Most messes comprised a long wooden table with a bench running down each side. At the inboard end of the table (the end furthest from the ship's side) would hang the mess 'fanny' in which eating utensils were washed. Cutlery and crockery would be stowed in a nearby locker. Each sailor would have a locker in which he had to keep all his kit. Clothes other than uniform were not allowed on board. The deck would usually be covered in corticene, a brown hard-wearing linoleum which was scrubbed daily as were the mess tables and benches.

After our four month period in *Wakeful* came to an end we were regarded as fully trained and ready to go to our first 'proper' ship. A 'proper' ship in the Navy is the one to which you properly belong and in which you fill a complement billet. Moving from one ship to another is done by being 'drafted' and in the hope that men would occasionally be drafted to a ship which would operate near to home the Navy was split into three Port Divisions, or Home Ports: Chatham, Portsmouth and Devonport. Most Londoners would expect to be in the Chatham Division although some belonged to Portsmouth. Each Division had immense pride in its ships and its achievements which was exemplified by the inter-Divisional rivalry at the annual Royal Tournament field gun competition. I was appointed to the Chatham Division.

CHAPTER 3

Chatham Barracks 1948

ON 29 SEPTEMBER 1948 my Service Papers noted that I was 'Trained' and I left *Wakeful* and joined Chatham Barracks – HMS *Pembroke* – on 2 October.

The barracks were opened on 30 April 1903. There were six blocks of buildings in the barracks. Each had taken on the names of Blake, Nelson, Anson, Grenville, Duncan and Hawke respectively.

The boy seamen had messes separated from the older men. Each mess was provided with trestle tables and benches. Meals were provided under a 'cafeteria' mess system. Between each pair of barrack blocks at ground level was a bathroom. It comprised showers, wash hand basins and larger basins for dhobeying (washing). Early risers might find some tepid water in the taps but late-comers had to make do with cold. Each boy had a kit locker and there were hammock nettings for the stowage of hammocks after they had been lashed up in the morning. Rails from which hammocks could be slung ran from side to side of the block. Hammocks were spaced twenty one inches apart.

The Daily Routine was only marginally less arduous than at *Bruce*:

0530	Call men under punishment
0600	Men under punishment muster at the main gate
0615	Call the Hands
0645	Hands to breakfast
0730	Duty Watch to muster
0750	Non-duty watches clean barrack rooms
0800	Colours (Summer)
0820	Clear barrack rooms
0830	Hands fall in (start work at allocated jobs)
0900	Colours (Winter)
1015	Stand Easy
1030	Out Pipes
1100	Up Spirits
1200	Hands to dinner
1255	Hands fall in (start work at allocated jobs)

1425 Stand Easy
1435 Out Pipes
1550 Secure
1630 Libertymen fall in
1845 Hands to Supper
2000 Clear up blocks
2100 Sunset
2225 Out pipes – Junior Ratings

On Sundays 'call the hands' was at 0645 and breakfast at 0715.

Every fourth night we would be in the duty watch. When not on duty it was possible to go on short weekend leave from noon on Saturday until Monday morning. Every fourth week there was a long week-end from Friday afternoon until Monday morning, known as a 'Friday While'.

Eventually the Boys from *Wakeful* had completed their joining routine and were allocated to various tasks whilst awaiting their draft to a complement billet. I, and one or two other boys, were instructed to help the barrack Shipwright. I don't think that he had asked for help as he didn't seem to know how to employ us. After some thought he took us outside and showed us an enormous pile of timber. It was lying against two very high outside walls set at right angles, and the pile rose to about twenty feet. Some of the timber was off-cuts, other pieces were from old ship's furniture and had been salvaged because of the quality and type of timber and as I recall some of it looked as though it had come directly from the saw-mill.

Our instructions were to tidy up the whole pile. Obviously this was going to take a long time. We spent the first day or two picking at the pile in a desultory manner and then during a stand-easy we decided that it was pretty pointless piling up the off-cuts that had no chance of being used because they were so small. It was also cold being outside all day in our working clothes. We decided to start a small fire and didn't consider that we needed to ask anyone's permission. Like most young boys, fires have always had a fascination for me; I could stand and poke at them for hours. Also, of course it is quite hard work keeping them going, and it's very comfortable just sitting round and yarning. Unfortunately on such an untidy pile it was quite difficult to get the short pieces without extracting the longer pieces first, and the longer pieces had to be stowed somewhere and we found it much easier to break them up and use them to replenish the dying fire.

This went on for several weeks and I began to worry whether the Shipwright, a Chief Petty Officer, had noticed anything amiss. He came and went from his workshop twice a day, but never came round the side of the workshop to monitor our progress.

The pile steadily diminished. 'He's bound to notice sooner or later,' I thought and had visions of being in 'chokey' before long. I was very grateful, after two months of this 'quiet number' which had developed into a nightmare, to receive a 'draft chit' to join HMS *Troubridge* in the Mediterranean.

But I had achieved something useful whilst in the barracks. I had passed the two academic examinations which were necessary before I could be promoted above the rank of Able Seaman. The first one was Educational Test 1 taken on 9 November, and the second, Educational Test 2, on 12 November. I also recall being one of three Boys who took an intelligence test. We weren't told why we had been selected. The tests were administered by a very attractive Leading Wren. Afterwards she told us that one of the Boys had performed exceptionally well but she didn't tell us which one. I didn't think any more about it at the time.

Several of my friends from *Bruce* also received draft chits to travel out in the same troopship. We were allowed two weeks embarkation leave before leaving for the Mediterranean. Before I left for my leave I went back to say cheerio to my two pals as they put the last pieces of timber on the fire.

I was looking forward to my appointment in the Mediterranean and had no knowledge of the conflict between Jews and Arabs or the problems developing in Egypt.

After my two weeks embarkation leave I returned to barracks and shortly afterwards made my way to Southampton to join the troopship.

CHAPTER 4

Two years in the Mediterranean 1949-50

I N SOUTHAMPTON I joined the *Empire Windrush* which was manned by the Merchant Navy but was contracted as a troopship running between Southampton and Singapore or Hong Kong.

We sailed from Southampton at 1230 on 8 December 1948. We had moderate seas through the Bay of Biscay, and we felt like experienced sea-dogs with all the authority of someone with three months' sea experience. It was a pleasant trip. The Army policed the ship and the Navy had very little to do except keep our own messdeck clean.

A day or two before we were due to arrive in Malta there seemed to be some confusion regarding the whereabouts of *Troubridge*. Eventually those of us bound for *Troubridge* were told to stay on board *Empire Windrush* in Malta and carry on to Port Said. On arrival at Port Said, we disembarked and found ourselves accommodated in the Navy's small transit camp, HMS *Stag*, which was situated on the bank of the Suez Canal. We weren't allowed to leave the camp.

Eventually we heard that *Troubridge* was in Cyprus and that the troopship *Empire Comfort* would take us there. *Empire Comfort* was an old corvette which had a few extra bunks added and all the guns removed. My bunk was in the fore ends. We sailed in the evening with a fairly strong wind blowing. I quickly discovered that the person who had named the ship *Empire Comfort* had a warped sense of humour. I had never been in a situation less comfortable. The discomfort caused by living as far forward as possible was aggravated by the paint fumes which had impregnated everything in the compartment. I decided I could stand it no longer and spent most of the night pacing up and down the upper deck being cooled by the salt spray.

The following day we arrived at Famagusta. Famagusta has a lovely natural harbour with beautiful sandy beaches. *Troubridge* was at anchor just outside the harbour. Eventually a boat took us out to *Troubridge* and as soon as passengers and stores were on board we weighed anchor and sailed for Larnaca on the other side of the Island.

Troubridge had been on the Mediterranean Station only a short time. She had relieved HMS *Saumurez* which had been mined in the Corfu Channel which led to a court case in the International Court of Justice. HMS *Volage* was involved in the same incident and had her bow blown off. Some wit proposed that the *Saumurez* and *Volage* should each be cut in half and the good halves welded together as HMS *Sausage*.

Troubridge's work in the Cyprus area related to the problems in Palestine and the newly formed state of Israel. Palestine had been governed by the British since 1918. Anti-Semitism, particularly in Germany, had created waves of Jewish immigrants into Palestine and the Arabs responded with a campaign of terrorism against the British and the Jews. In 1947 the UN General Assembly had voted to partition Palestine and set up a Jewish state. Until shortly before I arrived on board *Troubridge* the Navy had been carrying out a Palestine Patrol in an attempt to turn the immigrants back. These patrols were extremely dangerous for the men who formed the boarding parties as they were repelled with force. I was lucky to join *Troubridge* just at the time when these patrols had been abandoned.

Troubridge was commanded by Captain L.G. Durlacher OBE DSC who was Captain (D) of the First Destroyer Squadron. *Troubridge* was an Emergency Type destroyer built during the war as was *Wakeful*, my previous ship. She was one of those ships named after famous Naval officers. Perhaps the most famous ship of this class was HMS *Kelly* which was sunk in the Mediterranean whilst under the command of Captain 'Dickie' Mountbatten.

Our First Lieutenant was Lt. Cdr. J.B. (John) Burghfield DSC* who had spent a large part of the war as a prisoner of war in Germany and my Divisional Officer was Lt. R.F. White. *Troubridge* had a total of 18 officers.

After a while in Troubridge I was given the job of 'painter's mate'. The painter was an able seaman whose job it was to provide all the necessary equipment for painting. From time to time we would 'paint ship' which would require all hands. The painter had his store in the foremost part of the ship. It was an unpleasant place to work because of the fumes. There was also more intricate work to be done. On official visits the ship would present the local dignitaries with a ship's crest. It would be partly covered in gold leaf. I was sent on a course learning how to apply it and was made responsible for having sufficient ship's crests available for presentation on official visits.

Meanwhile I was progressing with various qualifications. I had already passed the two easiest educational qualifications ETI and ETII which would get me as far as Petty Officer, provided I also passed the professional examinations. To become an officer it was necessary to pass the Higher Education Test. A Branch Officer had to pass four HET subjects taken at any time, but to become a Commissioned Officer it was necessary to take four subjects at the same time which must include Mathematics and English. After settling down in *Troubridge* I decide to study for HET and Lt. White arranged for me to receive the necessary books and a syllabus and guidance notes for a programme of study. In March 1949 I took two subjects and obtained a second class pass in General Knowledge (65%), and Navigation (55%).

Lieutenant White was an ex-upper yardman which term needs some explanation. An upper yardman was a person who had been selected whilst still a junior rating on the lower deck as having 'officer-like-qualities' (or 'oily Qs' as they were known). Those who were able to pass all the different stages of training successfully could join the wardroom as a sub lieutenant. The term upper yardman comes from the days of sail when the best seamen worked the upper yards. In due course, after seeing that I was keen to make progress in the Navy, Lt. White kindly made out the papers for me to become a CW Candidate (Commission & Warrant) which would lead to upper yardman. To this day I haven't had the opportunity to thank him properly for putting his faith in me, which I now readily do.

On 27 May 1949 I reached the age of 17^1/$_2$ which entitled me to become an Ordinary Seaman. Of course I had to submit the usual request in writing – 'Request to see the Captain, through the First Lieutenant, through the Divisional Officer, to be promoted Ordinary Seaman'. Fortunately I hadn't blotted my copy book recently so my request was granted. My pay was increased to 4 shillings a day or £73 per annum. I had particularly looked forward to this promotion. The Navy had kept back a considerable proportion of my pay as 'credits'. I assumed that this had amounted to a tidy sum. I was distressed to discover that my credits came to about £2. I was convinced that a mistake had been made, but there was no way that I was allowed to look at the account.

The main item of news at this time was the escapade of HMS *Amethyst* in the Yangtse River. When Chinese communists ashore fired on the ship forty three of her ship's company were killed including the captain. On 30 July *Amethyst* made a 140 mile dash under cover of darkness down the flooded Yangtze River and reached the open sea safely. The first lieutenant Lt. Commander J.S. Kerans who had taken over command was awarded the DSO.

Life in the Mediterranean was very pleasant in those days. We would go to sea from time to time and exercise. Once a year the whole Mediterranean Fleet would exercise together. The exercises usually involved steaming along towards a fleet anchorage, probably Cagliari in Sardinia or Argostoli in Turkey. The submarines of the First Submarine Squadron would take up stations in patrol areas ahead of us and attack us as we sailed past. Short counter attacks would follow and we would then press on. At the fleet anchorage we would participate in inter-ship sports, particularly boat pulling and sailing races. At the end of the sports the winner would be declared 'cock of the fleet' and would proudly display the cock for the next year much to the other ships' companies' envy.

After the fleet gathering, more exercises would probably follow and we would then disperse and make our way in small groups of ships or individually to various ports for formal visits. These were great fun as we visited all the best places such as Villefranche, Cannes and Nice in the south of France and similar ports around the rest of the Mediterranean.

The great attraction of these visits was that whenever a British ship visited a foreign port the expatriates would gather together with the Anglophiles, and ships were usually inundated with so many invitations that it was difficult to find enough people on board to accept them all. Sailors had a glossary of terms for the different experiences. 'Up-homers' meant that you had met someone who accepted you into their home as one of the family. A 'Grippo' was an invitation which indicated that your host would pay for everything, which was also described as 'Strangling a Baron'.

Whilst in Villefranche another sailor and I accepted an invitation for a 'Grippo' and had a very enjoyable afternoon visiting the perfumeries at Grasse followed by a pleasant picnic tea. I remember the surprise on the faces of a group of British tourists when they saw a couple of jack tars taking in the luxuries of the south of France and ultimately being whisked away in a Daimler.

Before a scheduled visit to Trieste and Venice I had unwisely made a complaint to Lt. White that life for a Boy Seaman was rather unadventurous, so a few days before we sailed from Trieste I was told that a group of other boys and myself would be dropped off about 100 miles from Venice in a whaler and that we were to sail the rest of the way. I was very pleased to be offered this possibility of adventure. However for safety's sake Lt. White came with us.

Our whaler was lowered into the water in the middle of the afternoon. It was obvious that we wouldn't complete the journey that day and so in the evening we put the boat aground and waded ashore to make a camp. We knew that we were on the island of Burano. The rise and fall of tide in that area is about ten inches and we made no allowance for it. We slept lying on the mainsail and pulled the fore-sail over us for cover. When we woke the next morning we found that the level of the water had dropped but in terms of distance it meant that the tide had gone out about a hundred yards leaving the boat high and dry. We decided to use the boat's oars as rollers to roll the boat

A run ashore in Venice. Bryan on right.

down to the sea but the weight of the boat broke the oars. Eventually we got the boat into the water and managed to sail into the canals of Venice to reach our ship without further incident. The shipwright was not amused, and I determined not to seek any further adventure.

Not all our time was spent on cruising the pleasure spots of the Med. In May 1948 the Israelis had shot down an Egyptian Spitfire in the vicinity of Tel Aviv. The resulting tension had prompted the Admiralty to establish a standing guardship off Aqaba where Egypt, Israel and Jordan each had a stretch of coastline in close proximity. *Troubridge* was programmed to undertake one of these patrols and we set off looking forward to a new experience.

After passing through the Suez Canal we steamed southwards through the Gulf of Suez and then passed into the Gulf of Aqaba, leaving Mount Sinai on our port hand. The area looked so barren that it gave the impression that no one had set foot there before, although we knew that history had been acted out there since before biblical times. When we reached the head of the gulf we anchored in good holding ground which was about two miles offshore. Once there we settled down to a monotonous routine. We had been sent there in case trouble blew up although we could do little apart from bombard the shore or defend ourselves from air attack. I suppose we were sent there as a deterrent using the old fashioned gun-boat diplomacy, the same diplomacy which had put *Amethyst* in such a perilous position.

The port was strategically important to the Jordanians as it was the only coastline of their country. It stretched for only about two miles. It didn't appear that the Jordanians used it at all as a port and seemed neither to import nor to export goods from it. The Israeli stretch of coastline was even shorter.

Although we went to action stations each time we detected an aircraft it was always our friendly Dakota delivering mail to the soldiers encamped ashore.

The comforts of life are all relative. We felt very sorry for the British soldiers living ashore in tents, with water rationing, a plain diet, and very little amusement. Each evening we invited some of them on board for a fresh water shower, a decent supper, and a film show before sending them back ashore. To them it was living in the lap of luxury.

Perhaps we overdid the hospitality. One night when I was one of the sentries on duty with a Lanchester machine gun, I saw something moving in the darkness some distance from the ship. I blew my whistle and called out not to approach the ship or else I would fire. It had little effect. I was on the point of firing when I was blinded by light. The duty officer had gone up to the signal deck and trained the signal lamp on the intruder. We could then see that the boat contained an extremely drunken soldier who had been drinking all evening in the NAAFI beer tent.

My assessment of the strategic and commercial value of Aqaba was clearly wrong for we heard that King Abdullah of Jordan was to come on board and take lunch with the Captain. I assume that this was partly to thank the British for their support and possibly to confirm the bond between the two countries. There was naturally a great deal of scrubbing and preparation before this important visitor arrived. I was proud to be included in the piping party which would perform part of the welcoming ceremony. Piping on the bos'un's call is very impressive when well done, but some people cannot master it no matter how hard they try. If the calls are not blown in synchrony then the sound is a cacophony. We practised hard to ensure we worked well together.

After waiting excitedly for some time, His Majesty King Abdullah of Jordan came on board. Here was I, only two or three feet from the man who had ridden with Lawrence to evict the invading Turks, and while the peace conferences were taking place in London at which France expected to get her share of the Arab lands, he had calmly marched into Amman and set up his own government. The powers in London decided to establish Abdullah as the King of Transjordan for no other reason than they hadn't the capability of evicting him, and there he stayed establishing one of the most stable governments in the Middle East for generations to come.

My part in the ceremonies was now over until it was time to see the King back over the ship's side, but I would dearly have loved to know what took place around the lunch table.

On our return to Malta we learned that *Troubridge* had been scheduled to return to the UK, but as I had only been on the Mediterranean station for eight months I wasn't allowed to return in the ship. Instead I was to be transferred to HMS *Pelican* which I joined on 2 August 1949. Before I left *Troubridge* I was called to the First Lieutenant's cabin. Naturally I went with some apprehension thinking that I had done something wrong, but the First Lieutenant thanked me for painting the ship's crests so well. It was a very thoughtful gesture which I hadn't expected.

Pelican was an Egret class frigate built in 1938. She was the only one of her type but similar ships were known collectively as 'Bird' class. Captain W.G. Crawford DSC was in command. Once again I had been drafted to a Leader, in this case Captain (F) – standing for 'Frigate'. The routine was much the same as in *Troubridge*, the hands being called at 6.30 and 'falling in' at 7.30 to start the forenoon's work.

Almost as soon as I joined *Pelican* we moved into No. 2 Dry dock in Malta in order to undertake the unpleasant task of scraping the ship's bottom of algae and barnacles before repainting. Whilst in dock another unpleasant job befell the junior seamen. The fresh water tanks were drained and we had to go into the tank through an eighteen inch manhole and scrub them clean.

Some of the older men had their wives in Malta. Able Seamen and above were allowed to stay ashore all night, but Ordinary Seamen had to return by 2315 and Boys by 1900.

A month after I joined, the Captain left the ship and was relieved by Captain Christopher Bonham Carter. I was surprised that the new captain was heavily tattooed down both arms.

After we had completed our docking period we sailed for a short goodwill cruise. We spent the first three days of October in Philippeville in Algeria then after a 150 mile overnight sea trip we spent a further three days in Bizerta, Tunisia. The visits followed the usual pattern of the Captain calling on the dignitaries ashore and a cocktail party on the quarter deck in the evening. The sailors were entertained by a guided walk through both towns. There didn't

Troubridge leaving Malta.

seem much to attract us to go ashore again in the evening. After this short interlude we returned to Malta.

We had only been in Malta a few days before we sailed for Aqaba to emphasise Britain's presence in the area once again. We arrived at the beginning of November. Shortly after we arrived we were joined by the frigate *Peacock*. She had on board a contingent of soldiers to relieve those already on station. The routine was exactly the same as our previous visit in *Troubridge*. We maintained a watch alongside the ship's side for saboteurs or aircraft attack, but in good weather there was no need to man the guns continually. We continued to man the anti-aircraft guns in the middle of the forenoon when the scheduled mail plane was expected.

As soon as *Peacock* had settled into the routine we went on a short cruise in the area. We were never told why, but it made an interesting diversion. We went back down the Gulf of Aqaba and then north up the Gulf of Suez and anchored off the port of Suez. Leave was granted but as it was necessary to go ashore by boat, I didn't bother to avail myself of the opportunity. The next day we moved further south and anchored in Hurghada Bay in Egypt. We stayed there for a few days and held our Remembrance Day service ashore which aroused interest from the local populace. We left Hurghada on 10 November and returned to Aqaba the next day.

On 12 November the army offered us a trip to Petra. Because of the heat I decided not to go. Bearing in mind the popularity of Petra today, and the cost of such a visit, it has been a source of irritation to me that I turned down such a wonderful opportunity.

Having completed our stint on station we weighed anchor on 18 November and started our passage back to Malta. We arrived in Malta on 26 November. The next day was my 18th birthday. This meant that I started my 12 year engagement. Although all the boys had joined initially on a twelve year engagement, we were allowed to change this to seven years 'with the Fleet' followed by five years in the Reserves. Quite a few of the Boys who had joined with me opted to serve only the seven years. I was still quite firm in my mind that my career would be with the Navy. My pay remained at 4 shillings a day.

At the age of eighteen, a rating could decide whether he wished to draw his tot of rum. Until then he was marked in the ledger as 'UA' (Under Age). Those who declined to draw their tot were marked 'T' (Temperance), whilst those who drew it were marked 'G' (Grog). Those who were temperance received threepence a day in lieu of their tot. Rum was a great bargaining tool or method of showing appreciation. It could be offered in the form of 'sippers', 'gulpers' or 'see it off'. I became 'grog'.

Having arrived back in Malta it was decided that it was difficult for me to study for HET without proper tuition so I was then drafted to HMS *Forth*, the depot ship of the First Submarine Squadron. I joined on 30 November 1949. Both *Troubridge* and *Pelican* moored in Sliema Creek whilst in Malta, but *Forth* was in Marsaxlokk. Although *Forth* was a fully seagoing ship she only went to sea about twice a year and a series of pontoons were provided to form a walkway from ship to shore. This made life much easier than in Sliema Creek where all traffic to and from the ships was by boat or more often by *dghaisa*, the Maltese local craft not dissimilar to a gondola.

The Captain of *Forth* was Captain B.W. (Bertram) Taylor DSC, but it was also the Flag Ship of the Flag Officer (Destroyers) Mediterranean Fleet, Rear Admiral H.W.U. McCall CB DSO, so we had two diverse responsibilities. Our main task was to service the submarines in the Squadron which secured alongside when in harbour. On the other hand we attempted to keep the ship at a high state of cleanliness as befitted a flagship.

Occasionally I met a certain amount of resentment from ratings because I was hungry for promotion. I don't know whether that is why I was appointed as 'Captain of the for'ard heads' as soon as I arrived in *Forth*. The for'ard heads, or lavatories, comprised a large compartment with about 36 cubicles known as 'traps'. They were a very good place for 'loafing'. If a Petty Officer was given a job which had arisen unexpectedly he might not have enough hands to undertake it. He would then go down to the heads and bang noisily on the metal bulkhead whilst shouting 'Fire'. A number of sleepy sailors would tumble out of the 'traps' only to find themselves forming a working party under the Petty Officer's eagle eye.

It was several years later that Lt. Beattie, my Divisional Officer, told me that he noted the results of my intelligence test on my official papers. He told me it was called a T2 Mark. He had learned about this test on one of his courses and his recollection was that no one who scored below 180 had ever become an officer and no one who had scored over 220 had failed to become an officer. Apparently my score was above 220 so he decided to keep a particular eye on me.

I had been drafted to *Forth* to give me a better chance to study. *Forth* had three Instructor Officers on board, usually referred to as 'schoolies'. The schoolies didn't want to spend all their time on one particular student, so I was put under the charge of a 'Coder (Special)' called Willoughby. As his name might imply he was a well educated ex-public schoolboy. Coder (Specials) were national servicemen who could speak one or more foreign languages fluently. Not only were they trained in coding duties but they could also monitor foreign radio transmissions. They were a typical example of ratings who showed that there were those on the lower deck who were better educated than some officers. The following story illustrates the position.

A Coder (Special) was serving in a destroyer which didn't have a chaplain on board and so the first lieutenant took the Sunday church service. At the end of the service the first lieutenant granted absolution of the sins of all those in attendance. The Coder immediately submitted a request in the usual style, on the appropriate form, which read: 'To see the first lieutenant to state a complaint: that he absolved our sins when he is not a Clerk in Holy Orders.' The 'requestmen' procedure followed the usual ceremony. The Coder was in his Number One uniform with cap on. The Master at Arms ordered 'Coder "Bloggs", Quick march...Halt...Right Turn...Salute.' 'Coder Bloggs Sir, To see the first lieutenant to state a complaint that he absolved some sins when he does not have authority to do so.' The first Lieutenant then asked: 'And what have you got to say, Bloggs?' Bloggs then gave a long explanation of the different rites within different religious denominations which baffled most of those present. He concluded that in the Church of England only a Clerk in Holy Orders may offer absolution. This presented something of a quandary to the first lieutenant who didn't know what action he should take, if any, but the Master at Arms came to the rescue as is customary in these circumstances. In a firm voice to indicate that there would be no argument, he ordered: 'Sins not absolved…Salute…Right turn…Quick March.'

As well as studying for academic subjects to progress towards officer status, I also had to make normal progress as a seaman. Additionally it was necessary to obtain a 'non-substantive' rate and I qualified as a Radar Plotter 3rd Class (RP3). As the term implies this job split into two components. We operated both air and surface warning radar sets, reporting contacts to the operations room or Officer of the Watch. At other times we plotted the contacts to present a picture of their movements. The radar would also be used as a navigation aid.

I spent my first day at sea in a submarine, HMS *Sportsman,* whilst serving in *Forth.* We went out 'day-running' on a simple exercise acting as a target for a destroyer. After being shown round the submarine, life became rather boring. There was no likelihood of any of the ship's company allowing me to operate any of the equipment. It became apparent that every man trusted each other, but not someone who was outside their trained circle.

1950 began as a bad year for the Navy. On 12 January the British submarine *Truculent* sank after a collision in the Medway Estuary. She had been on trials after a refit in Chatham dockyard and was returning to Sheerness. Besides her normal complement there were 18 dockyard workers on board. As the collision occurred five men on the bridge were knocked overboard and were later rescued. Six men were killed in the collision but the remainder were alive when it sank in sixty feet of water. Sixty four of them escaped almost immediately but most were swept away before they could be picked up. The final death toll was 64. The loss led to the introduction of survival clothing to be worn by escapees and the fitting of an extra steaming light at the back of the fin on British submarines known as the 'Truculent light'.

Forth spent most of January in the dry dock with the ratings scrubbing and painting the ship's bottom. After coming out of the dock we returned to our normal berth.

On 24 March I passed HET in English History (55%), and Geography (65%). This qualified me for branch officer rank as I had already passed General Knowledge and Navigation in March 1949. But this didn't qualify me for commissioned rank.

July was the time for the routine summer cruise. We made plans to visit Navarin, Marmaris and Cyprus.

On 17 July, I passed professionally for Leading Seaman. The examination was entirely oral with one exception. We had to splice an eye into a wire rope.

At the time I was living in No. 1 mess on the large for'ard messdeck. The messdeck comprised about sixteen tables, each one being termed a mess. We had to fetch our food from the galley in the metal containers referred to as 'fannies'. Most of No. 1 mess were members of the 'rigging party'. They were the toughest sailors in the ship and maintained all the wire and manila ropes on board. Frequently when a severe wind rose in the night – a gregale – the wire pennants to which the submarines would secure their own lines would part. The rigging party would be called out and in adverse conditions they would splice a replacement pennant. When they discovered that I had to produce a wire splice they were all eager to do it for me. I had to be quite firm to persuade them not to. Apart from the cheating aspect it had also occurred to me that if I presented one of their splices to the examining board it would have been such a high quality that none of the examining officers would have believed that it was a result of my own efforts.

We also had in the mess the sailmaker who was a leading hand. He maintained the awnings and canvas covers for various pieces of equipment on deck but he followed a dying trade and must have been one of the last sailmakers in the Navy.

Another mess member was 'Pincher' Martin, an old and wizened Leading Physical Training Instructor. It was about this time that a concert party was set up. He persuaded me to join, as he was a leading light in the show. I found myself constructing and, in particular, painting the scenery. but I also had a small part in the show called *We've Heard a Buzz*. It was my first effort on the stage.

The show was produced by a Lieutenant who seemed to glory as a 'show-biz' celebrity with ideas above his station. When we were on watch as quartermaster or bos'un's mate he would often tell us to go into the wardroom and announce that there was a telephone call for him from Hollywood, or some other exotic place. I often wondered whether his wardroom colleagues realised what a fraud he was.

It was during the early preparations for the show that he sent for one of the ex-*Bruce* boys. He proposed an idea to the boy which he pretended was for an act in the show. It involved the boy systematically removing items of his clothing. When it had gone too far the young man made a hasty retreat.

'Make sure you don't tell anyone on the messdeck about my little plan,' said the producer, and the incident came to an end.

After our visit to Cyprus we sailed from Khryokhou on passage to Malta.

We arrived in Malta on 24 July and two days later Captain Taylor was relieved by Captain A.C.C. Miers VC DSO. We learned in due course that he was known by a number of different names including 'Tony', 'Gamp' and 'Crap'. He was a forceful character as one might expect from someone who had had such a distinguished wartime career. Life in *Forth* was never dull after he had taken command.

Tony Miers' father was a Cameron Highlander and was killed in action in France in 1914. Miers joined the Navy ten years later and volunteered for submarines. When war broke out he was appointed to command *Torbay*. Miers fought his war with extreme aggression, but took great care to calculate the risks he was taking. Each patrol is a story in itself but the most outstanding is his incursion into Corfu harbour which led to the award of the Victoria Cross.

In July 1942, Miers was summoned to Buckingham Palace to be invested with his Victoria Cross. Three of his officers were to receive DSOs and DSCs but the decoration of twenty four ratings with the CGM was indefinitely postponed. Miers informed the Lord Chancellor that his medical advisers insisted that his health would not allow him to wait upon His Majesty unless he could be decorated with the rest of his crew. Not only did Miers get his way but he also managed to overturn protocol. At normal investitures awards are presented in strict order of precedence. On this occasion, apart from other recipients of the VC, the procession into the throne room was headed by Miers and all his officers and men who were to receive an award. The story goes that Miers then took all those with him to lunch at the Savoy and sent the bill to the Admiralty.

Our new Captain (S/M) loved to fight and would think nothing of squaring up to an officer or rating and settling any disagreement with fisticuffs.

On 4 October we sailed for Tripoli, Libya, securing between two buoys on arrival the next day. We stayed until 13 October before returning to Malta. The highlight for Captain Miers must have been the evening of 10 October when the band of the Cameron Highlanders, his father's old regiment, Beat Retreat.

On 24 November I sat and passed the Higher Education Test in four subjects at the same time. English 78%, History 58%, Geography 63%, Practical Mathematics 59%. I was now educationally qualified as a Candidate for Commissioned rank – (CW) – (Commissioned and Warrant). I was an Able Seaman at the time.

On 27 November, my 19th birthday, HMS *Tyne* entered Lazaretto Creek. She had arrived to replace *Forth*. I was transferred to HMS *Phoenicia*, a shore base, as I had nearly completed my two years foreign draft and it would soon be time for me to go home.

I travelled home on board the *Empress of Australia,* a very old troopship. We sailed into Liverpool. I was very amused as we went through the customs after our arrival, when the customs officer said to one of the Army wives in front of me: 'That's not a very expensive coat, is it, ma'am?' The woman was quite hurt to think that she should possess a cheap fur coat. She didn't realise that the customs officer was giving her an opportunity to pay the minimum customs duty.

'Of course it is,' she replied, 'It cost me a hundred pounds.'

'In that case, Madam, I must charge you the duty on a hundred pounds.'

She had certainly talked her way into it.

We travelled by train to London and we arrived in a 'pea-souper' which certainly brought home to us the difference between the Mediterranean weather and that experienced in London. At the time all the buildings were black with soot, as coal was the only method of providing heat.

My leave entitlement was two days leave for every month spent abroad, plus two weeks for the Christmas which was approaching, so I had six weeks' leave to come. After a couple of weeks at home doing nothing I soon became bored and went to work at the Hounslow branch of the London Co-operative Society. My job was to load the furniture vans and then deliver to the waiting customers. I soon discovered that the driver was the 'Casanova of the Co-op'. After delivering the furniture, he would send me back to wait in the cab. It became apparent to me that he wasn't staying for tea and biscuits.

It was good to be home for Christmas with my mother and two sisters.

CHAPTER 5

Aircraft Carrier *Triumph* 1951

AFTER MY LEAVE I returned to Chatham Barracks for a short time and then I
joined the aircraft carrier *Triumph* on 13 April at Portsmouth. When you're
carrying a kit bag over one shoulder with a hammock under the opposite arm
and a ditty box in a spare hand, if you have one, you don't have time to
appreciate the grandeur or historical significance of the Royal Dockyard which
King Richard I ordered to be built at Portsmouth in 1194. As I trudged through
the Dockyard oblivious to my historic surroundings, Article of War No. 34 still
read: 'Every person subject to this Act who shall unlawfully set fire to any
dockyard, victualling yard, [etc.]…shall suffer death or such other punishment
as is hereinafter mentioned.'

In due course I found *Triumph* lying alongside and I made my way on board.

Triumph belonged to the Colossus class and was launched in October 1944.
She displaced 16,650 tons with a length of 694 feet and a beam of 112 feet. The
class was one of the most successful utility carrier designs ever built, but they
were soon to become obsolete because of the new generation of jet aircraft
coming into service at this time. Our Captain was Captain C.T. Jellicoe DSO
DSC*. The Commander was Commander Horace R. Law OBE DSC.

Shortly after joining, on 16 April, the British submarine *Affray* failed to
surface whilst operating in the English Channel. Apart from her full
complement, she also had on board an officers' training class. The total
number of lives lost was 75.

As soon as *Triumph's* full ship's company had joined we sailed to work up
before taking on board our first squadron of aircraft. The intention was that
our commission would be spent training pilots who at that time were flying
Sea Furies. We also trained observers who were being flown in Fireflies. Our
operational area would normally be in the approaches to the English Channel
when training observers, and in the northern half of the Irish Sea when
training pilots. In those days it was very unusual to have a helicopter on board
and we always operated with a destroyer, the 'Guard Boat', following on one
quarter to rescue any aircrew whose aircraft had fallen into the sea while taking
off or landing.

The allocation of jobs in a ship was made by means of the Ship's Watch and

The watchkeepers' messdeck in Triumph *– Bryan in left background.*

Quarter Bill. As a Radar Plotter, my job at sea when we were operating aircraft was to work in the Operations Room where we manned the ship's radars and radio circuits by which we spoke to and directed our aircraft. We would also plot them on a large vertical Perspex screen which we stood behind. The main qualification for this job was the ability to write backwards.

In harbour I acted as a member of a boat's crew when we were at anchor, and at other times I worked as a bos'un's mate and assisted the Quartermaster in running the ship's routine under the Officer of the Watch.

Boats' crews and Quartermasters had a special messdeck in view of the unsocial hours they worked. We were a happy team. One of the characters in the mess was Tim Durlacher. He was the nephew of Captain Durlacher under whom I had served in *Troubridge*. Tim had been at Dartmouth and it was rumoured that he had been asked to leave after making improper advances to the Captain's daughter, and as Tim preferred not to dispel this rumour he had become something of an icon. He then joined the lower deck and by the time I met him he had progressed to Leading Seaman.

At this time sailors were still paid cash fortnightly and Tim must have been one of the first ratings to have a cheque book. A rating who is scheduled for duty can go ashore if he can find a substitute to do his duty for him. As Tim was in the social whirl requiring maximum time ashore he offered anyone three pounds if they would 'do him a sub'. Although he had little difficulty in finding a taker, the 'sub' usually had great difficulty in cashing the cheque as he was unlikely to have a bank account.

Tim's car was an Austin Healey. It was widely believed that if you saw Tim going over the side with a bucket you should stand well clear because it probably contained aviation spirit for his petrol tank.

Sailors weren't allowed to proceed ashore in anything other than uniform, so Tim always went ashore with a most enormous suitcase which contained his civilian clothes into which he changed as soon as he was able.

Tim didn't have much time for dhobeying, so he had an arrangement with another Leading Hand, 'Cuddles' Cadle, to be his dhobey wallah or laundry-man. Unlike any other sailor on board Tim had two kit lockers. 'Cuddles' Cadle would put all his clean kit into one locker. The other was Tim's laundry basket from which Cuddles would extract the dirty clothes.

To ensure that Tim wasn't starving, his grandmother sent him regular food parcels from her estate in Scotland which required a third locker. This larder contained far more food than he could eat. We therefore had permission to make ourselves a venison sandwich whenever we were feeling peckish at night, or to help ourselves to a little Gentleman's Relish to put on our bread and scrape at breakfast.

'Cuddles' Cadle came from Harrow. At one inspection a visiting Admiral stopped for a brief word with every fourth or fifth man. On reaching 'Cuddles' Cadle he stopped and asked the usual question of how long he'd been in the Navy and then asked:

'And where did you go to school, my man?'

''arrow, Sir,' Cadle replied.

'What? Harrow-on-the-Hill?' asked the Admiral.

'No! 'arrow in the 'ollow', replied Cadle.

The Admiral moved on quickly with eyebrows bristling.

On 27 May I was promoted to acting Leading Seaman. My pay went up to 13 shillings a day, (£237 a year). I now moved up to being a quartermaster and a coxswain of a boat when required.

Our thoughts soon returned to the crisis in the Middle East when we were told to prepare to take out a contingent of soldiers to Cyprus. The operation was called 'Trimed'. There were 3,500 men from the 16th Independent Parachute Brigade Group, 'The Red Devils'. They were divided between *Triumph* and *Warrior*, another aircraft carrier of the same class.

There's many a joke about dockyard workers (mateys). There's an irreverent song which runs:

Triumph taking 16th Independent Parachute Brigade Group to Cyprus.

We're dockyard mateys' children, sitting on the dockyard wall.
Watching our fathers, doing f*** all.
And when we grow older, we'll be dockyard mateys too.
Just like our fathers with f*** all to do.

But this hides a great respect and fellow feeling that the Navy has for the dockyards. Frequently, when given an almost impossible deadline, the dockyards have managed to pull out all the stops and meet their commitments.

This exercise was a typical demonstration of how Naval dockyard staff can excel in a crisis. *Triumph's* complement of 120 officers and 1000 ratings was more than doubled by the 52 officers and 1,358 men who came aboard for the passage. They were strategic reserves for the Middle East. The men slept in the aircraft hangar, but makeshift washing and lavatory arrangements had to be provided. The troops embarked on 4 June. We were ready to sail as scheduled at 1340 on 5 June. We had all the Army's transport on the flight deck and there was natural concern about the weather. We sailed independently from *Warrior*. For the first part of the voyage we encountered rain and fog and then high winds which threw spray over the unprotected vehicles. On 10 June we joined up with *Warrior*. The weather improved and we arrived at anchor off Famagusta on the 12th having covered the 3,000 miles in eight days. As usual everyone was given a pep talk on how to behave when ashore. The advice was that 'Cyprus is one of the healthiest places in the Middle East,' but I don't recall the newcomers to the Mediterranean being advised about the excessive alcoholic content of the local 'hooch'. As a quartermaster I witnessed the return of our sailors after a night in the local bars. The log for 19 June reads that 'Nine ratings are in safe custody' or in other words they were in cells until they were no longer a danger to themselves.

We sailed from Famagusta for Malta on 14 June in a Force 7. Not a pleasant experience for those with a monstrous hangover.

We entered Grand Harbour, Malta on 16 June and stayed for two days before sailing for Gibraltar. We made this leg of the passage in thick fog arriving on 20 June. That evening the wind rose to Force 6 and then increased steadily to Force 13. The weather was so bad that tugs were necessary to hold us off the wall for a while to avoid damage to the hull. We sailed the next day for Portsmouth and arrived on 23 June feeling that we had completed a worthwhile job.

We barely had time to give the ship's company a weekend leave before we were back to our flying duties. Our programme took us to the SW Approaches in the company of our 'guard ship' *Ulysses*. Although we worked a long day at sea we spent the nights anchored either in Torbay or Weymouth Bay. At sea I would do my duties in the Ops. Room and in harbour I coxed the motor boat ashore with libertymen.

The 'observer' training was mainly without incident as aircraft were being flown by experienced pilots. We had on board an experienced Petty Officer pilot who flew one of the aircraft ashore each day to collect the mail. He only failed us once when his plane bounced over the side on landing and all the mail was lost. Fortunately he managed to get out of the cockpit before the plane sank, and he was saved by the guard ship.

We stayed in the SW approaches until 5 July when we took passage towards Bangor, Northern Ireland to change our programme to pilot training. This was the same day that the Admiralty announced a ban on 'snort' breathing masts on submarines after the snort mast on *Affray* was found to have fractured which led to her tragic loss.

At this time, aircraft were guided down on to the deck ('recovered') manually by a 'batsman' (or 'Bats') operating what looked like two table tennis bats. 'Bats' stood on a raised platform on the port side of the after end of the flight deck surrounded by dive-nets into which he jumped when an approaching pilot didn't get it quite right. The aircraft had an arrester hook hanging from its rear end which was intended to engage on one of the ten wires tensioned across the deck. Forward of the arrester wires were two vertical netting barriers in which any aircraft which missed the arrester wires would be ensnared. Occasionally the aircraft would miss the arrester wires and then bounce over the barriers causing havoc amongst the aircraft which were arranged on the forward part of the flight deck. It was dangerous for both the pilot and the flight deck crew.

We arrived at anchor at Bangor on 6 July and stayed over the weekend. *Ulysses* continued to be our guard ship. Our first day's flying on 9 July was rather eventful. The pilots of 737 Squadron flying their planes from RNAS Eglinton were making their first deck landings. Several aircraft crashed but fortunately no one was hurt.

Those of us on duty in the Ops. Room were situated immediately under the flight deck and we developed a rather childish habit of waiting for the planes to land, and then making an assessment judging by the severity of the landing whether or not it had been successful. At times we would call out 'Crash on Deck' before it was announced officially on the ship's broadcast.

When all the serviceable and damaged planes were safely secured we ceased flying for the day and made our way to anchor for the night. We managed to conduct flying operations for the next three days without serious incident, but Friday the 13th July was one of the most tragic days of the commission. In the early afternoon an aircraft missed all the arrester wires, bounced over both barriers and landed amongst all the parked aircraft. Every aircraft on deck was damaged. The CPO in charge of the flight deck was killed and one rating was seriously injured. We anchored off Bangor to land the CPO who had been killed and spent the night sorting ourselves out. The next day we proceeded to Greenock to unload the wrecked aircraft. As soon as that task was completed there was no point staying in the area as there were no aircraft left on which to train, so we transited the Irish Sea again and made our way to Falmouth Bay. By the time we arrived in the south, a programme had been arranged for trainee observers and we recommenced the tiring flying training programme. All went smoothly until 23 July when we had two crashes on deck but by this time those of us on duty in the Ops. Room had stopped calling out 'Crash on deck' each time an aircraft landed heavily on the deck above us.

When this training period ended the ship made its way to Portsmouth for a well earned leave and maintenance period. It was also time for the Captain to be relieved. We entered Portsmouth harbour on 30 July and the next day Captain Ughtred H.R. James CBE joined the ship.

Whilst we were in harbour a team of dockyard 'mateys' came aboard to work on our flight deck. At the time, aircraft would land on the deck in line with the fore and aft line of the ship. The dockyard workers painted out the fore and aft line and replaced it with a line at an angle of about twelve degrees to port of the fore and aft line. The theory was that this would give a clear landing space whereas, as we knew to our cost, the fore and aft method made aircraft parked at the forward end extremely vulnerable. With an angled deck a pilot who missed the arrester wires could simply increase power and fly off again.

After our month's rest in harbour we were back at sea to test the new flight deck layout. The idea was found to be a great success and the 'angled deck' was judged to be safer, and was universally accepted throughout the navies of the world.

Also at about this time, it was decided that the method of guiding aircraft on to the deck with a couple of 'bats' could be improved. This method was eventually superseded by the system of a light beam approach by which the pilot kept his aircraft within a visual beam and flew the aircraft on to the deck without assistance.

I had by now not only achieved the academic qualifications to become an officer but my Divisional Officer decided that I was ready to undertake the Admiralty Interview Board which would decide whether I was to go forward for further training as an officer. I only remember the event vaguely.

Like most examinations and interviews, there is a certain technique in convincing the officers on the board that you have Officer-like-qualities ('Oily Qs'). As well as looking for young men who have the right academic qualifications, the board is constantly watching for signs of initiative and leadership. Conversely they are watching for indications of a defective character. These are most likely to be revealed by what the candidate says, and questions are frequently posed with that in mind. For example, the questions might go something like this:

'How did you travel here this morning?'

'By train, Sir.'

'What was the number of your carriage?'

The candidate doesn't know whether to tell a lie and rattle off the first number that comes into his head knowing that it is unlikely to be proved incorrect, or to say that he doesn't know because he regards such matters as irrelevant.

There's one story which relates that an officer on the board told the candidate to turn with his back to the board and then asked:

'Now, how many members of the board have beards?'

The candidate is alleged to have replied:

'Two have got beards and one hasn't shaved this morning.'

The story doesn't relate whether he passed or failed.

In my case, I had been to the ballet a few days earlier and eventually we came round to discussing my interests. I explained that I enjoyed the theatre and that my most recent visit had been to the ballet. I then received a barrage of questions about ballet and it was painfully obvious that my knowledge of ballet was only superficial. I came out feeling like a sponge which had been wrung out to dry, and when the Chief Petty Officer in charge of administering the interviews asked me how I had fared, I explained why I hadn't done too well. He smiled sympathetically, and told me that the officer in question was married to a well known ballet dancer and obviously his knowledge of the subject was extensive.

I returned to *Triumph* and was not surprised, but nevertheless disappointed, to be told that I had not passed the Board. But I hadn't failed completely. I was offered the possibility of going for a second attempt in a year's time.

On 24 September we completed our rest and maintenance period and left harbour with Capt. James in command. We were destined yet again for flying training in the SW Approaches. Our faithful guard ship *Ulysses* had gone off to other tasks and we were due to join up with *Grenville* to take her place.

At sea, the quartermaster takes the wheel of the ship or he supervises the bo'sun's mate. When entering or leaving harbour the Chief Quartermaster usually takes the wheel. Occasionally if the Chief was unavailable or if there was a long passage in confined waters I would take his place. On this occasion when leaving Portsmouth harbour I was on the wheel. Portsmouth has a very narrow entrance with a narrow channel beyond. During our departure I nearly put the ship aground. In confined waters the ship is 'conned' by giving direct orders on how much rudder to use. The helmsman follows these instructions without question. As the ship gets into more open water the officer on the bridge orders the helmsman to steer a set course. On this occasion having been conned into the middle of the channel I was given a course to steer. As soon as the ship swung off course I put the appropriate helm on to come back on course, but the more helm I put on, the more the compass showed that we were swinging wildly the wrong way. The officer of the watch, realising that something was wrong, conned me back into the middle of the channel and again gave me a course to steer. Once again as we swung off course I did my best to correct the situation. but again I completely lost control. Eventually we realised what was wrong. An Electrical Artificer had been working on the compass repeater and had reversed the wires when he had reconnected them.

Consequently the compass card was rotating in the wrong direction. I'm sure that those watching from ashore must have thought there was a drunken helmsman at the wheel as we left harbour.

Another character in the mess at that time was a cockney leading hand called 'Chunky' Reynolds. He and I ran a 'radio' show which we broadcast over the ship's Sound Reproduction Equipment (SRE). The programme lasted half an hour and came 'on the air' once a week at dinner time (noon). It tended to highlight events of the week but to a degree poked harmless fun at a number of ship's characters. There was great apprehension amongst the officers when we started to produce the show and we had to have our scripts vetted before they could be transmitted. The ship's Master at Arms ('Jossman') was an enormous man and had a fearful reputation as a bully. When the ship's official discipline didn't suit him he took young ratings into his cabin and beat them up. He was never upbraided by any officers because that would have undermined his position. As we imitated a number of voices on our programme and rarely spoke in our normal voices he was never sure who was responsible for what he considered to be an outrage against the ship's discipline. At the time there was a popular song whose first line ran 'Rose, Rose, I love you!' The Jossman was particularly partial to bread rolls for breakfast. The ship's company had to make do with bread but he ordered the galley to bake bread rolls entirely for his own consumption. We then rewrote the song whose first line now ran 'Rolls, Rolls, I love you!' He started a witch hunt to identify the perpetrators and mistakenly settled on a young sailor who lived on our messdeck but had nothing to do with our broadcasting efforts. The poor lad took a beating although he was swearing his innocence. Chunky and I decided that it was time to stop broadcasting if people were going to take us that seriously.

As I had failed my first Admiralty Interview Board I was very keen to broaden my experience as much as possible. I had seen an article in Admiralty Fleet Orders (AFOs) inviting applicants to a two week course at Hartford College, Oxford. It was intended to give people in the services a wider knowledge of world affairs and this particular course was arranged for students to discuss the situation in South Africa. I applied for the course and to my surprise was recommended by the Captain and was allocated a place. I took the train to Oxford whilst the ship was preparing to visit Guernsey.

I was the only rating on the course and as we wore uniform I was rather conspicuous, but I did my best to hold my ground. I had only been on the course for a couple of days when a telegram arrived on 2 October saying that I had to report on board immediately at Devonport. I learnt on my way back that *Triumph's* guard ship, *Grenville*, had been in collision with an Italian merchant ship and that one rating had been killed. *Grenville* was so badly damaged that she had to be towed back to harbour.

I arrived to find *Triumph* secured to a buoy in Plymouth Sound. A Board of Enquiry assembled on board on 3 October. The next day one officer and three ratings had to report on board *Vanguard* for a second Board of Enquiry. Fortunately as I had not been on board during this incident I was able to keep well clear of any recriminations which might occur. As is so often the case our Captain, as the senior officer, took the blame. I recall that the prosecuting officer at the court martial used the phrase: 'Order, counter order, disorder.' Apparently it summed up accurately the entire train of events.

Our next duty was to act as a safety ship for HRH Princess Elizabeth when she flew across the Atlantic with her husband the Duke of Edinburgh. King George VI was scheduled to make a Royal tour of Canada but he was suffering from a blood clot in his foot and he required a major lung operation. Instead of cancelling the tour, Princess Elizabeth and the Duke of Edinburgh took the King's place.

This was the first time that a royal tour had used aircraft to cross the Atlantic in preference to a sea passage. As a result, careful preparations were made in case the flight got into difficulties.

We sailed from Plymouth for our station on Friday 5 October. The sea was calm with light winds and a sunny sky. The newspapers had reported on our preparations for departure. They credited us with having all the latest search and rescue equipment on board when, in fact, we had only one ill-equipped helicopter. The next day was dull with rough seas and towards the end of the day the port sea boat was washed away. The next day was calm and sunny with light winds and we thought that the worst had passed, but the weather forecasters ashore diverted the route of the royal aircraft off its programmed track to make for Reykjavik and then to Goose Bay. On Monday 8th, the day of the flight, the barometer dropped 50 millibars within $1^1/_2$ hours. The wind rose steadily up to 100 knots with very rough seas. We were desperately trying to head northwards to get underneath the new aircraft track. I spent the early hours of the morning going round the ship with the Commander, Horace Law, trying to secure loose fittings to prevent them doing further damage. The booms which were used to secure the boats in harbour were swinging wildly and beating rhythmically against the ship's side each time we rolled. We could do little but report the damage to the bridge as it occurred with no hope of relieving the situation. As the ship made its way northwards the bows rose high above the waves and then pitched into them sending a volume of water rolling along the flight deck as far as the bridge superstructure. Down below, steel girders supporting the decks above were visibly twisting and all loose gear was being smashed to pieces as it slid from one side of the ship to the other. Inevitably some water had got below onto the messdecks and was sloshing to and fro. It was certainly the worst weather at sea that I had experienced.

As the Royal Flight passed our nearest point we were still a hundred miles from it, and shortly afterwards we received the signal releasing us from our duties. In due course we heard that Princess Elizabeth and the Duke of Edinburgh had arrived safely.

On the way back to harbour we received a message, relayed through the Admiralty: From Her Royal Highness: 'My husband and I would be grateful if you would convey our appreciation to all ships stationed in the Atlantic during our flight to Canada.'

By now we had no serviceable boats on board and we were ordered to Belfast to sort ourselves out and to take new boats on board. We weren't given very long because by 10 October we were back to our flying training duties. As we had lost *Grenville* our new guard ship was *Wizard*.

We soon settled down again to the routine of flying training and spending the nights at anchor in Bangor Bay.

We had a bad day on the 15th. One of the aircraft had a defect but the pilot was able to make it to the shore base at Sydenham. Then an aircraft crashed over the side and the pilot was lost, and finally there was a crash on deck but the pilot was unhurt. We anchored in Bangor Bay and held the inevitable Board of Enquiry into the day's tragic events. We then weighed and proceeded to Plymouth.

On 19 October, British troops seized the Suez Canal in a swift dawn raid. It was revealed that some British troops had landed by parachute two nights earlier. Britain had offered a Middle East pact backed by France, Turkey and the US which would include Egypt in a five nation defence organisation. Egypt would in due course hand over her base to the new organisation. Egypt rejected this olive branch. As a result four British warships entered Port Said on 21 October and more British troops were heading for the Canal Zone.

Our flying training continued until we were ordered to return to Portsmouth. There we soon discovered that we were to take another contingent of soldiers to Cyprus. The dockyard hurriedly replaced all the fittings which we had on board during the previous trip and we commenced embarking the advance party of Army personnel on 2 November at the same time that more British troops were being flown into the Suez Canal Zone. During the next two days we embarked a contingent of the Royal Inniskilling Fusiliers complete with their mascot and their colours. We sailed on the 5th and arrived without incident on the 12th and anchored at Famagusta. *Illustrious* was there on arrival but sailed soon after. There was no shore leave given that night. I never discovered whether that was because of the behaviour of those ashore during our previous visit or whether it was because the political situation was so tense. The disembarkation of the soldiers and their vehicles commenced immediately. On 14 November General Stockwell, the Senior Army Officer on the island, came on board, presumably to thank the Captain for getting the men out speedily and safely. As soon as he departed we weighed anchor and sailed for Port Said.

Most sailors have a yearning to obtain a medal of some sort, even if it is only the Naval General Service Medal. It had been given to those operating in the Cyprus area until just before I arrived to join *Troubridge* in December 1948. We thought we might get an opportunity this time as we were on the brink of war. But that was not to be.

On arrival at Port Said on the morning of the 15th we secured to head and stern buoys. The cruiser *Gambia* was also in harbour. I don't know whether we obtained diplomatic clearance to enter harbour. I presume that the British thought they had a right to enter. Nevertheless we took particular care to make sure we weren't vulnerable to attack. We assumed Security State 2 which meant patrol boats constantly going round the ship looking for frogmen or other means of attacking the ship, and security sentries stood guard on the upper deck. Mere sailors were never told the purpose of our visit, but we sailed in the evening for Portsmouth. Alas, our hopes for a medal were thwarted once again. We arrived at Portsmouth on the 23rd, and after two days in harbour we were back to our flying training programme off the Devon and Cornish coasts.

On 29 November we made passage northward through the Irish Sea. On Saturday 1 December I had a memorable 20th birthday party run ashore. There was a very good train service from Bangor to Belfast. I rarely went ashore but on this occasion, as it had been my 20th birthday three nights before, a few friends and I decided to see the city's attractions. Our first task was to find a place to stay and we found a Bed & Breakfast not too far from the city centre. There was a very good theatre in the form of the Belfast Opera House. Its name belied the fact that it was a variety theatre. The star attraction that night was Joe Loss and his orchestra. He introduced an Irish vocalist whom he had just engaged, called Rose Brennan. She rose to become an international star. After the show we had 'big eats' and then considerably more alcohol than was good for us. I recall turning in at our lodgings. Our landlady had thoughtfully put a stone hot water bottle in our beds, but at that time in the morning mine was stone cold. I found it very difficult to get up after a couple of hours' sleep and we missed our train. We arrived at Bangor as the ship was weighing anchor but fortunately one of the boat's coxswains had loitered off the jetty with his boat and he rescued me and my shore-going chums just in time to get us back on board and we avoided the Commander's defaulters table.

On 13 December we flew off 736 and 738 Squadrons and proceeded to Portsmouth for Christmas leave arriving on 18 December. Unfortunately I wouldn't be having Christmas leave that year because I was under punishment. This resulted from a situation which was quite ridiculous and which demonstrated my unwillingness to give way when I was convinced that I was right. Next to our messdeck, which was quite open, was a Chief Petty Officers' mess which was enclosed. The CPOs were therefore quite comfortable even in the coldest weather. The access to the upper deck above us was a large hatch about 5 ft. by 3 ft. This was intended for loading stores and bulky pieces of equipment. Within the large hatch was a smaller hatch. If the large hatch was closed and the small hatch open there was sufficient room for a person to pass through it. That was its very purpose. This combination made our mess much less draughty. But the senior CPO wanted the hatch open at all times 'so that he could escape in the event of the ship sinking'. The conflict between my mess and that of the CPOs ran for some time but followed the usual naval procedure that we 'always obeyed the last order'. When the CPO ordered me to open the hatch I obeyed, but I would then go to the Officer of the Watch and ask permission to shut the hatch. On receiving his permission I complied. As soon as the CPO found the hatch was shut he would order me to open it, and although I obeyed his order, the procedure of approaching the Officer of the Watch started once more. In due course the CPO charged me with disobeying an order. When I appeared in front of the Commander, Horace Law, we both told our stories. The Commander was put in the awkward position of deciding whether to support me or the CPO. As was customary in the Service, a mere Leading Seaman couldn't be seen to get the better of a CPO, so I was found guilty of disobeying a senior rating's order and was sentenced to fourteen days stoppage of leave. My mother, who didn't have much money, came down by train to visit me on Christmas Day when I was one of the few people left on board. At midnight on New Year's Eve I obtained permission to go ashore to the Dockyard Church to take Holy Communion. I found myself in a pew sitting next to the Commander. We didn't exchange seasonal greetings although I did wonder what he was thinking.

CHAPTER 6

My second year in *Triumph* – 1952

For *Triumph* the boring but important life of training naval aviators continued. We were back at sea on 21 January with the ship's flight on board. We made our way to the northern Irish Sea with *Zest* as our guard ship. As well as experiencing frequent flying accidents we also had a problem at one point with one of our cutters which had gone aground in Bangor Harbour. A salvage party was sent ashore to recover it. Fortunately I wasn't the Coxswain at the time.

On 12 February Sub Lieutenant Lentaigne left the ship. He had been in charge of the boat parties and in that respect was our boss. One of the dodges that we in the boat's crews would get up to when he was in charge was to get one of the junior ratings to lock us inside the boat equipment locker on the upper deck. In this way anyone looking for us would see that the locker was locked and go and look for us elsewhere. It was a safe place to kip ('snooze') or play cards although if a fire had broken out it is unlikely that anyone would have rescued us. We thought that this was a well kept secret until one day Sub Lt. Lentaigne asked to be locked inside with us as he was in need of some respite. We were not sure whether Sub Lt. Lentaigne's successor, Lt. D.J. Wright, was equally amenable and we sought other places to make ourselves unavailable.

We resumed our flying training in the SW Approaches with *Ulysses* initially acting as guard ship and then replaced by *Zest*. We returned to Portsmouth on 29 February where we were due to be docked for maintenance.

We undocked on 18 April and moved out to anchorage at Spithead on the 28th for a short period before weighing anchor and taking passage to the northern Irish Sea with *Zest* in company.

We remained operating off Bangor until 8 May and then moved south to the SW Approaches.

This period of flying in *Triumph* was marred by a number of crashes, one of them resulting in the death of the pilot.

The next day I had completed a full year as an acting Leading Seaman and was confirmed as Leading Seaman. Fortunately the punishment which I had endured over the previous Christmas period appeared to have been ignored. I had an increase of pay of 6 pence per day.

A run ashore in Guernsey – Bryan second from right rear.

This unhappy period of flying training concluded and we proceeded to anchor off St. Peter Port, Guernsey for a short spell of relaxation.

As soon as we were at anchor and everything was made ship-shape the Captain prepared to call on His Excellency the Governor, Sir Philip Neame VC, and the Bailiff.

Tim Durlacher's job was to drive the Captain's motor boat, usually the fastest boat in the ship, and Tim had the necessary panache to make quite an impression as he swept alongside, stopping at the precise place for the Captain to disembark. I only recall him making a mistake once, and that was during this trip to Guernsey. The Captain's first duty would be to call on the Governor and as we were at anchor he needed to be taken ashore in his motor boat. The boat had just left the gangway with the Captain wearing his Number Ones (best uniform). Unfortunately Tim didn't swing out away from the ship quickly enough and with the wind on his starboard side he ran all down the ship's side at a distance of a few feet. He passed under all the heads and bathroom outlets and an amount of the discharged waste was deposited all over the Captain. Pandemonium broke loose as soon as the Captain hurriedly returned on board so that he could be cleansed and shifted into his second best uniform in time to make his appointment with the Governor. We presumed that the call was a success as HE the Governor returned it and came on board for lunch. He was entitled to, and received, a 17-Gun salute.

Tim Durlacher was hoping to become an officer via the Upper Yardman scheme but hadn't yet acquired a sufficient number of HET passes, but he saw his chance when a new scheme for recruiting pilots from the lower deck was announced which would lead to a commission in the Fleet Air Arm. Tim had the three subjects in HET that were required and after passing the selection board he went off to do his flying aptitude test. Unfortunately he discovered that he had sinus trouble and left the Service. I haven't seen him since our *Triumph* days, but a year or two later I was idly leafing through a copy of the *Tatler* in a dental surgery when I saw a photo of him standing on the steps of a large country mansion with a caption which read: 'Mr Timothy Durlacher exchanges a joke with the Earl of Derby.'

We were off to sea again on 4 June and did a short trial with a Vampire landing and taking off. This was our first experience of handling jet aircraft. We then went into Portsmouth for the week-end but were off to sea again on 9 June. We experienced one particularly difficult crash on deck with the aircraft hanging precariously on the edge of a sponson with the after W/T mast holding it in position. We managed to extricate the pilot who was trapped but the aircraft was ditched over the side.

On 14 June we received a report that an airliner had ditched off Le Havre. *Zest* was detached at best speed to go to its assistance.

It was also on 14 June that the USS *Nautilus* was launched, the world's first atomic powered submarine.

We then commenced a passage to Antwerp for an official visit. As we approached the Belgian coast on 16 June, pilotage became particularly difficult. The area was still littered with wrecks left there since the war, but more particular was the problem of the countless number of mines which still remained. Channels had been swept through these minefields and were marked by buoys, but it was easy to lose one's way with so many hazards to avoid.

We made our approach to Antwerp during the hours of darkness taking our first pilot on board to make the approach, receiving him off Flushing to take us up the Schelde. I was nominated to relieve the chief quartermaster on the helm during the last stages of our passage upriver. To make sure that everything would go smoothly an electrical artificer came up to the wheelhouse to check over the gyro repeaters. In the meantime we steered by magnetic. After he finished this check he went below and we started steering by gyro. It was unbelievable that he had repeated the mistake which had been made earlier when leaving Portsmouth harbour and had connected the wires to the wrong terminals. Once again the ship was weaving wildly from one side of the channel to the other until we sorted the situation out.

Eventually we arrived alongside at 0900. *Zest* had accompanied us. This was the first visit to Antwerp by a major warship since the war and much importance was attached to it. The Captain first made his calls, then a wreath laying ceremony was conducted at the war memorial. A guard had been training during our passage and its members accompanied the Captain and other officers for this ceremony. Although I had been up most of the night I was appointed as quartermaster on the gangway for the forenoon watch. As afternoon approached all the VIPs returned the Captain's calls. These included the British Naval Attaché, the Ambassador, the General Officer Commanding Antwerp, the Area Burgomaster and the Governor of the Province This was a tense period. We had to decide the appropriate way to greet them. Did they warrant a pipe, a bugle call, or what? At one point a man came up the gangway wearing a rather scruffy uniform and cap. I had no idea what he was entitled to, so to be on the safe side I piped him over the side. He laughed as he came on board and explained that he was the Chaplain to the Missions to Seamen. Anyway, no harm was done.

We left Antwerp on 19 June and crossed the North Sea to visit Sheerness. As *Triumph* was a Chatham ship this was a welcome visit, giving members of the ship's company who lived locally an opportunity for a night at home.

After visiting Sheerness we moved back to Portsmouth where we stayed until 1 July when we took passage to the Bangor area with *Zest* in company. This was an important date because on 1 January and 1 July each year the Admiralty broadcast its promotion signal. All the officers of Lieutenant Commander and above who were in the zone for promotion would be waiting anxiously to see if they had been selected for advancement. On this occasion Cdr. Law was selected for promotion to Captain. The promotion was immediate and obviously he would not be able to stay in his present post in his new rank.

We stayed in the Bangor area until 10 July with only one crash occurring. We made our passage to the Portland area. On 14 July we said goodbye to *Zest,* our faithful guard ship, and welcomed *Wilton* as her replacement.

On 22 June I appeared in front of a Board which passed me professionally for Petty Officer, but I would have to wait for a vacancy to occur before attaining that rate.

I kept a number of watches as quartermaster with Lt. Peter Tostevin. The quartermaster's job in harbour was to run the ship's routine supervised by the Officer of the Day. Quartermasters came to know these officers quite well.

Lt. Tostevin, who was an ex-upper yardman, was quite amoral. During his period of duty he was responsible for the safety of the ship including prevention of theft. A Royal Marine did duty as keyboard sentry. When Lt. Tostevin was on duty, he would order the quartermaster to draw the keys for the officers' galley in order to take food, and if there was none in the galley we were told to raid the store rooms. He had a particular liking for a mixed grill, but we were all expected to share in the spoils and were therefore equally culpable. It was particularly unpleasant going into the cockroach infested galley at night. Whenever I raided the galley I was always in fear of being caught by the Commander. However, Tostevin came to a sticky end before I was caught.

The Motor Fishing Vessel (MFV), which was attached to the ship, assisted in landing libertymen when *Triumph* was at anchor. The MFV followed the ship from port to port. As an ex-seaman, Tostevin, who by now had become a Lieutenant Commander, skippered the MFV. Whilst he was making the voyage from Torbay to Portsmouth conditions were foggy and the MFV ran aground on Chesil Beach. Communication was lost and a frantic search was mounted. The MFV was ultimately found high and dry on the beach with no one on board. At the Court Martial which followed, the excuse offered was that Tostevin had sent a rating ashore to find out where they were. The sailor found a pub so he had stopped for a 'quickie'. As he didn't return to the ship, Tostevin sent a senior rate ashore who also took liquid refuge in the pub. This happened in turn until Tostevin went ashore to investigate. The Court Martial paid little heed to his story because the naval search party reported that he, too, had a drink in his hand when found.

We arrived at Portsmouth on 25 August for the summer leave period. I had now served my year since failing my previous Admiralty Interview Board. I was told that after my leave I would be going to Dartmouth for a second attempt.

The President of the Board was a captain with a number of commanders assisting him. There was also a psychologist serving as a full member of the board. I always believe that I passed this board by a stroke of luck. The psychologist asked me what my hobbies were. I wasn't going to be caught out this time and get involved in a long discussion on ballet.

'Reading, Sir,' I answered.

'What was the last book you read?' he asked.

'Here we go again,' I thought, but answered truthfully, '*The Colditz Story*,' thinking to myself, I'm glad it's still fresh in my mind.

'Who wrote it?' he persisted.

'P.R. Reid, Sir.'

And then he became entirely informal and he chatted to me about 'Pat' Reid. He revealed how they had been at school together and they had been great chums. All formality disappeared and I became totally relaxed. Then another curious coincidence came to light.

'I see you went to Hampton Grammar School,' he said.

'Yes,' I replied.

'What do you know about the Lady Eleanor Holles School?' he asked.

I explained that it was situated next to my old school and that we had a master called 'Jammie' James who was very keen that we should all learn ballroom dancing. He arranged joint dancing lessons between the boys and girls from the two schools. This was the only approved fraternisation between the two schools. Apart from that we were caned if we were caught within ten feet of the dividing chain link fence.

The psychologist explained that his wife was an old girl of the school and this seemed to cement our relationship.

But the interviews were not the only hurdles which we had to negotiate. After these we moved to the gym where we undertook a number of 'command' tasks. In turn, we were each put in charge of a group of about five fellow candidates with which to achieve a given task. An example would be to be shown two parallel chalk lines on the floor about twelve feet apart and be told that these marked the edges of a bottomless pit. We would be given two lengths of rope, a plank of wood ten feet long and a fifty gallon oil drum. We would be gathered on one side and told that our task was to get all the people and the equipment across the chasm without mishap. Some of the tasks were almost impossible, but the board members were more interested to see how we controlled men and whether we kept a cool head rather than whether we completed the task. Members of each team were also watched to see how well they worked with others. I had three attempts at my task and failed each time.

Another candidate was given a task involving ropes suspended from the ceiling. Somehow he managed to get himself upside down at the top of a rope suspended only by his legs. Eventually he could support himself no longer with his legs and he slid slowly head first down the rope until he banged his head on the imaginary minefield below, but the floor was hard enough anyway. He lay there exhausted for a moment. When he stood up, his comment was: 'I'm doing all this to become a sub-lieutenant. I think they ought to make me a f***ing admiral.' He caught the next train out of Dartmouth.

Our visit to Dartmouth ran over the weekend and we were invited to go beagling on the Saturday. We weren't familiar with this activity and fell into the trap of attempting to follow the beagles. After we had exhausted ourselves we noted that the more experienced followers went to the top of the nearest hill to monitor the chase. They remained there until it was time to move across to the next hill. But while we were chasing along after the beagles we came across a closed farm gate with a dishevelled fellow standing by it. As each individual approached he kindly opened the gate. After I passed through I thanked him. It was only after I had gone on a little further that I realised that it was the President of the Board. We were still being closely observed!

Eventually the board completed its deliberations and the members retired to make its decisions. After some time we were called in individually and I was relieved to hear that I had passed, but I had to return to *Triumph* to await being called for training.

As soon as the leave period was over we left Portsmouth and started a further flying training programme. On the first day of flying one of our aircraft ditched into the sea some miles away. We turned towards and increased speed but fortunately the M/V *British Diligence* was nearby and was able to take the pilot on board and reported him fit and well. He was an RAF Pilot Officer who was on exchange duty.

We spent a few days in the Irish Sea before making for the Clyde estuary to assemble for Exercise Mainbrace. It was the first major exercise in which we had participated and began on 12 September.

The exercise gave us a much better understanding of a wartime carrier's role. All the pilots on board were experienced and we had far fewer accidents. Our only serious accident was on the 13th when a Naval Airman got his leg trapped in the after lift causing him serious injuries. We exercised to the north of Scotland. As one of the major ships in the exercise we were subject to frequent attack from Sea Hornets and other jet aircraft which our propeller driven aircraft were unable to match in aerial combat. Once more we found ourselves battling against heavy weather. On the 18th we were struggling through a Force 8 gale but on the 19th we were released from the exercise and made our way towards Rosyth.

CHAPTER 7

Upper Yardman Training,
HMS *Hawke* 1952-53

WHEN WE ARRIVED at Rosyth on the 20th, there was a 'draft note' waiting for me and I was ordered to proceed to Victoria Barracks in Portsmouth for Upper Yardman training. At the barracks I met up with a group of seamen who came from different ships but who had all got to the same stage as me in their quest to become an officer. We had to undertake a four month preparation course before moving to Dartmouth for our final year's training. We were now Upper Yardmen as opposed to being CW candidates. We had to wear a white flash on our shoulders to make us more distinctive so that the officers could monitor our every move. We also lived in our own mess.

Victoria Barracks was a typical barrack block of the time with no central heating and an inadequate boiler to heat the water for washing. There was a cast iron cylindrical coal burning stove at one end of the room. We were rationed to one bucket of coal per day. If we tried to eke out the coal it would burn inefficiently and fill the mess with smoke. We preferred to burn it quickly and generate heat for a short time whilst putting our mugs on top to get enough water for a decent shave.

Our training was almost entirely academic but there were diversions to broaden our minds and to give us a greater understanding of activities outside the RN. The officer in charge of us was Lt. Basil Mosenthal.

On one occasion we were given a talk on the magistracy and then taken to Portsmouth Magistrates Court to witness the Court in action. By chance we heard the case of an ex sailor who had allegedly stolen a bicycle. The annual conduct assessment system in the RN has five levels: V.G., Good, Fair, Indifferent and Bad. There was a further assessment of V.G.* for those who had only transgressed once during the year.

The case started with an explanation from the police, then the person who was originally in possession of the bicycle told his story, and then the alleged offender explained his position. As he put his side of the story he explained that when he came into possession of the bike he understood it was 'hot'. The chairman of the magistrates stopped him and asked him to explain what 'hot' meant. We found this rather amusing. Having listened to all the evidence the magistrates found him guilty but noted from his service records that he had been discharged from the Navy with a 'Fair' character. The magistrate observed that it was obvious that he had been highly thought of in the Navy and so he was discharged with a warning. Little did the magistrate understand what you needed to do to be discharged with a 'Fair' character.

On another occasion it was decided that we would all be put through an initiative test. A variety of tasks were placed individually in envelopes which we drew out of a hat. My task was to obtain the signature of someone who had been awarded the Victoria Cross. I knew that my old Captain of *Forth*, Tony Miers, was now the Captain of the Royal Naval College at Greenwich but felt that I should attempt to obtain a signature which presented a greater challenge. I knew that there was a Brigadier Smyth who was a member of the House of Commons. Having obtained his address from *Who's Who* in the library I set off for Dolphin Square, Westminster, to seek him out. Unfortunately when I arrived at his apartment there was no reply to the doorbell. Somewhat reluctantly I decided to go to Greenwich. Knowing of Miers' reputation I knew that he might set me a task before giving me his signature. He might be in the mood for a scrap and I knew that I wouldn't be a match for him. Fortunately when I arrived he was at his desk. I was shown in by his secretary and was offered a glass of beer. After a short chat he gave me a note which said: 'This rating has behaved entirely satisfactorily whilst speaking to me and I have no hesitation in giving him my signature.' He then signed it. I set off back to Portsmouth with much relief.

Victoria Barracks also housed National Servicemen who were doing their initial training. The Upper Yardmen had the responsibility of looking after them out of working hours in order to guide them along the right path of Naval ways. We did rounds of their messdecks at 2100 after they had cleaned through. On one occasion one recruit complained to an officer one morning after I had told him that the messdeck was unsatisfactory. He explained to the officer that he wasn't going to have another seaman telling him what to do. He soon learnt!

We left the barracks and went on Christmas leave before reporting to HMS *Hawke* at Dartmouth on 26 January 1953 for the Upper Yardmen's Course which would last a year.

Hawke was in the grounds of the Britannia Royal Naval College but we lived 'down the hill' from the main college building in a small establishment commissioned as HMS *Hawke*. A group of seamen started their course each term and alternately each term we were joined by a group of electricians, engineers or supply ratings whose course only lasted for one term. Totally at any one time we numbered about thirty with a staff of officers of about six. We lived in the wardroom as officers although we still wore ratings' uniform with the distinguishing white shoulder flash. Our CO was Cdr. L.R. Lawford, the Executive Officer Lt. Cdr. George Cussins DSC, and a third Seaman Officer Lt. R.A. Stephens. The Instructor Officers ('Schoolies') were Lt. Cdr. H.C. Malkin, Lt. Peter Brown and Lt. Robin Budgen.

Our routine was rather like being back at school. We mustered in the morning for divisions and prayers which we took in turns, The colours ceremony followed and we then went to instruction for the forenoon. The subjects comprised Mathematics, Mechanics, Electricity, English, History, Geography and Navigation.

We played sport every afternoon and had instruction again in the evening until about seven, when we were allowed ashore. There were some very good hostelries in the area.

We had the use of all the sporting facilities at the college, but mainly played rugby and cricket. Our fixture list for these two sports took us right across the southern half of Devon. I have never been good at sports but I was occasionally picked for the rugby team and at other times was a touch judge. I never made it into the cricket team but acted as umpire throughout the season.

There was also a very good fleet of boats at Dartmouth to which we had access. As well as using them for recreational purposes, we also used the larger offshore picket boats to learn and practise manoeuvring and station keeping by flag hoists. Although radios were coming into play for this purpose in the Navy, the flag hoists had the advantage that manoeuvres could be carried out without breaking radio silence.

Great emphasis was placed on ensuring that we had the ability to express ourselves orally and in writing. To this end we had to keep a journal. Each day we had to write an article. We could choose any subject we liked, but the writings were scrutinised meticulously and any errors were pointed out.

Without doubt, the main event during our year at Dartmouth was the Coronation of Queen Elizabeth II. King George had died on 6 February of the previous year, and the massive organisation necessary to plan a coronation swung into action.

We were appointed as the First Platoon of the First Battalion of the Naval party. We trained initially as a platoon at *Hawke*. Our orders were written down meticulously and included every detail. Each man was issued with a new pair of boots. A diagram showed how the studs were to be placed in the soles and we were told on which days we were to wear the boots and for how long. The purpose was to ensure that our boots would be comfortable on Coronation Day but would not have lost any of their newness. We naturally spent many evening hours developing a good shine. At the same time, programmes of physical exercises were distributed to bring us to a high state of fitness. Those of us, like myself, who followed the instructions to the letter were extremely fit on the day.

Our CO, Commander Lawford, was to be the platoon commander and as such would carry a drawn sword for long periods. Platoon officers were advised to strengthen their forearms and practise carrying the sword. This was because the forearm has to be extended horizontally forward from the body and the sword held pointing vertically upward. Commander Lawford spent some time each day walking through the Devon lanes carrying his walking stick as though it were a sword 'at the carry'. On one occasion he met a lady walking towards him who assumed he was threatening her and reported the incident to the police. Thereafter he had to confine himself to the college grounds lest he get a reputation as a deranged man threatening the local populace with his walking stick.

We were told that we would be in The Mall lining the route of the Coronation procession. A number of phenomena about this role were explained against which we were advised to take precautions. First, it was explained that blood circulation is affected when one stands still for long periods which might lead to fainting. To ward against this we had to 'waggle' our toes from time to time and also to flex and relax our fingers without, of course, making this apparent to the civilians who would be thronging the route.

We were also told of the difficulties which affect the balance if you watch a stream of traffic, such as a procession, going in one direction for a long time. Once the procession has passed the people standing on the opposite side of the road appear to be moving in the opposite direction to the procession. If one isn't prepared for this one can become completely unbalanced and fall over.

We also received a communication that each platoon would be allocated two Coronation medals between them and we decided to draw names out of a hat to decide the lucky recipients. Jim Lucas' name came out first, and mine followed.

Several days before the Coronation we moved to Plymouth and lived in the Royal Naval Engineering College at Manadon. After practising at battalion strength on the parade ground at Plymouth barracks we then moved on to London.

In London we lived in the old air raid shelters which were still available at

Clapham South underground station. The whole of Clapham Common was marked out with white tape to represent the streets of central London and we were able to have two rehearsals as though we were in our proper places. This was not easy because we were marching on grass which makes it difficult to get a good marching rhythm. During the last rehearsal the First Sea Lord inspected us with the usual entourage of senior officers. The First Sea Lord at the time was Admiral of the Fleet Sir Roderick MacGregor who was quite short. He appeared to be about five feet two inches tall. The lacing on his sleeve comprised one thick stripe with four stripes above that, and the uppermost stripe had a curl above that which reached well up to his elbow. As he walked past I distinctly heard a sailor behind me mutter: 'Who's that funny little man with the yellow sleeves?' We did our best to contain our laughter and fortunately the Admiral chose not to hear.

It was during our occupation of Clapham South tube station that we were instructed when we should have our last alcoholic drink before the event. Additionally we were told not to have any sexual experience within forty eight hours of the great day. My girl friend at the time often met me in the evenings so that we could go into central London and see the sights. On the evening just before the cut-off period she stood waiting for me at the station entrance. Almost every sailor who came out of the station accosted her. It seemed that they had misconstrued her reason for waiting at the station entrance and also the orders which they had assumed to mean that they were obliged to have a sexual experience forty eight hours before the Coronation.

On the great day, 2 June, we were up at the crack of dawn and were in our London Transport hired buses by 0530 to take us to the Embankment. From there we marched up Northumberland Avenue, across Trafalgar Square, under Admiralty Arch and into our positions for lining The Mall. It was a miserable day, drizzling for most of the time, but we were trained to the peak of fitness and had no difficulty in staying properly at our posts whilst the processions went to Westminster Abbey.

To add to the excitement of the day the newspaper billboards declared that Everest had been conquered, being scaled by Edmund Hilary and Sherpa Tensing.

We remained lining the street during the Coronation Service until it was over and the processions returned to Buckingham Palace. By the time we got back to Clapham we were exhausted but exhilarated. Everything had gone to plan. But the order 'Splice the Mainbrace' had been given by Her Majesty and so we were rejuvenated by our normal daily 'tot' complemented by another. After getting out of our sodden uniform, Tony Mitchell and I went off to St.

George's hospital to chat to the patients. We told ourselves that we were doing charitable works but Tony's acquaintanceship with one of the nurses appeared to have had some bearing on the chosen venue.

The rain had caused all the white blanco to run into our best, Number One, uniforms and we were told initially that we would be issued with new uniforms to replace them, but eventually we were all given £2 and told to get them cleaned.

We only returned to Hawke for a short time because the Coronation was to be followed by a Fleet Review at Spithead. Everyone at Dartmouth, both the cadets and the upper yardmen, were to proceed by special train to Portsmouth to embark on board the aircraft carrier *Implacable* from which we would witness the Fleet review.

The 32,110 ton *Implacable* was large enough to absorb the complete train load from Dartmouth as well as a large number of cadets from Pangbourne. There were slight problems with the catering arrangements. The dress of the Dartmouth cadets was almost identical to that of the cadets from Pangbourne. The Dartmouth cadets were supposed to have first sitting for meals followed by the Pangbourne boys. Many of the Dartmouth Cadets went round twice leaving the Pangbourne cadets without food, causing a great deal of consternation among the ship's caterers.

There were one or two other amusing incidents which made our visit worthwhile. At a Fleet review there is usually an event known as 'cheer ship'. It is all done to a precise routine. Officers and men remove their caps, and holding them up in the air with the top facing outboard they give three cheers whilst making a circular motion with the cap. As this isn't done very often it usually leads to a number of explanatory signals until everybody is working together. For example there is inevitable discussion whether the circular motion should be clockwise or anti-clockwise. Then it has to be decided whether we all shout 'Hooray' or 'Hoorah'. The steam past went well and in the evening there was a massive firework display. The next day the party was over and we boarded our special train to return to Dartmouth and to work.

At the end of each term at *Hawke* we had a passing out parade for those who had completed their training and who were to be promoted to acting sub lieutenant. At the end of my second term there, the Admiral Superintendent, Devonport Dockyard, Vice Admiral Sir Philip Enright KBE CB was due to take the passing out parade. He was an ex-Boy Seaman. A message was received that his Royal Marine driver didn't know his way around the college and that some directions would be helpful. At this time I rode a BSA Bantam 125 cc motor cycle and it was arranged that I would meet the Admiral's car at the westernmost gate of the college grounds and lead it down the hill to HMS *Hawke* where the commanding officer and the assembled ship's company would be waiting. The car was a few minutes late but stopped at the gate. I approached the driver to tell him where to stop when we arrived at *Hawke* but the Admiral was impatient and said, 'We know, we know. Get on with it!' So I mounted my bike and moved off. I led the car through the college grounds and down the hill to the waiting line of officers. I gave the recognised hand signal for slowing down with the intention that the car would stop at what seemed to be the obvious point. We even had a rating standing by to open the car door for the Admiral. I then accelerated to get clear of the parade and ran about two hundred yards down the road, and turned left into an area behind the galley which wasn't too tidy with a collection of refuse bins. I dismounted thinking that I'd done a good job, took off my crash helmet, turned round and found the car still behind me containing a very cross Admiral and a puzzled Royal Marine driver. Neither of them were amused to arrive eventually at a formal inspection in reverse gear.

Although I was concentrating on becoming an officer, my career as a rating was still in progress. On 27 November, my 22nd birthday, I had completed four years 'man's time' and was awarded my first Good Conduct Badge. Then, only two weeks before I hoped to be commissioned, my name came to the top of the roster of those waiting to be promoted to Petty Officer and I was duly promoted. My pay rose to 16*s*. 6*d*. a day (£301 per annum)

The final examination at *Hawke* was entirely written. Having been told that we had passed we had a few days before the passing-out ceremony. My mother was able to come down for the ceremony and the dinner and dance which we gave in the evening. We were allowed to wear our officers' uniform for the dance although we wouldn't be commissioned officially until 1 January 1964. We spent most of the afternoon before the dance discovering how to tie a bow tie.

After the dance we were sent on Christmas leave and told to wait at home for our appointments to arrive by post. We knew that we would all be posted to a destroyer or small ship for four months, after which we would be appointed to the Royal Naval College, Greenwich for two terms to undertake the Junior Officers' War Course. Those who qualified with me were Horace Caisley, George Claydon, George Kemp, Paddy Lake, Tony Mitchell and Mike Sorsbie.

CHAPTER 8

HMS *Crossbow* 1954

O N THE MORNING of New Year's eve I received a telegram saying that I was to report on board HMS *Crossbow* immediately. This sounded exciting. I couldn't imagine that the Navy would send for me in such haste unless there was a crisis brewing and so I hurriedly got my things together and went straight off to Chatham. My mother was still living in Hampton Hill just outside London and so I travelled by train and took a taxi from Gillingham station and was making my way on board *Crossbow* within about four hours. When I found *Crossbow* at her dockside berth she certainly didn't look as if she was making preparations to go to sea. On my arrival, there was considerable activity and before my kit was unloaded from the taxi a baggage party arrived on the jetty and officers appeared on the quarterdeck. I left my kit in the care of the baggage party and I was received on board.

Before I could say anything, the Officer of the Day enquired, 'You must be the new First Lieutenant, Sir?'

'No. I'm acting Sub Lieutenant Smalley,' I responded.

With that, all the deference being shown by the reception party vanished and I thought for a moment that I would have to go back over the ship's side to collect my kit. As there was obviously some confusion I took out the telegram which had ordered me to report on board which was passed around with some puzzlement. It appeared that the ship was completing a maintenance period and wouldn't be ready to leave the dockyard for another two weeks at least. After that the ship would first go to Portland for a work-up and then join the Home Fleet on its Spring cruise to Gibraltar. My expectations of excitement were shattered.

There was nowhere for me to sleep on board. I was told that the present acting Sub, Mike Ortmans, would be leaving the ship shortly to join the RN College at Greenwich and as he was in London for the night I was told to use his bunk. I learned that Mike Ortmans was a term ahead of me.

I was told that the officers were going to have a light supper on board and then they were going to the Naval barracks where the New Year's Eve Ball was being held. They suggested that I should put on my mess undress and join them at the ball even though they were still extremely apprehensive about my presence, as the only authority I had for being on board was a telegram which by now had become rather crumpled. This put me in something of a predicament. I was aware that I hadn't paid for a ticket to the ball and technically I was still only a Petty Officer until midnight. I felt rather like Cinderella in reverse. In the end I took the bull by the horns and went to the ball and had a thoroughly enjoyable time.

I hadn't been at the ball very long before I was approached by a Shipwright Lieutenant who had brought his wife and his unmarried daughter with him and he was pleased to find a partner for her. It was a memorable transition from rating to officer.

After the ball was over we returned to the ship. Goodness knows what time it was, but I had already been allocated a bunk and soon fell soundly asleep. I was in the deepest of sleeps when I was shaken violently by a rather angry Mike Ortmans who had driven back from London expecting to find a bed to fall into, but instead had found an unknown body snoring away peacefully. He claimed his bunk and I spent the rest of the night in an armchair.

My promotion to Petty Officer a few weeks before being promoted to acting Sub Lieutenant led to an interesting situation regarding my pay. An acting Sub Lieutenant's pay was 15s.6d. a day (£283 a year). As a Petty Officer I received 16s.6d. a day (£301 per annum). Therefore my pay might have decreased on promotion, but there is an overriding rule that a person being promoted cannot suffer a pay loss, so I kept my pay as a Petty Officer for the time being. This gave me one shilling a day more.

My contemporary Upper Yardmen and I had now joined up with the other acting Sub Lieutenants of the same seniority who had joined directly through Dartmouth at the age of sixteen. After each of us had gained four months' experience in a small ship we would then meet up at Greenwich.

Crossbow was a Weapons Class Destroyer attached to the 6th Destroyer Squadron. She was armed and equipped as a fleet anti-submarine escort. There should have been a good number in the class but the last 16 were cancelled at the end of the war. Her armament comprised 4 x 4" guns in twin mountings on 'A' and 'B' turrets, 6 x 49 mm AA Bofors and 2 x squids. The squids were three barrelled depth charge mortars in 'X' position which entailed firing them over the mast if the ship was steering towards the submarine's position. There were also 15 depth charges and 10 x 21" tubes in quintuple mountings.

On board *Crossbow* I was given the responsibility of looking after the boats and I spent a considerable amount of time understudying the Officer of the Watch on the bridge when at sea.

On 21 January the lower deck was cleared of all ratings for the yearly inspection of their Service Documents. This was the same day that the USS *Nautilus* (the world's first nuclear powered submarine) commissioned.

We ammunitioned ship on 26 January on completion of our maintenance period and moved round to Portland the next day. Our purpose in visiting Portland was to 'work up' all our systems and the ship's company to an efficient fighting unit. We were given ten days to do this. Apart from the seamanship aspects such as running the boats, practising towing another ship ('prepare to tow aft') or being towed ourselves ('prepare to tow for'ard') we also checked all methods of operating our sonars and conducted damage control exercises and fired our guns, torpedoes and squid (anti-submarine mortars). A number of submarines were based at Portland and they provided realistic opposition during exercises.

Once we were pronounced efficient we departed for Gibraltar to meet up with the Home Fleet for the Spring exercises.

On the way south we joined up with *Battleaxe* and *Scorpion,* our sister ships in the Squadron. As an 'evolution' we were towed from aft by *Scorpion*. Further south we met up with *Decoy* and *Aisne* and in turn took on extra fuel from a Royal Fleet Auxiliary (RFA) tanker.

Before we arrived in Gibraltar, the CinC decided to have some fun-and-games in the form of evolutions. When we were about ten miles from Gibraltar he ordered each ship to lower a whaler and sail it into harbour. Needless to say, as the junior officer I was put in charge of *Crossbow*'s whaler. At the same time we had the aircraft carrier *Eagle* in company and some of its jet aircraft decided to beat us up. One of them came so low that he just missed the top of my mast. I was watching it carefully as it approached as I thought I might have to jump overboard. Fortunately it passed overhead only a foot or two clear. When I looked back into the boat I found I was alone. All my crew had decided it was safer in the water. The wind was only light and they soon scrambled back on board, hopefully unnoticed by the officers in the watching flagship.

By the time we made harbour, all the niceties of such an important occasion such as saluting the flag of the CinC Home Fleet had been completed and I found *Crossbow* secured in the destroyer pens alongside *Verulam*. Instead of being allowed a 'quiet' run ashore, we found all hands 'turned to' as the CinC had decided to inspect us at 0900 on the following day.

After the inspection was over I was standing on the quarterdeck watching a pinnace manoeuvring just off the stern. Having had my attention drawn to the boat I then realised that the coxswain was 'Cuddles' Cadle with whom I had served in *Triumph*. I had a hurried word with him over the guard rail and in spite of officers being discouraged to go ashore with ratings we arranged to meet ashore that night and cross the border into Spain and have a quiet drink together. Naturally we had a lot of news to catch up on and we drank rather more than we should have. Cuddles had married since we last met and he had a flat in Gibraltar. Cuddles drank too much and I took him back to Gibraltar in a taxi but on arrival at his door I couldn't summon up the courage to meet his new wife. I leant him against the doorpost, rang the bell, and beat a hasty retreat. I haven't seen him since.

On 17 February our visit to Gibraltar came to a close and we slipped and headed for sea to undertake short exercises known as Casexes. We were thus able to return to harbour each evening. Having been to sea on 19 February we returned and were all in our mess undress after dinner when the CinC decided to hold 'harbour life-saving evolutions'. We were told that there was some 'imaginary' crisis on the other side of the harbour and we had to send assistance by whaler. This meant rowing across the harbour and once again, I was the obvious choice to take the boat over. To me this was all in a day's work and our boat was the first to arrive gaining the ship a 'Bravo Zulu' – the traditional flag hoist meaning 'Manoeuvre well carried out', or put more simply, 'Well done'.

We were allocated an official courtesy visit to Setubal whilst the Home Fleet was at Gibraltar. We arrived at Setubal on 26 February and secured alongside *Scorpion*. Setubal is about 25 miles south of Lisbon at the mouth of a large bay famous for its salt flats. It also boasted a fish canning plant. At the time there was no bridge over the Tagus and so we were quite remote from the capital. The previous year a Royal Navy ship had visited and a car had been sent to collect the ship's officers to take them to a civic reception. On leaving the ship the driver had driven off the jetty and all the occupants had drowned. This made our visit a rather sombre occasion. In spite of the tragic events of the previous year, a ball was organised to honour the occasion. The invitation said quite clearly that the ball would start at 8.00 p.m. and we dutifully set off to arrive a short time after this in order not to keep our hosts waiting. When we arrived at the town hall we found a few people setting out some music stands for the band, and one or two others tidying up the hall, so we returned to the ship for a couple of drinks and returned about an hour later. This time there were a few more people there although the hosts had not yet arrived.

In due course the Mayor and his wife arrived with a number of other dignitaries and introductions were made. Then the band started to play what I thought was a waltz and I turned to one of the ladies intending to ask her for a dance when I realised that everyone else was standing to attention. I followed suit but the band was more than halfway through its rendering before I was able to recognise it as our own National Anthem.

The Ball in Setubal. Bryan in foreground.

Quite a number of beautiful young girls had been invited to the ball but they were all chaperoned. The chairs in the hall were set in two rings around its perimeter. The chaperones sat on the chairs in the outside ring and the young ladies whose honour they were protecting sat in front of them in the inside ring. After each dance they shot back to their places as though they were attached to their chaperones by elastic. Surely they didn't think that officers of the Royal Navy would take undue advantage?

An equivalent number of university undergraduates from Lisbon had also been invited. The young ladies were beautifully dressed, but the young men wore their gowns. Some of the gowns were in shreds. We didn't know at the time that it was customary for Portuguese university students to put a small tear in their gown for every young lady they had conquered. It became obvious that there was a real need for chaperones, unless of course, the undergraduates were prone to exaggeration.

One girl with whom I was dancing asked me if I knew the Queen. She was quite disappointed when I replied that I didn't know her personally but I had seen her on Coronation Day.

After a pleasant visit we rejoined the Home Fleet in Gibraltar and remained until the end of March.

On our passage home we participated in Exercise Loyalty and then arrived at Chatham on 1 April. Easter was approaching and my time in *Crossbow* was drawing to a close. I was given two weeks' leave before taking up my new appointment.

The system of reporting on officers' competence and behaviour was different to that of ratings. Before leaving *Crossbow* the Captain was required to write a comprehensive report on a Form S.206. This was a confidential reporting form which was vital to an officer's promotion prospects. A combination of textual comments and marking points for various personal qualities gave an overall picture and score which was used to make up a ranking list when one was in the zone for promotion. If there were any serious deficiencies in the officer's ability or behaviour which it was within his power to correct, they were underlined in red ink and were shown to him. The report would also be reflected in a much shortened version which was given to the officer to keep. These were known as 'flimsies'. The best flimsy will start: 'This officer has behaved entirely to my satisfaction', and will then go on to mention the officer's particular strong points. Slightly lower down the scale, the flimsy would read: 'This officer has behaved to my satisfaction.' Officers writing reports are well aware that they tell as much about the officer writing the report as they do about the officer being reported on. Even so, many captains, feeling that this is an opportunity to get their own back on an officer who has not served them well, cannot resist the temptation to say in a few short words what they really think about the officer concerned. Examples which are alleged to have been written about some officers include:

'Men would follow this officer anywhere even if only out of curiosity,'

'This officer has behaved entirely to his own satisfaction,'

'He sets low personal standards which he is unable to meet,'

'This officer will go far, the farther the better!'

and probably the most damning of all:

'I would not breed from this officer.'

My flimsy at the end of my period in *Crossbow* reads:

This is to certify that Acting Sub Lieutenant B G Smalley RN has served under training in HMS *Crossbow* under my command from the 1st Day of January 1954 to the 12th day of April 1954 during which period he has conducted himself entirely to my satisfaction. Has taken a very keen interest in the every day life of the ship whilst under training. Is developing good seamanlike qualities.

Signed Hubert D.M. Slater Captain HMS *Crossbow*.

So my first report as an officer boosted my confidence considerably.

CHAPTER 9

RNC Greenwich and
'Subs' courses' 1954-55

AFTER TAKING my leave at home I then joined the Royal Naval College at Greenwich. Acting sub lieutenants had arrived from all corners of the world.

The course at Greenwich was called the Junior Officers' War Course but it had the wider purpose of broadening the students' horizons both educationally and professionally. In addition to the JOWC we also followed academic studies as well as liberal studies. Within liberal studies we could choose to study one subject of our choice and I chose to learn Portuguese. This had the advantage of taking me out of the college to the Regent Street Polytechnic. I also used some of my free study periods to take driving lessons although at that time I didn't have the wherewithal to buy a car. The driving lessons brought home to me one of the differences between being a rating and an officer. As a rating I would have had to write out a request for permission to leave the establishment, but as an officer I could just walk out of the gate. Provided I attended the scheduled lectures I was free to come and go as I wished, but every time I walked out for a driving lesson I had a pang of conscience as though I had committed some misdemeanour. As I hadn't driven a car before, I was petrified when the instructor at my first lesson, without any formal tuition, made me get into the car and drive it away. To coincide with my last lesson I arranged a test. For this the driving school recommended a half hour's warming up period before the test. During this warming up period I made every mistake possible including stalling the car in the middle of a very busy crossing. At the end of the examination, the examiner would give the examinee one of two certificates. A 'pass' was printed on paper of one colour and a 'fail' on a different colour. Fortunately I managed to pass and I saw the look of horror on the instructor's face as I walked towards him when he saw that I had passed.

For our liberal studies our tutor was Bryan 'Shaky' Ranft, a historian of some repute. We also had a military tutor, an old Etonian Guards Officer, Major P. J. Eastman Nagle, RHA which led to a certain amount of leg pulling.

One of the important things this course was meant to teach us was the need to think problems through logically by first analysing the problem, then comparing all the possible options, and finally deciding which solution should be adopted. This should then lead to a logical course of action. In the services this is called 'appreciating the situation'. Conversely some people will first decide what to do and then write a report attempting to justify it. This is jokingly referred to as 'situating the appreciation'.

'Of course,' our course officer told us, 'you don't write an appreciation of the situation every time you make a decision. In war there isn't time. You probably do it on the back of an old envelope.'

Taking our cue, the next time we had to do an exercise for him we wrote it out on the backs of old envelopes. The jape fell rather flat because he didn't seem to notice. He just marked them and returned them to us without comment.

Whilst we were at Greenwich, we took some time off our studies to witness the *Cutty Sark* being towed into the dock in which she was to be preserved.

One of the great pleasures of living at Greenwich was dining in the Painted Hall. It is a beautiful room in its own right but it is at its best when laid for dinner with all the silver glistening in the subdued light.

My report on leaving Greenwich in December 1954 reads as follows:

War Course – 'Has worked hard and made good progress, but must learn to be more methodical and write more clearly.'

General Education – 'Has worked very hard indeed and produced some excellent results. He can express his ideas better in writing than orally, although he is potentially a good lecturer.'

Mathematics – 'Good.'

Applied Mathematics – 'Satisfactory.'

Science – 'Good.'

Voluntary (Portuguese) – 'Started Portuguese in 'A' term and worked very hard, spending his long leave in Portugal. Just failed to obtain his preliminary interpretership after two terms work.'

General Remarks – [These were written by the Major who was my War Course tutor in a hand which is barely legible!] – 'A very likeable, loyal, well mannered, but not yet entirely confident officer. Has worked very hard and made good progress, but his thoughts are still inclined to sprawl as much as his handwriting. When he has learnt to marshal his ideas and to be more methodical he should develop into a very sound officer. Has been a loyal and regular helper in college games.'

The report was signed by Captain C.H. Hutchinson who had relieved Captain Miers as Captain of the College.

The amusing part of the report was the reference to my poor handwriting.

The major's writing took far longer than mine to interpret. The reference to sport also has an amusing side. As I am no good at games my contribution was merely to act as scorer to the First XI cricket team.

It was just before we completed our course at Greenwich that an invitation was placed on the notice board asking for a number of officers to attend a party at the Constance Spry Finishing School in Windlesham, Surrey. Constance Spry was renowned as a flower arranger. I put my name down and Peter Deller kindly offered to take me in his open topped sports car. Peter Deller wore a duffel coat. On arrival we were met in the entrance hall by a number of beautiful girls who had been detailed to act as hostesses. There was a bar with a few bottles of beer and one or two bottles of wine. The fruit cup was in a crystal bowl set on a table covered with the best damask. Our hostesses only offered us the fruit cup, so we danced the night away in an unusually sober condition. On our way home we came to a road block and a policeman ordered us out of the car and then searched it. When we were given permission to proceed we asked what the police were looking for. It appeared that they were looking for stolen Christmas trees. Once we were well clear I said to Peter that I was pleased that we had nothing on our consciences when the police stopped us. 'That may be so in your case,' replied Peter and as he did so he revealed his duffel coat pockets which were full of beer bottles which he had helped himself to on the way out.

At the end of the year I went home again for Christmas leave before moving back to Portsmouth for the next stage of our training. This was a series of nine 'Technical Courses', which included: Navigation, Gunnery, TAS (Torpedoes & anti-submarine), Communications, Air, Divisional, ABCD (Atomic Bacteriological & Chemical Defence), Amphibious Warfare, and Electrical. They were more commonly referred to as 'Subs' Courses'. These were all very practical courses and, as well as giving us an insight into the different specialisations in the Navy, they would also help us decide which sub-specialist branch we would wish to join at a future date. The courses lasted for different lengths of time depending on the amount to be learnt and the depth of knowledge required. There was an examination at the end of each course with passes at first and second class levels. At the end of these courses our results could give us additional seniority which would mean less time serving as a sub-lieutenant before being promoted to lieutenant.

Because the Royal Navy has a worldwide reputation for the quality and thoroughness of its training, it attracts students from many different countries to take its courses. It was always difficult to imagine what one officer from one Navy thought of another, particularly when some of the countries were virtually at war with each other.

During our time on these courses we had Australians, Canadians, Indians, Pakistanis and Southern Irish. Generally speaking we got on very well with each other as young apolitical people tend to, but there was some unnecessary leg pulling by inconsiderate British officers.

One of our earliest courses was on Amphibious Warfare. It was held at Poole, Dorset. We were there when the country was experiencing severe weather conditions. The Training Centre was new and the heating system and other facilities were not working. We spent most of our time trying to survive which is probably why I earned the noncommittal report which read: 'Obtained a good knowledge of the subject.'

The ABCD (Atomic, Bacteriological and Chemical Defence) School was one place where some fun was had. This had been aptly named HMS *Phoenix*. When this newly created branch of the Navy was formed, quite a number of Lieutenant Commanders who had been passed over for promotion volunteered to join the branch on the assumption that as it developed they might gain late promotion. This meant that this branch had quite a number of officers who, to put it mildly, weren't 'the sharpest knives in the drawer'.

One of the ruses played on these officers related to the use of mustard gas. We were taught about all the possible gases that might be used against us at that time, and the culmination of this instruction was to have a small drop of mustard gas placed on our hands. We then had to remove the droplet using the approved technique. Mustard gas is liquid and is scattered in droplets. The approved way to remove a droplet is to take a swab of cotton wool and with a light twisting motion lift off as much as possible. The emphasis is that it shouldn't be rubbed into the skin. The small amount of gas remaining can then be treated with a cream which is lightly applied to the affected skin. This cream comes with the respirator which all officers and men have in their kit. Whilst the instructor was still passing down the line, carefully placing a blob of gas on each pupil's hand, some members of the class would quickly go through the proper cleansing procedure, then taking a fresh piece of cotton wool rub it vigorously on an unaffected part of the hand. This could always be guaranteed to make the instructor go apoplectic or in Naval terms 'go ape'.

Another part of this course was Damage Control. Its purpose is to teach the techniques for repairing damage sustained in a ship whilst in action or possibly by collision. The aim is to keep the ship afloat whilst still engaging the enemy. At *Phoenix* there was a mock ship's compartment. Under normal circumstances this would be watertight. We were taught the techniques of shoring up weakened bulkheads and plugging holes. We were then placed in the compartment with the bulkhead door shut behind us. We discovered that the compartment had a number of holes through which water began pouring, slowly filling the compartment which we occupied. We then had to set about stemming the inrush of water. Fortunately, if we failed in our task the instructors turned off the water supply shortly before there was no air left to breathe, but any incompetence would be marked against us at the end of the course. This exercise did not lend itself to any form of skylarking.

The fire fighting section was also interesting with plenty of practical exercises. They could be both spectacular and at times quite frightening. We were taught the different ways to fight fires depending on their type and severity. We were given the confidence to walk through a large fire using the water as a shield. After learning of techniques such as this, we were trained in the use of breathing apparatus. There was a metal compartment built like a maze. We were told to don our breathing apparatus and were then pushed into the entrance. Not being able to see a thing we had to feel our way through the maze and come out on the other side. Those who wished to skylark attempted to disorient others in the compartment. A student would often emerge from the place where he had entered, to his surprise. I never heard of an accident in this device although it was not unknown for instructors to go in and rescue students who had become totally confused.

My report when I left *Phoenix* read: 'A cheerful keen officer who achieved a good grasp of most subjects.'

On 7 March 1955 there was a significant change to the officer structure and uniform in the RN. Until that date all officers other than 'executive' wore colours between their stripes to show their specialism and used a suffix after their rank such as Lieutenant (E) for Engineer. This particularly caused dissent amongst the specialists who perceived that the executive officers regarded themselves as superior. From 7 March the suffixes and colouring between the stripes were abolished and 'executives' became seamen officers.

As a general rule, our flying course didn't lend itself to practical joking. On completion of our short courses, anyone who wished to join the Fleet Air Arm (Royal Naval Air Service) and take up flying as a career would move straight on to his flying course. There was therefore a wide range of interest amongst the students. Those who wanted to fly loved the practical side of the course. As for myself, one who likes to keep his feet firmly on the deck of a ship, I enjoyed it, but no more than that. We flew two types of aircraft, the Seafire, a Naval version of the Spitfire, and the Sea Venom, one of the early jets. Usually on our first training flight, our instructor did very little except throw the aircraft around in a series of aerobatics. This usually ended up with the pupil being sick into his face mask.

Bryan on the Air Course.

The course was properly called the Junior Officers' Air Course which was abbreviated to JOAC and was pronounced 'Jowac'. On one occasion one of our group, Keith Brunton, was up with his instructor when they had a 'flame out', that is the engine died and there was no ignition to light the fuel which was being injected into the engine. Consequently there was no thrust and such a heavy aircraft does not lend itself to gliding. On these occasions the drill was to make a quick survey of the terrain below, decide on the flattest and least obstructed area, and put the aircraft down as best possible. Fortunately there was a large cornfield in sight and they were soon back on terra firma amidst the corn. A farm hand who had been working in the next field came over to see what was happening. The rather shaken couple asked him whether he could lead them to a phone so that they could inform their base that they were safe. 'We're from "Jowac",' they explained. 'Aar,' he said. 'We get a lot of you'm foreigners hereabouts,' and with that he climbed back on board his tractor and got on with his work.

My report from the Air Course read: 'A very cheerful young officer who was interested in practical flying but he is not keen to specialise. He worked hard for the examinations.'

We then moved on to HMS *Excellent* at Whale Island, the Royal Navy's gunnery school. Gunnery officers regarded themselves as the élite of the Service. They based this presumption on the fact that the guns were the main armament. They assumed that all other branches only existed to enable the gunnery officer to bring his guns into action.

The Captain was W.F.H.C. Rutherford DSO and Lt. David W. Leach, an Australian, was our training officer. He marched everywhere, even off duty, and we nicknamed him 'the mechanical man'.

Whale Island had a reputation for being tough, and one of the ways of smartening up classes was to make them double round the island. This is a highly organised routine and the instructor sending his class round the island would warn the other instructors by telephone that his class was coming their way. The instructor would await the arrival of the class on his patch and then 'about turn' them a number of times. In this way, although the island is probably only a couple of miles round its perimeter, the class could cover any number of miles as it doubled backwards and forward during its progression.

The subs' course at Whale Island was one of the longest: seven weeks, if I remember correctly. At the end of the course we would have our passing out parade at Friday's Divisions with everybody at Whale Island present. It had been the custom in the past for subs' courses to play some sort of prank as they left Whale Island. The stories of the pranks that had been played are legion but the following examples show the sort of things that had happened relatively recently.

One class had a member who owned his own aeroplane. He bombed the parade with bags of flour as his class were marching past with the Captain standing imperiously on his podium. Another involved a class which, on the night before their passing out parade, had bricked up the store in which the cutlasses were kept for ceremonial parades so that when it came to issue the cutlasses there was no way in to the store.

The group which passed out just before us appeared to have done nothing, and were consequently regarded as being rather dull. But a few days after they departed their joke became apparent. They had written in large letters on the lawn with weedkiller 'STEADY THE GUARD'. This oft repeated order on ceremonial divisions remained for some months.

These pranks had become rather too much for the Captain. As soon as we joined the course he addressed us and told us that practical joking was to stop and that any practical jokers would be dealt with severely.

At the time our course was coming to a close a circus was appearing on the stage of the Portsmouth Empire. By shoring up the stage from below it was possible to get the elephant on to the stage to perform. Although we had been instructed not to play practical jokes we couldn't resist the temptation to do something with this elephant. We made enquiries about borrowing it from its owner. He was very pleased to co-operate on four conditions which were: first, a guarantee not to harm the elephant; second, the provision of a large bag of buns; thirdly, payment of a fee of £5; and finally, to ensure that the circus got maximum publicity.

On the appointed day, Donk Read and I were up early. We left Whale Island wearing our battledress uniforms covered by civilian raincoats and took with us the battledress of Courtenay Hobday who was unable to march owing to a bad foot. We returned with the Singhalese mahout astride the elephant wearing Courtenay's uniform looking like a very old sub-lieutenant.

The approach to Whale Island is via a bridge and access is controlled by sentries. Inevitably we were challenged by a Petty Officer who denied us entry, but we identified ourselves as officers and he phoned the Duty Lieutenant Commander to report the situation. We had overlooked the fact that it was 1 April but the Duty Officer hadn't. On being told by the sentry that two officers were attempting to bring an elephant on to the island he assumed it was an April Fool's joke and told them to carry on. We took the elephant behind the drill shed out of view of those attending divisions. After the class had marched past properly they joined up with us and proceeded to march past again.

When a march past is taking place the inspecting officer's eyes are usually on the class in front of him, and as it moves away all eyes turn to the left to look at the next approaching class. We were well on to the parade ground before anyone noticed that anything was amiss. When the Captain realised what was happening he dashed his silver topped cane to the ground and the instructors shouted: 'Get rid of that elephant!' A general shemozzle ensued.

After we had marched off the parade and dismissed the elephant trainer and his elephant, Lt. Leach had a few words. 'Privately I would like to say "Well Done",' he said, 'but the Captain thinks differently; you are all under stoppage of leave until further notice.'

In due course we appeared as a class before the Captain in the room specifically furnished for defaulters. He stood on a podium looking down at us. We stood in two ranks facing the podium. The Captain reminded us that he had forbidden us to play pranks at the end of our course. Therefore, we were guilty of behaviour unbecoming to Naval officers and had directly disobeyed an order. This was a court martial offence. He then ordered the two officers who brought the elephant on to the island to take a pace forward. Donk and I, who were standing in the front row, obeyed. 'And now I would like to know

Marching the elephant off the parade ground – April Fool's Day, 1955.

what steps were taken to stop this happening.' He then said that the class leader and his deputy should have stopped us and ordered them to take a pace forward. Donk and I took a further step forward. The Captain's eyebrows bristled and he clearly was not amused. We were dismissed.

We then spent several days waiting to hear what would happen. After about a week we were eventually mustered, given another good talking to, and told to go on our Easter leave which should have commenced on the evening of the day when the misdemeanour occurred. We never knew what went on behind the scenes but we did hear that his office was bombarded with telephone enquiries asking if he would take a trunk call.

In spite of our unpopularity with the Captain, my report from the gunnery course read: 'A very cheerful, alert and intelligent young officer. Although his bearing and standard of dress leave room for improvement, he has a good power of command and takes charge well. Completed a most satisfactory course. Recommended for Gunnery.' It was the only course which I completed with a first class pass.

I was confirmed in the rank of Sub-Lieutenant on 1 May.

Our next course was the Divisional Course which only lasted two weeks and was held in Portsmouth Barracks. Its purpose was to ensure that we knew all the procedures and paper work required when looking after the ratings below us. It wasn't a particularly inspiring course which may be why my report read: 'His personal appearance is inclined to give a bad impression. He lacks complete confidence. Nevertheless he tried hard to gain full benefit from the course.'

On 16 June the British submarine *Sidon* tragically sank in Portland harbour after an explosion. At the time experimental torpedoes fuelled by High Test Peroxide (HTP) were being loaded when a torpedo's engine accidentally started. Thirteen people lost their lives including a Surgeon Lieutenant who went on board to render medical assistance.

On 20 June Britain signed an agreement with the USA regarding the exchange of nuclear information.

We moved on to the TAS Course which was important because both torpedoes and sonar were becoming more sophisticated. On the other hand the Gunnery Branch was moving into the rocket era. The TAS course was held at HMS *Vernon* which was situated at the eastern side of the entrance to Portsmouth Harbour.

Then followed the Navigation Course at HMS *Dryad* in what had been a country estate in Southwick. It was there that the Normandy invasions were planned in 1944.

The Communications course followed. That, too, was held in what had once been a country estate but was now aptly named HMS *Mercury*. Much of the course concerned radio communications, both the technicalities and the procedures to be used. We practised the Morse code by flashing light and by hand key. We also practised semaphore and the use of flag hoists. To drive the message home we even marched using flag hoist techniques. When a flag order is hoisted it goes to the top of the yardarm. As each ship sees the signal it hoists it to half mast until it understands its meaning at which time it too takes the signal up to the yard. When the senior ship executes the order he pulls the signal down. At *Mercury* as we marched round the establishment we raised our right arm above our heads and pulled it down when the executive order was given. Thank goodness people outside the gate weren't able to see us or they would have thought it was a lunatic asylum.

In due course we reached the Electrical Course, our final one. That was on another large piece of real estate outside Portsmouth. The course was purely technical.

After we had completed all the subs' courses we went our separate ways. Those who wished to join the Fleet Air Arm went off to do their flying course. My friend Harry Bond was one of those who chose to fly. I volunteered to join submarines and joined the Submarine Service on 7 November.

CHAPTER 10

Submarine Training 1955

THE ALMA MATER of the Submarine Service was HMS *Dolphin* at Gosport. It was on the Western side of the entrance to Portsmouth Harbour. It was also the establishment where the Flag Officer, Submarines (FOSM) Rear Admiral G 'Guy' B.H. Fawkes flew his flag. The Captain of *Dolphin* and Flag Captain was Capt. E.F. Pizey DSO, but he was relieved shortly after we joined by Capt. G.D.A. Gregory. The submarines operating out of *Dolphin* comprised the 5th Squadron. In overall charge of training was Lt. Cdr. Bob Garson whom I had met before when he visited Dartmouth whilst commanding *Astute*. The title Training Officer was shortened to TROFF. We were simply called the SOTC (Submarine Officers Training Class).

Directly responsible for our training was Lt. P.R (Richard) Compton-Hall, the Officers' Training Officer (OTO).

All the officers above us had had interesting experiences, but probably none as dramatic as CPO Cox'n Gordon Selby DSM and Bar, BEM, who undertook much of the instruction and administration. Of the submarines in which he served with distinction during the war, four were sunk by enemy action. After he left *Upholder* in February 1942 she was sunk on her next patrol. His next submarine, *P39,* was sunk by enemy bombing whilst in Malta Harbour. He then joined *Olympus* which hit a mine and sank. His fourth submarine, *Sickle*, was mined and sunk in Greek waters a few months after he had left her. He was someone whom we held in great awe.

Our course comprised S/Lts George Barr, David Barrow, Neil Boivin RCN, Alistair Bruce, Keith Brunton, Ken Forbes-Robertson, Peter Godley, Ryan Harman, Nigel Laville, Doyne Nicholson, Charles Pope, Jim Rose, Mark Ruddle, myself and Neil Warneford.

The loss of the *Affray* in April 1951 was particularly crippling to the officer structure in the Submarine Service because as well as losing an entire ship's company, the *Affray* also had on board an entire officers' training class, and so a total of twenty five officers were lost. Since then the number of officers volunteering for submarines had dropped off and the Navy was forced to conscript officers into the Submarines Service for a three year period after which they could return to General Service, but to my knowledge they all remained in submarines.

Our class formation was interesting because we were all volunteers.

At our introductory meeting Bob Garson told us what he expected from us and how the routine worked. He also boasted about his athletic prowess and challenged any one of us to knock him off his position at the top of the squash ladder. Nigel Laville was a very tall gangling sub lieutenant. He never seemed to move with any great urgency and at normal times he rather gave the impression that he didn't have complete control over his limbs. But he could play squash! Nigel took up the challenge and knocked Bob Garson down to second place. I don't think he ever forgave the entire class for its apparent temerity.

Our submarine course consisted mainly of technical training. At the end we were expected to understand the intermingled mass of pipework, electrical cables, valves and switches which at the beginning we found incomprehensible.

There were one or two highlights to the course which broke the normal daily classroom routine. We would go to sea occasionally for the day to put what we had learned into practice. On one occasion we were going to sea in an 'A'-boat and were told that we would be sailing at 0815. We were to be on board in plenty of time by 0800. I was the first member of the class on board and waited in the fore ends as instructed. I felt rather smug as I was the first to arrive. By 0810 none of my class had arrived, but the fore hatch had been shut so I couldn't see what was going on. Eventually by about 0814 I turned to the fore-endman and enquired: 'This is *Artemis*, isn't it?' 'No,' he said. 'This is *Aeneas*.' I had to make a mad scramble through the boat to the control room, up into the conning tower, and down on to the casing. I then had to leap over to the adjacent submarine a few seconds before she slipped her moorings.

Included in the course was a visit to the RN Physiological Laboratory at Alverstoke. It was run by an apparently idiosyncratic professor-like scientist. His brief was to research into the effects of depth charges on sailors who were swimming in the sea after their ships had been sunk. It had been discerned that during the war many sailors had survived from a sinking ship only to receive severe injuries from explosions whilst in the water. After giving us an interesting lecture the 'professor' invited us all to put a hand in a water tank and then dropped in a hand grenade with devastating effect.

Another variation from the classroom routine was the two days spent in the submarine escape tank. The tank is a hundred feet deep with a compartment at the bottom representing a section of a submarine. Trainees can enter through a side door and, having shut the door behind them, they then flood the compartment until the water pressure is equal to that in the tank above them.

When the pressure is equalised it is possible to open the hatch and make an escape to the surface a hundred feet above. But this procedure is the last event in a two day course. There are lectures and escapes from thirty feet and sixty feet before making the final one hundred foot escape.

The lectures covered the use of all the escape equipment and physiology so that students understood what was happening to their lungs under pressure. All the instructors were submariners and delivered their lectures with the customary light hearted approach renowned of Service instructors. I recall our instructor saying: 'Now don't forget that you do not inflate your lifejacket until after you have reached the surface. The last chap who inflated his lifejacket before making his escape came out of the water so fast we're still scraping him off the deckhead.'

Included in our classroom studies was the provision of fresh water. Submarines had two distillers to make fresh water at sea. I recall our instructor explaining that they were capable of making '15 gallons of fresh water – per distiller – per hour – per-haps!' The distillers were extremely noisy and it was always a calculated risk whether to run the distillers on patrol with the risk of detection.

Whilst I was on the course I had my 24th birthday. At this time it was felt that officers had become too old for Submarine Service at sea by the time they reached the age of 32.

Towards the end of the course we spent a week at sea in a submarine. Once again we were allocated *Artemis*. The CO was Lt. Cdr. James Pardoe. Also on board was a National Service midshipman J.P.B. O'Riordan. James Pardoe told us that when we were on watch we were to be subordinate to the midshipman and obey his orders. The midshipman's qualification as a submariner put him above us as trainees.

At the end of the submarine training course we had an examination. There were a number of appointments available and the sub lieutenant who came first in the exams was allowed to choose his appointment and so on until we all had an appointment. I came about a third of the way down the list and chose *Acheron*, but I was appointed to the submarine spare crew at Rothesay until *Acheron* was ready to receive me. Peter Godley who had been in the same class was also appointed to *Acheron*. Everyone in the class passed and we dispersed to our various appointments. As soon as I took up a submarine appointment I would receive submarine pay of 9s.6d. a day, an additional £173 per annum.

CHAPTER 11

Learning the hard way! 1956

I JOINED THE submarine depot ship *Adamant* on 12 March 1956. *Adamant* spent most of its time anchored in Rothesay Bay off the Isle of Bute. It was supported by a floating dock which was anchored in Port Bannatyne, the next bay to the west. The Captain of *Adamant* and the 3rd Submarine Squadron was Captain Norman Jewell who had been my First Lieutenant at *Bruce*. I discovered that the French had forgiven him for the deception that had been played on General Giraud when he was taken off the North African coast in a submarine which he thought was American. In August 1952 the French authorities had installed him as a 'Chevalier d'Honneur'.

The Commander S/M was Commander Challis but he was relieved shortly after I joined by Cdr. Tony Troup. The RN had six submarine squadrons at the time based as follows: 1st in Malta, 2nd at Portland, 3rd at Rothesay, 4th in Sydney (Australia), 5th at *Dolphin* and the 6th (HMS *Ambrose*) in Halifax, Nova Scotia.

Submarines which were just out of refit, or more rarely from the builder's yard, worked up their efficiency whilst allocated to the 3rd Submarine Squadron. There were eighteen submarines in the squadron when I joined.

Each squadron had a spare submarine crew whose purpose was to provide replacements in submarines if for any reason a crew member was unable to go to sea. The spare crew commanding officer was Lieutenant John Fieldhouse.

I hadn't been in the spare crew long before I had to relieve the navigator in *Scotsman*, 'Stumpy' Hodgson, who had broken his leg.

Scotsman was an old 'S' boat which had been converted to enable the Admiralty Research Laboratory (ARL) staff to carry out trials. The main engines had been removed and had been replaced with additional batteries. All torpedo tubes and armament had been stripped out and the hull had been completely streamlined. There was a small auxiliary engine which provided enough power to propel the submarine on the surface at about seven knots. This auxiliary engine would have taken an eternity to recharge our batteries, so an 'A' class submarine accompanied *Scotsman* wherever she went. After a day's work conducting trials, the following night would be spent recharging *Scotsman's* batteries. This involved 'humping' very heavy cables from one submarine to the other. For that reason and also because the 'A' boat's engines would be running all night this was not an assignment which the 'A' boat's crew cherished.

Scotsman's CO was Lt. Cdr. Harvey R. de C. Dutton, best described as a piratical eccentric. His eccentricity was accentuated by his enjoyment of the occasional glass or two of alcoholic beverage. The ship's company did their best to enhance their CO's reputation.

The other officers were Lt. Ken Cadogan-Rawlinson (1st Lt.), Lt. Mike Reeder, and Commissioned Engineer Ken Evans.

Accommodation on board *Scotsman* was minimal and we had been allocated a barge which gave us some room to stow our personal belongings. This barge had no propulsive power and had to be towed by tug to wherever *Scotsman* happened to be operating. The barge was called 'Harvey's Ark' in respect to the CO.

As this was my first post where I had not been appointed 'additional for training', I took my appointment seriously. My first passage which I had to plan was from alongside the depot ship at Rothesay to Inveraray. It didn't involve going more than about three miles from land at any one time and I now realise that it was nothing more than a 'pilotage passage'. Nevertheless I intended to start as I meant to continue, so I mustered all the charts and navigational stores. This didn't take too long as most of them were missing. Nor were there any of the necessary publications. Having searched in all the obvious places and asked questions of Ken Cadogan-Rawlinson and Mike Reeder, I decided to report to the Captain that I was unprepared for sea at present because I didn't have a nautical almanac on board and I was missing one of the charts which I needed for the passage.

'You don't need a chart, you clot,' said Harvey. 'You just keep in the middle of the loch. And what on earth do you need a nautical almanac for?'

'I need it to work out the time of sunrise and sunset at Inveraray, Sir,' I said.

'You don't need to work out sunrise and sunset, boy. Every month the Squadron Navigator works out sunrise and sunset for Rothesay and distributes it throughout the depot ship. Go and take the copy off the wardroom notice board, add a couple of minutes and you've got the answer for Inveraray. In any case there's nobody at Inveraray to check to see whether you pull the ensign down at the right time. Push off and stop wasting my time,' he said, reaching for his glass.

I staggered away, totally confused; this wasn't what they'd taught us at *Dryad,* the Navigation School.

Neil Boivin, my Canadian contemporary, joined *Andrew* under the

Scotsman *taking passage to trial area.*

command of D'Arcy Burdett. When Neil went to sea for the first time he had problems with sunset and sunrise too. On his first evening at sea the boat was on the surface with Neil on watch. He sent the customary message to the captain: 'Five minutes to sunset, Sir. Navigation lights tested and correct.' The answer came back from D'Arcy: 'I am the Captain of this ship and I decide when the sun will set. Remain on the bridge until I determine that the sun has set.' Neil remained on the bridge a considerable time before being relieved

Back in *Scotsman* our time had come to slip and we made our way at best speed to Inveraray. Harvey's Ark had gone ahead by tug but we also had another boat which came under Harvey's command. This boat had a fairly roomy compartment for'ard with a coal stove. It was manned by the second coxswain known as 'Scratcher'. The scratcher's responsibility was to maintain the fittings outside the submarine's pressure hull. Our scratcher was even more piratical than the Captain. He had a bushy unkempt beard which he continually clawed, giving the impression that it was infested with living creatures. He carried a few bottles of wardroom whisky on board. When he managed to restrain himself from drinking the whisky he would barter it for coal from the Clyde puffers. Alternatively he would swap the whisky for fish.

At Inveraray we secured alongside the 'A' boat which would charge our batteries.

Scratcher's boat was used as a liberty boat until midnight and would then remain secured alongside the jetty. Libertymen who missed the last boat back had a coal stove to keep them cosy until the morning.

The trials that we were undertaking were all related to noise. There was some variety. Sometimes we would go deep and run at high speed measuring the vibration of the hull. We also had a specially installed window in the after-ends through which the propeller could be photographed. Much of the Navy's knowledge of cavitation was derived in this way. Cavitation is the noise created when air bubbles caused by the propeller blades collapse. It makes ships and submarines susceptible to detection.

Loch Fyne is very deep and about a mile wide so it was very useful for trials of this type. At the northern end of the loch where we did most of our trials, Loch Fyne veers off to the north-east with the smaller Loch Shira going off to the north-west. On the headland between the two we placed an orange incandescent marker as a point to steer towards when we were doing our runs. We also placed markers on the shoreline down the side of the loch. These told us when to go deep to start the run.

At the start of a northerly run we would compare the magnetic and gyro compass readings in case the gyro went wrong. We would steer towards the marker on the headland and go deep as we passed the appropriate marker on our starboard beam. Having gone deep our method of calculating the distance run was by stopwatch hanging from a lanyard round the Captain's neck. Obviously, it was important to keep the stopwatch well wound. Having run for the required time we would come back to periscope depth, check on our position and turn round for a southerly run.

One of my most frightening experiences in *Scotsman* was on one of the northward runs. We had gone deep and the Captain had just broadcast to the Auxiliary Machinery Space (AMS) to start the recorders for another run, when one of the boffins' head appeared through the hatch to say that he wasn't ready. Harvey then engaged in a long haranguing session. Eventually he remembered that he was running on a stop watch and on looking at it he ordered: 'Periscope depth,' and on reaching it: 'Up periscope.'

He was looking through the periscope as it broke surface and cried, 'Jesus Christ. Full astern together!'

The boat vibrated horribly as the propellers churned up the water and we waited with baited breath. Eventually all the way had been taken off the ship and Harvey ordered: 'Stand by to surface.' On reaching the bridge the Officer of the Watch was able to see how close we had come to running aground at full speed.

The shoreline of the loch had a roadway running along its edge. Ironically, there was a police car traversing the road at the precise time that we broke surface. The driver was so shaken on seeing this monster apparently about to leap out of the water at him, that he swerved off the road and ended up in a ditch, doing considerable damage to the car. We never heard how he explained his accident to his superiors.

After we managed to get ourselves back into a safer part of the loch, Harvey decided to call it a day and we secured alongside the charging submarine and took ourselves ashore to the George Hotel for some nerve soothing refreshments and relaxation. I soon discovered that there was a good relationship with the Clark family who owned the hotel but that didn't stop the daughter, Fiona, from charging me five pence for a bath.

When that series of trials was over, we returned to the depot ship in Rothesay for maintenance. Stumpy Hodgson was still unfit so I had to remain on board for the next series of trials. These trials were in Kilbrannan Sound, another area of deep water in the mouth of the Clyde. We followed much the same programme as before but would spend each evening at a buoy at Lochranza on the northern shores of Arran. We were there for the weekend when the Brodick Highland Games were held which included the Goat Fell Race. Our ship's company entered in every event possible and actually managed to be placed in some of them. We were greatly helped by Mike Reeder, our very fit third hand, who, I seem to remember, came sixth in the Goat Fell race. Goat Fell is 2867 feet high.

The Captain was invited to join the panel which chose Miss Brodick 1956. Also on the panel was the Dowager Duchess of Hamilton whose home was at Brodick Castle. Having entertained the Duke of Argyll whilst we were in Inveraray, Harvey was now enjoying his acceptance within the Scottish social scene and invited the Duchess on board for tea. She came a few days after the invitation was offered, and I was sent ashore with the 'scratcher' to help her into the boat. We had done our best to tidy up the scratcher's boat and had washed some of the coal dust into the bilges. She had a Highland terrier with her and brought it out to the submarine. Harvey had spruced himself up by turning his sweater inside out. As we were about to help the Duchess on board, Harvey said: 'I don't think we'll take the dog. We don't want it doing a george in the control room.' I prayed to God that the grand old lady wasn't aware that 'to do a george' was the naval term to defecate. The Duchess didn't stay long, but we were proud to have had her on board. When we returned to

Scotsman. *Photograph courtesy of Royal Navy Submarine Museum.*

the depot ship, Stumpy was declared fit for sea and I returned to the spare crew.

The school holidays had begun and Captain Jewell's children had come home to their parents. Harvey decided to take them on a 'banyan' in the scratcher's boat. I was asked to go along too with one or two other officers. Harvey decided that we would do the job properly and hoisted a white ensign. As he didn't have an ensign the proper size for the boat, he flew a submarine ensign which was totally out of proportion.

We set off to the north west passing through the Colintraive narrows and made for the jetty at Tighnabruich. There was a pub at the end of the jetty and Harvey decided it was time 'for a wet'. This was entirely unnecessary as he had already arranged for an ample beer supply on board. But the captain's word is law and so we secured alongside without mishap. We had hardly started our first drink when one of the locals arrived and asked us to move our boat as the daily Clyde ferry was due alongside at any moment.

'Certainly not,' replied Harvey. 'We are a British warship and no one has the right to ask us to move!'

'But it's carrying passengers and mail,' replied the local who was beginning to doubt Harvey's authenticity.

'Well, tell it to come back tomorrow,' responded Harvey adamantly.

Whilst this argument was taking place the rest of us maintained a diplomatic silence. The ferry appeared round the headland and the ferry skipper started calling us through a megaphone.

Eventually Harvey allowed our boat to be moved, but unhurriedly in order to make it clear that we were only moving as a favour.

The ferry came alongside about fifteen minutes behind schedule.

I think Harvey had forgotten the object of our trip because he took the boat straight back to the depot ship and that was the end of the 'banyan'. I shuffled round the depot ship furtively for the next couple of days hoping not to bump into Captain (S/M) in case he asked me what had happened on our trip.

The wardroom bar in a depot ship served as an ideal meeting place. Rather than wander through the ship looking for someone it was preferable to wait till lunchtime when the person you wanted to speak to would almost certainly be present. There were some who said that they did all their business at the bar. These were the people who rarely got promoted because they had ill defined boundaries between booze and business. The traditional drink in the Navy was 'pink gin'. That is a splash of angostura bitters with a measure of gin topped up with water to taste. Ice was rarely available. The favourite brand was probably Plymouth gin, but during the war the distillery in Plymouth had been bombed and after the distillery came back into use, the gin didn't compare with its predecessor. It was a mildly yellowish colour. Nevertheless it was still drunk because it cost only a penny a tot. In due course it was impossible to maintain the price and the younger officers changed their preference to the 'Horse's Neck' – brandy with ice and a slice of lemon, topped up with ginger ale

When ashore in Rothesay we often frequented the Glenburn Hydro where the rich Glasgow businessmen brought their families for the weekend. On Saturday evenings there was always a dinner dance and the rig was naturally 'black tie'. We would walk in properly dressed and the staff assumed we were resident. In this way we made contact with some of the most eligible girls in Scotland. We called ourselves 'The Glenburn Harriers'.

It was not yet time to join *Acheron* and I found that while I had been away Peter Godley had played an unkind trick on me. The next exercise which was being planned under NATO jurisdiction was to be called 'Exercise Fishplay' and was to be held in the western Atlantic with the 'wash-up' in Bermuda. The Depot ship *Adamant* was to go over to Bermuda to provide maintenance facilities after the exercise. *Scotsman* and *Explorer* (a brand new steam driven submarine with High Test Peroxide (HTP) as fuel) would be left behind in Rothesay.

Whilst I had been at sea in *Scotsman*, John Fieldhouse had sent for Peter Godley to explain that one of the sub lieutenants would go to Bermuda in *Adamant*, whilst the other would stay behind to look after the assorted collection of remaining vessels. Without hesitation Peter told John Fieldhouse that I had slight problems at home as 'I had to look after my ageing mother'. He was confident that I wouldn't wish to go abroad for an extended period. So the cunning blighter talked his way into this coveted foreign 'jolly' whilst I would remain behind.

Several submarines were attached to the Squadron undertaking trials of new equipment. *Totem* was one of these. It was doing trials on a new development termed the 'dual pressure torpedo firing gear'. I was put in charge of a Torpedo Recovery Vessel and told to take it round to Loch Long and act as Safety and Torpedo Recovery Officer to *Totem*. I had a crew of one stoker and one seaman but this didn't diminish my pride in having my first command. On my first day we started work at about 0800 and I was told by radio to lie off in the centre of the loch. I was assuming that torpedoes would be fired fairly soon, but lunchtime came and went, and nothing happened. By tea time I couldn't bear the inactivity any longer so I sent a signal which I thought was a masterpiece for its brevity. It read: 'What is the delay?' This seemed to have an electric effect in the submarine. Suddenly hands appeared on the casing and I received an even briefer signal which said: 'Come alongside.'

I went alongside and scrambled up on to the casing. An anxious second coxswain said, 'The Captain is in his cabin and he wishes to see you, now.' I could detect from his tone that I was in some sort of trouble.

I found my way to the Captain's cabin and met Lt. Cdr. Brian Mills.

'Smalley,' he said, 'sub-lieutenants don't send signals to commanding officers of major war vessels asking them what is the delay.'

'No, Sir,' I grovelled.

'Well', said the Captain. 'It so happens that I've received a letter from shore from a certain Mr Roy Cordiner of Ardmay House. It seems that this Saturday the Scottish Conservative and Unionist Association will be holding its Annual Ball in the Arrochar Hotel and Mr Cordiner is unable to find a young man to take his daughter to the ball. He wants to know if one of my officers would like to accompany her. I shall be writing to him to tell him that Sub-Lieutenant Smalley will be delighted to take his daughter to the ball. Make sure you're smartly turned out and a credit to the Service.'

'Aye Aye, Sir,' was the automatic reply, but my mind was in a whirl. I was relieved that my punishment was apparently so light but on the other hand who was this Cinderella who couldn't find a man to take her to the ball?

'Oh, and by the way,' the Captain finally remarked, 'a car will be on the jetty to collect you at 1930.' I'm still not sure whether there was a twinkle in his eye when he said this.

When the appointed time arrived I was waiting anxiously on the casing when a highly polished Rolls Royce hove into view. After parking alongside the jetty a delightful young lady stepped out from the driving seat and introduced herself. And so began my punishment in grand style. On our way to the ball I established that my partner was known as 'Winkie' and we developed our relationship. On arrival at the dance, I had some difficulty in finding the right knob to open the door from quite a large selection, but apart from that I succeeded reasonably well in giving Winkie the impression that I was quite accustomed to travelling in such style.

The ball was quite a success but I did notice that even by submarine standards everyone seemed to consume a fair amount of alcohol.

After a time we came to know the Cordiners quite well. Ardmay was a beautiful house a mile or two down the loch. I discovered that it was customary to invite the Cordiner family and friends on board submarines whenever one was in the loch undergoing trials. Roy Cordiner ran Ardmay as a very up-market hotel. At some point, someone obtained an Ardmay House brochure. It was noted that one paragraph offered a tour of one of Her Majesty's Submarines 'when available'. After that, the relationship became rather more formal.

When I returned to Rothesay, *Adamant* had sailed for the exercise and I was left in charge of what remained. Things weren't as quiet as we had hoped. The experimental submarine *Explorer* had to be docked on a number of occasions. *Explorer* was on its first commission. It had been built to explore the possibility of using High Test Peroxide (HTP) as a means of propulsion. The idea had first been proposed by the Germans, but as the war came to an end they hadn't reached the position where they were able to decide on its viability. At the end of the war it was realised by the Allies that we needed submarines that could go faster and remain submerged for much longer without the need to rely on air drawn from the surface, which was necessary for combustion engines and for breathing. There were a variety of options which could be explored, and wide divisions on which would be most easily achieved. Some wanted to improve the batteries' capacity by changing from lead/acid cells to something different, possibly nickel/iron plates. Others wanted to take up the German idea of HTP propulsion, and some favoured the development of nuclear power. In the end the British came to a reciprocal arrangement with the Americans that we would work on HTP whilst they would concentrate on the development of nuclear propulsion. It was fortunate for the Americans that they had Hyman Rickover, an aggressive Rear Admiral who pushed their project ahead in spite of many obstacles and doubters. The HTP which *Explorer* used as fuel was extremely volatile and reacted with anything organic. The theory was that this reaction could be controlled by means of a catalyst. The reaction created oxygen and steam which was then passed into a combustion chamber where it was ignited with kerosene and used to drive a steam turbine. The fuel was stored in thick polythene bags secured outside the pressure hull, but within fairing plates forming the streamlined surface of the outer hull. Organic substances, usually salt water, frequently got into the bags causing an explosion which tended to blow off the outer plate. Fortunately the pressure hull was strong enough to withstand the force of the explosion close by. The intention was that these teething problems should be resolved during *Explorer's* first commission. Then during her first refit the fuel tanks would be placed within the pressure hull. One only had to talk about the possibility of this happening to stir up rebellious mumblings from the ship's company.

Another of my duties was to maintain relationships with the local authorities which led to my first contact with the Scottish police. I was asked to go to Gourock to bail out one of our stokers who had been charged with being drunk and disorderly and resisting arrest. I was horrified when I collected the poor sailor. He was black and blue. I asked him what had happened. His story was that he had been drunk and was asleep when the train arrived at the terminus. The next thing he knew was that he was being manhandled by the police. Of course he may not have been telling the entire truth but it did seem that the force used to arrest him had been excessive.

I was promoted to acting Lieutenant on 1 June 1956. My basic pay increased to £1.10*s*. a day (£547 a year) plus my submarine pay of 9*s*.6*d*. a day (£173 p.a.).

I joined *Acheron* as navigator on 17 June. I relieved Lt Richard Campbell who had decided to leave the Submarine Service to qualify as a Naval hydrographer. As soon as I was in this position on board a submarine I was entitled to 'hard lying money' when I slept on board. The rules regarding hard lying money read: 'Hard Lying money is payable when living and sleeping in ships employed on mainly sea service at full rates when the living and sleeping conditions are not superior to those in a trawler.'

Lt. John Fieldhouse had taken command by now and the First Lieutenant was Lt. George Hayhoe with Lt. Dick Horner the third hand. I joined as the fourth hand.

Although my experience in *Scotsman* had given me some practical idea of the workings of a submarine I was still without a watchkeeping certificate and I had

Lt. John Fieldhouse CO of Acheron – *on the bridge.*

to spend a period of time under the watchful eye of the Captain until he was prepared to give me my ticket.

As soon as I arrived on board we slipped and went to sea for a period. I can still vividly remember my first night at sea on watch by myself. We were on the surface off the north coast of Ireland and the Captain had written in his night orders that he had to be informed if a ship was going to pass within one mile of the submarine. I relieved Dick Horner on the bridge and he handed over to me taking care to point out that there were some faint white lights fine on the bow, probably fishing vessels. With a friendly warning to report them early and make sure we didn't foul their nets he disappeared into the warmth below. I spent the whole of my two hour watch taking bearings of these lights to see if the bearings moved whilst at the same time trying to assess whether they were getting any closer. They were still relatively in the same position when Peter Godley relieved me two hours later. It took a long time before I developed the ability and the confidence to appraise the situation whilst standing alone on the bridge at dead of night.

At sea we kept two hour watches because conditions were frequently so bad that after two hours our efficiency dropped right off. Frequently we went below soaked to the skin and frozen stiff. Quite often we weren't thawed out again before it was time to go back on the bridge for the next watch. It was naturally in our interest to develop waterproof clothing and we were issued with Ursula suits named after the submarine whose officers had pioneered their design. They only kept the water out for a limited period of time.

Underneath them we would wrap a towel round our shoulders, but in due course the towel would be saturated and you would feel the water slowly penetrating your undergarments, but worst of all was the icy trickle down the small of the back. Conditions below weren't much better. Submarines, being cigar shaped, tend to roll uncontrollably, making it necessary to expend a lot of energy maintaining your balance. When the seas were washing over the bridge, quite a lot of water would make its way down the conning tower. To collect this water, a canvas tube was hung below the conning tower in which the water could be collected and pumped out from time to time. This was referred to as the 'elephant's trunk'. When conditions were even worse we would lace a large piece of canvas under the elephant's trunk which had sides all round. It looked like a makeshift swimming pool which was known with typical submarine understatement as the 'bird bath'. In these weather conditions it was a great relief when we were able to dive and clear up the sodden mess and settle down to what was, relatively speaking, a more comfortable life. Even so submarines still tended to roll heavily when dived and I have fallen out of my bunk with the submarine at a hundred feet.

On this occasion, my first trip to sea in *Acheron*, we were scheduled to exercise in the Londonderry exercise areas and were in a position to rendezvous with the other units at first light of day. On completion of the exercises we made our way up the River Foyle to Londonderry and secured alongside HMS *Stalker*, a rather decrepit old Tank Landing Ship which had been modified to accommodate submarine crews in harbour.

Londonderry had been used for some time as the Joint Naval and Royal Air Force Maritime Warfare School. On looking back, the area in which we operated didn't have a great deal to recommend it. The water in which we operated was littered with hazards. A number of wrecks were lying on the bottom, and worse still there were a number of rocky shallows on which we could quite easily ground when dived. In poor visibility there were few navigational aids, and at the end of the week's exercises we had to make our way up the River Foyle and round a very nasty bend at The Crook just before securing alongside. We would usually take a pilot on the first two or three trips up the Foyle in such tricky circumstances but several submarines managed to get stuck on the mud whilst making the passage. The rise and fall of tide was considerable and so when a submarine got stuck 'on the putty' on a falling tide, the captain knew he was going to be very conspicuous for at least twelve hours.

One of the great advantages of a visit to 'Derry was the hospitality of its inhabitants. For those entitled to leave, there was an abundance of girls. As linen was produced in the area, there were a number of shirt factories which employed mostly female labour. The girls liked dancing and so did the sailors.

After a short rest we exercised again in the 'Derry Areas, but instead of going into 'Derry for the next weekend the Captain decided to spend the weekend at anchor off Douglas, Isle of Man. We were able to arrange a boat to take us ashore and we were royally entertained by the local dignitaries and townsfolk. As is often the case we were also given free access to a number of recreational facilities administered by the local authority including free rides on the horse drawn trams which ran up and down the sea front. John Fieldhouse spent most of the Saturday afternoon in one of these trams going backwards and forwards at no expense. This laid him open to a certain amount of leg-pulling about the tightness of his wallet.

After I had been in *Acheron* a short time George Hayhoe left the ship to take his Commanding Officers Qualifying Course – the 'Perisher' – and those who were left behind all moved up a peg. Dick Horner became the first lieutenant. I became third hand and Peter Godley fourth hand. At this time John Fieldhouse was still a lieutenant.

Our engineer was a Senior Commissioned Engineer, Joe Mullard, within the Branch Officer system. On 1 January 1956 the Admiralty had issued AFO 1/56 (Admiralty Fleet Orders) which totally reorganised the Branch Officer system. These officers were now to be called Special Duties Officers and were to wear sub lieutenants' stripes. Senior Commissioned Officers were to wear lieutenants' stripes. As a result Joe Mullard became a Lieutenant (SD) from 1 July 1956, and until 1 October 1956, when John Fieldhouse was promoted to Lieutenant Commander, every officer in the submarine was a lieutenant from the captain down.

Our next exercise area was in a position to the south of the Isle of Arran. At night we secured alongside the jetty at Campbeltown.

Campbeltown had the reputation of being the best run ashore in Scotland or probably the whole of the UK. On arrival we were always met by the harbour master, Captain MacShannon. He enjoyed his whisky but never overstayed his welcome. The jetty was relatively small and was intended for the use of fishing boats. The depth of the water alongside it was suitable for the fishing boats but submarines would sit on the bottom at low water. The navigator had to watch the tides carefully otherwise he would find the submarine firmly aground when it was time to slip and proceed to sea.

The nearest watering hole to the jetty was the Royal Hotel. It was very hospitable to visiting submarines, owing to the revenue they brought with them rather than the conduct of the ship's company. There was a public hall in the town named the Victoria Hall. As soon as a submarine was seen approaching the harbour, a dance was hurriedly arranged, and as my Canadian classmate, Neil Boivin, used to say in his mock Scottish accent: 'Aye, they'll be piping the whores down from the hills.' The Victoria Hall had a balcony and, having imbibed sufficient alcohol, one of the sailors' pastimes would be to jump from the balcony onto a dancing couple below. The authorities eventually closed the balcony when submarine dances were in progress.

During my first visit to Campbeltown, Peter Godley had badly twisted an ankle and felt unable to walk as far as the Royal. I overcame the problem by taking a fish cart and transporting Peter to the hotel in rickshaw fashion. The area by the jetty was not unlike a French town square with a public lavatory in the middle. I was passing the lavatory when a Scottish policeman came out. He was the standard size for Scottish policemen, being about six feet three inches. He stopped us and said: 'I suppose ye'll be Naval officers.' We had to admit that was the case but wondered why we had been so easily identified. Perhaps it was because by using the fish cart we had demonstrated initiative. We explained that Peter was *hors de combat* and that we intended returning the cart when we had finished with it, and he let us proceed to the Royal Hotel. We shared an enjoyable evening in the company of the *Alcide*'s officers as it was also in harbour. The engineer of *Alcide* was an extremely tall fellow called Freddie Costello. As we left the hotel I managed to get Peter Godley back onto the fish cart and we were joined by Freddie. Then the policeman approached us and a conversation took place. At one point Freddie explained to the policeman that he had a hobby.

'Oh, what is that?' asked the policeman.

'I collect different caps,' replied Freddie.

I now became suspicious and wondered whether I would have to leave Godley to his own devices sitting on the fish cart.

'And, unfortunately,' went on Freddie, 'I haven't yet acquired a Scottish policeman's cap with a diced headband.' He was looking at the policeman's hat all the while. I got ready to run. To my great relief Freddie decided not to try to relieve the policeman of his cap and we managed to get back on board in one piece. I couldn't help thinking of the treatment which the poor stoker in Gourock received in the hands of the police.

We also spent a couple of weeks running out of Rothesay. As well as acting as target for some of the working-up submarines we had some time to carry out our own evolutions and drills. One of the most interesting was learning how a submarine could sit on the sea bed. First, the chart had to be perused to ensure there were no wrecks in the area and that the sea bed was suitable, preferably sandy. The submarine had to be in good trim, and speed would be reduced gradually until the submarine was hovering just above the sea bed. With all the way off, water would be flooded gently into the trimming tanks, and the submarine would settle on the bottom. The waters to the south of Arran were ideal for this exercise.

We were at sea on 10 August and at three hundred feet when there were reports of a leak in the engine and motor room. We quickly came up to a hundred feet and having ascertained that it was safe to do so we came up to periscope depth. At this depth we couldn't find the leak so we returned to three hundred feet and there was no doubt that there was a fine spray throughout the compartment but we were unable to identify its source. So we had to return to Rothesay where the squadron experts did their best to determine where the leak was located. They were unsuccessful and so on 15 August we had to sail round the north coast of Scotland to Rosyth dockyard.

From a navigational point of view the easiest passage to Rosyth would be to sail through the Minch which lies between the Inner and Outer Hebrides and then on to the North Minch. The narrowest part of this passage is over ten miles wide so it is simple and less worrying for the captain.

But it is possible to take a shorter 'inner route'. John Fieldhouse decided to take the inner route. Apart from being the shortest and the most attractive passage, it exercised our skill in pilotage so I planned the passage which in some areas took me back into the waters which had impressed me so much in my first experience at sea in *Wakeful*.

After following our usual passage down the Clyde and round the tip of the Mull of Kintyre we went northward through the Sound of Jura, a most beautiful passage about half a mile wide at its narrowest point. We then turned northwards again passing Colonsay and into the Firth of Lorne until we had Oban on our starboard side. Then we negotiated the Sound of Mull passing Tobermory and going round the bleak and sparsely populated Ardnamurchan on the starboard side. Then into the Sound of Sleat which separates the Isle of Skye from the mainland. This was the trickiest part of the passage, with the tide running swiftly as we went through Kyle Rhea with a ninety degree turn to port. After that there was only the Kyle of Lochalsh to negotiate and then we were in the Inner Sound between Raasay and the mainland after which it was a relatively easy run up to Cape Wrath.

After passing Cape Wrath we turned eastward and had only to negotiate the inner sound of the Pentland Firth between Stroma and the mainland and the difficult parts of the passage were all behind us.

On our arrival at Rosyth we were placed in dockyard hands. The constructors tried magnetic crack detectors and x-ray equipment but they were hampered by all the equipment and pipework which prevented them getting close to the hull. Eventually they asked us to isolate the engine room and put a pressure of air inside it. They then sloshed soapy water over the hull and when we saw the bubbles emerging we knew we had found the leak. We had a hairline crack in a weld. It had to be cut out and re-welded and then, after a trial dive in a dockyard basin to ensure that the repair was watertight, we became operational once more.

It was while we were in Rosyth that international tensions with Egypt reached crisis point. British Reservists were called up and on 29 August British and French troops sailed for Suez.

We sailed from Rosyth on 16 September and as soon as we were in deep water we dived to our maximum diving depth and then returned to periscope depth and snorted for a period. Having decided all was well we surfaced and made our passage back to Rothesay. We then began a period of rather tiring day running out of Rothesay and then went south into the approaches to the English Channel for more day-running, spending each night at a buoy in Falmouth. At the week-end we went back to Gosport for the benefit of the Gosport 'natives'.

Once we'd finished our commitment in the Falmouth areas we returned to Rothesay to prepare for an extended period at sea in an area north of Iceland. At this time the Navy was developing a vast number of new equipments and these had to be tested in all weather conditions. Our task was to take some of these gadgets into Arctic waters to see how they performed. *Acheron* had undertaken some similar trials shortly before I joined and had experienced very rough weather.

One of our trials concerned food. Because of the long periods spent dived and therefore without sunlight, submariners were allowed extra rations to make up for any vitamin deficiencies which resulted. These were known as 'submarine comforts'. They consisted of very strong grapefruit juice, usually referred to as 'battery acid', and sardines and herrings in tomato sauce, usually referred to as HITS. But the naval victuallers were keen to modernize and we were issued with a number of pre-cooked frozen meals which were in their infancy at that time. We had two or three different dishes manufactured by Joe Lyons, one of which was 'Chicken Supreme'. An 'expert' came on board to brief us and instructed us to issue half a portion per man twice a week.

Our Coxswain 'Ruby' Ayres was in charge of catering. To be given free food in addition to his normal expenditure allowance was a godsend enabling him to reach an even higher standard than normal.

We completed storing and sailed on 20 November. Ruby decided that he wasn't going to fiddle about with half a portion per man so each man had a full portion. Everyone on board agreed that the meal was excellent but thought that the portions were inadequate It was decided to repeat the meal the next day but to issue double portions.

We had remained on the surface to get to our operational area more quickly. The weather was not at all rough so it was a comfortable passage. On the third night out, not long before we expected to make a landfall off the southern coast of Iceland, I had the 'two to four' watch which is one of the most miserable. At about three in the morning the rather muffled voice of the Captain came over the bridge intercom saying:

'Turn round and steer a reciprocal course.'

I thought quickly and couldn't understand the logic behind this order, so I assumed that the Captain had been dreaming so I replied: 'Say again, Sir.'

'Turn round and go the other way,' came back the rather impatient order.

I was now convinced that this order was the result of a dream and that the Captain had woken and given me a totally false instruction so again I said:

'Do you want me to turn round and steer back towards the UK, Sir?'

'Of course I do, that's what I keep telling you.'

So round we went and steered the reciprocal course heading for home. I was naturally anxious for my relief to get on the bridge so that I could find out what was going on. When I got below I discovered that owing to the political situation, there was a feeling that we could be going to war in the Middle East and we had been ordered to return home to disembark our experimental equipment and bring our torpedo outfit back to full strength.

Fortunately I didn't get bawled out for this. In fact I don't recall John Fieldhouse ever bawling anybody out which was a different cry from my time in *Scotsman*.

There was no point in keeping our experimental pre-cooked frozen meals on board as they would have to be unloaded on return to harbour, so we ate them.

When we arrived back, one man whom we didn't recognise came on board and explained that he had come up from London to collect our report on the catering trial and to take back the uneaten food. He was pretty cross when he was told that we had eaten all of it and we hadn't had time to write a report.

War didn't break out and we spent some time alongside the depot ship until a new programme was devised, and in due course were scheduled to go back to the 'Derry Areas. We moved up river to secure alongside *Stalker* in 'Derry on 27 November, my 25th birthday.

Officers frequented the Northern Counties Club for their relaxation where we were accepted as honorary members. To obtain admission we had to sign the visitors' book. After Peter Godley and I had celebrated my birthday in various bars we decided to conclude the run ashore in the Club. I have always asserted that whenever I went ashore in company with Peter I got into trouble, so I regard him as the instigator of our misdemeanours. On this occasion I started the ball rolling by signing in as 'The Earl of Hampton Hill'. Not to be outdone, Peter adopted a grander and rather offensive title. We hadn't finished our first drink when an apoplectic club secretary came storming over and threw us out. With cries of 'We've been thrown out of better joints than this', we staggered off to another hostelry and thought no more about it. The next morning we were sent for by John Fieldhouse who had received a letter from the secretary with the offending page torn out of the visitors' book. He was naturally upset that we should let him down so badly by our behaviour and stopped our leave for the rest of our stay. At least it kept us out of further trouble.

We spent the next two weeks operating in the 'Derry Areas.

The choice of navigation instruments was extremely limited at this time. The basic aids were bearings of shore objects, the echo sounder and the hand held sextant. The only two external aids were radio direction finding beacons and a system known as Consol. The Consol system radiated signals from a central source. Depending on the position of the recipient, a series of 'dots' followed by a series of 'dashes' were received. Having counted these they were supposed to give a line of bearing from the transmitting source which could be plotted on the specially printed Consol chart. In practice, the sound of the dots faded away and after a period of time the dashes slowly became audible. The perceived bearing on which the recipient was lying had an error of up to ten degrees. The transmitter which served the 'Derry Areas was at Bushmills. After striving to make sense of the Consol system during all my time in *Acheron*, I came to the conclusion that the only useful thing which came out of Bushmills was its whiskey.

Snorting at night was frequently difficult particularly in rough weather. On a moonless night we had no hope of seeing the horizon or nearby ships or fishing boats. Red lighting is provided throughout the submarine for use at night at sea to dilate the eyes' pupils to improve 'night vision'. On one occasion off 'Derry it was so dark outside that all the red lighting was switched off. The only light in the control room was that from the instruments which allowed the helmsman and planesmen to control the submarine. The ship's log which was made out the following day in my handwriting says: 'Courses and speeds as requisite. The log was not kept because: (1) No spare hand available, (2) Insufficient light in control room.'

We returned to *Adamant* on 7 December as *Acheron*'s commission was coming to an end and she was due to be refitted. After each refit a Safety Certificate is signed. This expires after two years after which the submarine is no longer permitted to dive.

We were due to refit at Cammel Laird's at Birkenhead but had to go to Portsmouth first so that we could disembark the stores which would not be required during the refit. We sailed for Gosport on 13 December.

On preparing for sea the First Lieutenant would be on the bridge in overall charge. The navigator would also be on the bridge. When it was time to go to sea the CO would be piped over the side and go straight on to the bridge where he would expect to find everything ready.

On this occasion we were ready in plenty of time and Dick Horner and I were talking about the idiosyncrasies of various captains. Then we puzzled over any idiosyncrasy which John Fieldhouse might have. We could only think of one and that was his constant perception that there was a slight list on the boat.

One of the First Lieutenant's most responsible duties is to calculate the trim on the submarine which he does before going to sea. Its aim is to ensure that the submarine is neutrally buoyant when it dives, that is, it should be heavy enough to sink when the main vents are open but not so heavy that it plummets to the depths and possibly hits the sea bed. The main vents are at the top of the external ballast tanks which keep the air in the tanks when the submarine is on the surface and conversely allow the tanks to fill with water when dived. The diving trim is 'put on' by filling internal trim tanks to the required amount to achieve a 'trim'. Most of the work in calculating a trim relates to the fore and aft trim, but there is also the athwartships trim which one wouldn't normally bother to calculate. If the submarine is listing to one side, it is only necessary to transfer water from one side to the other until the list is removed. We were usually upright as near as made no difference but it was never to the Captain's satisfaction. We all agreed that John Fieldhouse's only whim was his concern about a list on the boat. Having come to this conclusion we heard the shrill pipe of the bos'un's call as the Captain came on board. He climbed up to the bridge and after a brief 'Good Morning' he turned to Dick and said: 'Can't you get rid of this list, Number One?' All those on the bridge including the signalman, who had overheard our conversation, fell about laughing while the Captain stood there totally dumbfounded as to what he had said.

On arrival at Gosport John Fieldhouse went to see the Drafting Commander on the Flag Officer Submarines staff to arrange our next appointments. As it was the end of a commission I naturally wondered what sort of report I would get from John Fieldhouse. John Fieldhouse sent for me one day and gave me a very good flimsy but also, much to my surprise, he told me that he had recommended me to serve as the navigator of *Porpoise*. This was an honour indeed, as *Porpoise* was to be the first operational submarine to be built since the war and would incorporate a number of new ideas, some of which were quite revolutionary.

The final act of significance to me in 1956 was when John Fieldhouse awarded me my watchkeeping ticket after six months in *Acheron* on 31 December. This asserted that I was capable of keeping a watch on the bridge without supervision. I was also confirmed in the rank of lieutenant on the same day but my pay remained the same.

On 14 January we sailed from Gosport and had an uneventful trip to Liverpool, taking a pilot on board to take us to our berth at Cammell Laird's yard in Birkenhead. We were met by a host of shipyard managers, all keen to get started, so one of our priorities was to get all our personal belongings out of the boat. There were other Naval members already at Liverpool who were able to give us guidance including recommending a suitable hotel. After booking in we returned on board to return those stores which we had needed to steam the ship round from Portsmouth. We handed the submarine over to the shipyard and after we had concluded all the paperwork it was early evening and a rather wild party developed. There were quite a number of opened bottles of wine and spirits in the wardroom wine cupboard. Initially it was possible to mix the normal drinks, gin with tonic, brandy with ginger ale and so on. But as the evening wore on the choice became limited and as our palates became less choosy drinks such as Crème de Menthe with tonic and Cointreau with ginger ale were being poured. Eventually I decided to call it a day and I weaved my way back to the hotel leaving my colleagues to finish off what was left.

Understandably I fell into a deep sleep. At about four in the morning I awoke slowly. Being in an unusual bed it took time to work out where I was, and then the realisation came to me that I had been woken by a scratching noise outside the bedroom window. Thinking that I was in no fit state to apprehend a burglar I made my way cautiously over to the window until I could make out the bulk of a man's figure outside. At about the same time, the intruder started calling out for assistance and I recognised the voice of Dick Horner, the first lieutenant. I opened the window as hurriedly as possible and helped him into the bedroom away from his precarious hold of the drainpipe. He had managed, with the help of others, to finish the contents of the wardroom wine bar but had been locked out of the hotel on account of the late hour.

The next morning I took the train back to *Dolphin* to collect my kit and make my way to my new appointment at Barrow. There was a natural feeling of apprehension. In the 3rd Squadron I had made a number of friends, but now I was joining a new team none of whom I knew, and I was going to a town which I had never visited before. I had no idea what would be expected of me as the navigator of this brand new submarine. It was a completely new start.

CHAPTER 12

Vickers Armstrongs, Barrow – Standing by *Porpoise* and trips up north in *Tabard*

A s THE FIRST operational submarine to be built since the war, the new *Porpoise* was naturally an entirely new class of submarine. She was the second submarine to bear the name. The first *Porpoise* was a minelayer built by Vickers Armstrongs and launched in August 1932. She carried out a number of successful patrols in the Mediterranean in the early 1940s in which she sank 7 enemy vessels which earned her ship's company 1 DSO, 2 DSCs, 4 DSMs and 5 Mentions in Dispatches. She was then moved to the Far East where she was bombed and sunk by Japanese aircraft in the Malacca Straits on 16 January 1945. She was the last British submarine to be sunk in World War II.

There was natural concern right up to Board level that this programme should be a success, and to achieve this FOSM established the Porpoise Class Submarines (Building) Group in April 1956 based at Barrow. Cdr. James Pardoe was the Commanding Officer. Others in the Group were Lt. Cdr. Roger Presley and Lt. Cdr. John Grove together with a number of senior Chief and Petty Officers. Eight submarines were to be built: three at Barrow, three at Cammel Lairds (Birkenhead), and two at Scott Lithgow's (Glasgow). Whilst looking after *Porpoise* at Barrow, members of the Group made regular visits to the other two yards. John Grove had also been appointed to take over as Electrical Officer of *Porpoise*. Roger Presley was already in post as the Engineer Officer. As the boats progressed Lt. Cdr. Mike Collis joined *Porpoise* whilst Roger Presley remained with the Building Group until it disbanded. *Porpoise* had been launched in April 1956. She was named by Mrs Luce, the wife of Rear Admiral J.D. Luce, the Naval Secretary to the First Sea Lord. The second submarine of the class, *Rorqual*, had also been launched before I arrived in Barrow. When I joined, Lt. Basil Whitecross had been appointed as First Lieutenant and Lt. Sandy Woodward as Torpedo Officer (Third Hand).

I had just found myself a lodging in Barrow when I was told that I was to be loaned to the submarine *Tabard*.

Tabard was about to take what submariners called at that time 'a trip up north' and for this reason she needed an extra officer – a fifth hand. I suppose it was felt that I didn't have much to do at Barrow and it was probably thought that I needed more sea experience. So I packed all the kit that I would require at sea and went back to Gosport to join *Tabard* on 18 February 1957. She was attached to the 5th S/M Squadron and ran out of Gosport. The CO was Lt. Cdr. Peter Samborne with Lt. John Brockman as 1st Lieutenant, Lt. Dick Heaslip as Navigator and Lt. Tony 'Red' Miller as Torpedo Officer. The two technical officers were Lt. Ted Edwards, mechanical engineer and Lt. Mike Hosking, electrical.

Being the junior 'boy' I was appointed duty officer on the evening before we sailed for our patrol. This wasn't an auspicious occasion for me. At about 2100 the submarine is cleaned through and the duty officer does 'rounds'. I wasn't aware that the duty electrician had been under-performing. As well as being under stoppage of leave he was told that if he didn't pull his socks up he would be thrown out of submarines. When I arrived in the motor room he was standing facing me as I walked aft. It was customary to report: 'Motor room cleaned up for rounds, Sir. Motor room bilges dry.' As he was standing facing me in the middle of the passage, I stopped a few feet in front of him and he sprang to attention, saluted, and gave the correct report. I stopped, returned the salute, took a pace forward and disappeared into the bilges. In his enthusiasm he had lifted the deck-boards so that I would have a clear view of the dry bilges. Unfortunately I cracked my shin against one of the remaining deck boards as I fell and suffered quite a large wound. With the wound being dirty as well as bloody I made my way to *Dolphin*'s sick bay and asked for treatment. I was told that the duty doctor was watching a television programme and would see to me when it had finished. Although my leg was sore for the first few days at sea I was fortunate in that it healed without complications. The incident is an example of the different attitudes adopted by members of the Naval Medical Service. Some of the doctors in the Service were of the highest calibre whilst at the other end of the scale we had our share of the dregs of the medical profession.

We sailed the next morning. An incident as we slipped from the jetty brought home to me the trustworthiness of submarine ratings. One of our ship's company was missing, but the Captain decided to sail without him. We had let go all lines and the Captain was swinging the stern out from the jetty so that we could leave Haslar Creek stern first. Our bows were about six feet from the jetty when the sailor appeared running at top speed. With one enormous leap he jumped from the jetty and was caught by one of the casing party who saved him from falling over the side. I discovered later that he was not only a sonar operator but also the boat's chief wit and cartoonist.

Tabard was one of the 'T' Class submarines which had been so successful during the war. But *Tabard* hadn't been completed until 25 June 1946 and had therefore not seen any active service. Immediately after the war the Admiralty was keen to build a new class of submarine in order to incorporate all the lessons learnt in the previous conflict, but this would take time. In March 1949 it approved a programme to convert welded 'T' boats into Fast Battery Drive (FBD) submarines which became known as ' T-conversions' or 'Super Ts'. The conversion required having the hull cut in two with the two sections being pulled apart making room for two extra motors and extra batteries. The propulsion system changed from direct drive to diesel electric. The underwater speed doubled to 15 knots. The original casing and the bridge structure were replaced with a smooth even plating creating a large fin housing 2 stainless steel periscopes, 2 radar masts, 2 snort masts and a telescopic wireless mast. Another welcome feature was the 'periscope roundabout' comprising an electrically driven seat connected to the periscope which increased the efficiency of the look-out by several orders of magnitude. Another new feature was the ability to control the opening and shutting of main vents by means of electric solenoids.

We also had automatic depth keeping equipment ('George') in the control room similar to that in an aircraft. It was rarely used because of its unreliability.

We set off on the surface and ran north until the Captain felt that we needed to dive to avoid detection by surface or air forces. We remained dived until we withdrew from the patrol area. We had on board an American submarine officer. I learned that this was customary practice. We also had on board a Lt. Cdr. Anthony Mays from the Naval Intelligence Division. He was an Observer in the Fleet Air Arm but was with us as a Russian interpreter. He was an extremely convivial messmate.

Lt. Cdr. Mays had a fund of amusing stories which he declared to be true. One which I remember, related to his training as a Russian interpreter. The course started in a London classroom. Once the student reached a certain standard he was sent to live in Paris because that was the place in Western Europe where there was the greatest concentration of Russian speakers. They were mainly White Russians who had escaped during the revolution. Mr Mays had a compatriot who teamed up with a female in Paris and moved into her apartment. They spoke in her language all the time and he naturally thought that when he returned home for his final examination, he would pass with flying colours. After his oral examination his tutor said to him: 'Very good, but there is one slight problem. You are actually speaking Serbo Croatian!'

Lt. Cdr. Mays had great difficulty in operating the heads (lavatory) which involved operating a series of valves in the correct order. He never mastered the sequence and invariably suffered the embarrassment expressed as 'getting your own back'.

With a full ship's company and the extra passengers on board we had to ensure that we had ample food for the trip. We went to sea with crates of food lying in the passages which made a false deck. We worked our way through these boxes until the deck resumed its normal level. We also had on board as much bread as could be stowed. The loaves were wedged into any overhead space which could be found. The damp and smelly atmosphere soon caused the outside crust to go mouldy. When this occurred the crust would be cut off and the inside eaten.

I quickly learned that I was in the hands of a thoroughly competent captain and learnt many lessons from him. Rather like John Fieldhouse he seemed to have only one idiosyncrasy. His was a passion for tinned sweet corn. Fortunately we had taken sufficient on board to keep him happy throughout the trip.

The air in a submarine soon becomes foul and smoking is restricted. At times when the captain feels that smoking may be permitted temporarily, he will give the order and the broadcast 'One all round' is made. This gives permission for each crew member to smoke one cigarette. When the submarine is deep and about to come to periscope depth, the Captain will order the sonar operator to make an 'all round sweep' on the sonar to make sure that the submarine doesn't collide with any surface vessels above. The sonar operator who only managed to jump on board at the last moment would occasionally play a trick. After the Captain had ordered an all round sonar sweep, the operator would report on the broadcast: 'One all round…(long pause)…sweep carried out, Sir.' By the time he finished the report, most of the crew would have lit up and taken their first satisfying drag.

Dick Heaslip was probably rather more finicky than the average submariner and liked to keep his charts as clean as possible. Whenever Ted Edwards passed through the control room going for'ard from the engine room, he would stop and pore over the chart discussing the ship's position with keen interest. When he continued for'ard there would be a large oily thumb print on Dick's chart which infuriated him and which had, of course, been implanted for that very purpose.

Whilst we were returning from this patrol we were told to pass a specific distance to the west of the Shetlands. Although we didn't talk about this we knew that the Americans had been laying a network of cables on the sea bed to detect Russian submarines and surface craft as they made their way out of their Northern Fleet bases into the Atlantic. The system was called SOSUS (Sound Surveillance System). These large low frequency fixed arrays enabled the Americans to detect submarines at extremely long range. It was very effective in detecting and plotting the Russian submarines as well as other shipping.

Our patrol lasted for seven weeks at sea which was the longest period that I had been at sea at the time. I remember thinking half way through the trip, when spirits were probably at their lowest ebb, that when we got back to harbour we would probably spend our first night ashore as far from each other as possible. To give an idea how close we lived together, I was 'hot bunking' with Mike Hosking. That means that when he got out of bed to go on watch, I got in between the same blankets which he had just vacated. As this situation prevailed for seven weeks our bunk was odorous, but certainly not fragrant.

When we got back alongside at *Dolphin* I took the opportunity in the early evening to take a long stroll along the sea front towards Alverstoke. By the time I got back to *Dolphin* I had blisters on the soles of my feet which brought home to me how little we had walked whilst at sea. That didn't stop me from going ashore to a pub with the rest of the wardroom. We found ourselves playing darts squashed together like sardines even more closely than the conditions we had found discomforting at sea.

I expected to return to Barrow after this patrol but Peter Samborne requested that I should stay on board for a little longer as *Tabard* was programmed to take part in an exercise followed by some more secret activities.

Whilst we were waiting for our orders to sail Mike Hosking and Ted Edwards spent their evenings relaxing in their favourite Southsea pub. As Gosport is on the other side of the harbour they had to rely on a boat to ferry them back to *Dolphin*. This was inconvenient because it curtailed their drinking hours, until one day they hit on an idea which seemed to be infallible, particularly as they were in their cups. Before leaving the pub they phoned the quartermaster who ran the boat routine. One of them explained that he was an admiral who had travelled down from London. He asked for the boat to wait for him until he arrived at the jetty on the Portsmouth side. The quartermaster wasn't in a position to argue so he agreed, but being alert he informed the Officer of the Day and the Duty Lieutenant Commander so that the Admiral could be properly received.

Eventually, some time after the boat was scheduled to depart, Mike and Ted staggered down to the jetty and after boarding the boat ordered the cox'n to 'Carry on'.

'I'm afraid I can't go yet, Sir, until Admiral Bloggins [or whatever name they had given] arrives.'

After a period of waiting Ted and Mike realised they had talked themselves into an inextricable position. They had to admit that the cox'n was waiting for a mythical admiral and after some persuasion the cox'n took the boat back to *Dolphin*. The senior officers waiting to greet the Admiral were naturally unamused and Mike and Ted suffered the consequences the next morning.

Before we sailed for our next patrol sometime in May '57 it was decided that we would give a cocktail party on board to thank the squadron officers for all they had done for us. All the senior officers and the staff and their wives were invited. Mike and Ted were naturally ashore the night before saying goodbye to their drinking friends. One of Mike's particular friends was a maintenance man at Billy Manning's funfair by Southsea pier. His job at the funfair was to replace defunct bulbs in the illuminations. He was known as 'Sparky'. Being in the electrical business 'Sparky' and Mike had an affinity. Consequently Mike invited Sparky to the cocktail party. The receiving officers on the casing could hardly believe their eyes when this apparition appeared on the casing, waiting his turn to go down the ladder into the submarine with the gold-braided guests. Sparky was dressed in brown shoes with no laces, a pair of flannels which were probably grey under the grease and a tattered and torn blue polo necked sweater. But the Navy is trained to deal with the unexpected and to have the ability to make conversation with a wide cross-section of people, so Sparky mingled with the guests, had his glass topped up from time to time, and generally made the party a bit different from usual.

The drink which *Tabard* served at cocktail parties was rather strong, even by submarine standards. The boat had previously made a visit to France and had taken on board a supply of *fundador* (a type of 'firewater' brandy). They served it with a sugar cube with a dash of Angostura bitters in each glass, then a large slug of *fundador* topped up with cheap champagne. It went under the name of 'elephant's breath'. This was quite a change for Sparky who usually stuck to Watney's Red Barrel.

The next day we took our hangovers and the submarine to sea. We took passage up the North Sea and entered the Baltic via the Kiel Canal. At this time the North Sea was littered with mines and it was necessary to navigate with extreme care to keep in the swept channels. Our duty in the exercise was to attack ships of the Home Fleet. When it ended we visited Stockholm. This followed the usual pattern of foreign visits. We laid alongside *Maidstone* which was the flagship of the CinC Home Fleet.

On the first evening in harbour the customary cocktail party was held on board the flagship. The senior guests frequently brought their daughters who were quickly assessed by the junior officers. In this case all eyes were on the daughter of the senior Swedish admiral present, a most beautiful Scandinavian blonde. After a certain amount of jockeying for her favours it seemed that the CinC's flag lieutenant was emerging as the clear favourite. It appeared that the Swedish admiral's daughter had accepted the flag lieutenant's invitation to go on to an expensive restaurant for dinner. But I persevered amongst the other potential swains and asked her whether she would like to come on board *Tabard* after the party to see over the submarine. That was a lucky stroke! I hadn't realised that in the Swedish Navy, ladies were not allowed on board submarines under any circumstances. Even though she was an admiral's daughter this beautiful girl had never seen the inside of a submarine. After weighing up the pros and cons she opted to come on board the submarine with me. We were still able to go on to a less expensive meal afterwards and enjoyed each other's company during the rest of the visit. Stockholm therefore still holds many pleasant memories for me.

After a few days of social activity we sailed for a patrol in the eastern waters of the Baltic. Our participation in the exercise had really been a ruse to get us into the Baltic without suspicion. We had great difficulty when diving in catching our first trim owing to the difference in salinity of the water in the Baltic to that of the Atlantic to which we were accustomed. Once we had caught the trim we settled down to an interesting snooping activity on the Soviet Baltic Fleet.

On completion of this patrol we visited Copenhagen, mainly, I think, to justify to prying eyes our continued presence in the Baltic. We were instructed to leave the Baltic at night and to dive and remain so until after we had passed through the narrows of the Kattegat. Once again we assumed that we were testing the efficiency of the SOSUS system in that area.

We returned to *Dolphin* and after we had tidied up a few loose ends I was told to return to *Porpoise* in Barrow. I arrived back on 4 July to find that a new CO, Lt. Cdr. Brian (Nobby) B.W.M. Clarke, had taken over command on 13 March.

Now that I was back at Barrow my task was to learn about the intricacies of *Porpoise's* systems and oversee its building programme as far as my responsibilities as navigator and communications officer were concerned.

A civilian shipbuilding yard has a number of marked differences to a Naval dockyard. Vickers was an enormous yard. In addition to *Porpoise* they were also building two more Porpoise class submarines; the submarine *Excalibur;* the aircraft carrier *Hermes*; an oil tanker and a number of other craft. The *Porpoise* officers had a small office in the yard which we could use for perusing drawings, dealing with correspondence (of which there was a great deal), and holding countless meetings. As well as training ourselves in all the new systems, the senior and junior ratings were also learning the systems and were converting the ship's drawings into diagrammatic form for printing in the Porpoise class handbook for use at *Dolphin* by those being trained in the Porpoise systems. Very often they would discover design errors and we would then talk these through and propose modifications to the constructors based at Bath and with Vickers' managers.

The building work was progressing slowly. The slow progress was not always the shipbuilder's fault. As the submarine was being built, alterations and additions were periodically being approved by the Admiralty and where possible the shipbuilder incorporated them into the programme. But eventually the shipbuilders could only incorporate the modifications if they were given additional time for completion of the building programme. This process leads to the inevitable consultations and bargaining until the Admiralty declares a moratorium after which no more modifications are accepted.

Although the submarine was not yet complete certain systems were ready for testing. The engines and generators were ready and trial runs were undertaken. The propulsion system was a completely new concept in *Porpoise*.

Previously most British boats used the 'direct drive' system. These boats had twin propellers with an engine on each side of the submarine. The engines at the forward end of the engine room were connected by means of engine clutches to their motors. The motors were connected by means of tail clutches to the propeller shaft which passed through the pressure hull by means of hull glands. This gave a variety of propulsion and battery charging combinations which would meet all the submarine's requirements. To propel the submarine through the water by the engine both the engine clutch and the tail clutch would be engaged. To propel the submarine by means of the main motor, the engine clutch would be disengaged and the tail clutch engaged. In harbour, when it was necessary to charge the battery, the engine clutch would be engaged with the tail clutch disengaged and the main motor would then be used solely as a generator. This was a system which had proved thoroughly reliable over the years and in which submariners had great confidence. There had been some modifications in this traditional system in the 'T' conversions of which *Tabard* was one.

The system in *Porpoise* was described as 'diesel-electric'. Each engine was connected to a generator as a completely separate system, and a motor was connected to the propeller as another completely separate system. The arrangement was duplicated with one system to port and the other to starboard. The Navy had made a decision some time earlier to make their submarines as quiet as possible. The diesel-electric system was a step in that direction. Noise reduction was further enhanced by mounting the diesel engines on flexible mounts. When we eventually tested the propulsion system it was found that our submarines were significantly quieter than their American counterparts.

The engine was a completely new design known as the 'Admiralty Standard Range – One' (ASR1). The 16 cylinder engines were all built in Chatham Dockyard. The smaller cylinders made the submarine even quieter.

Not only were John Grove and Mike Collis highly competent technicians, they were also resourceful in resolving problems, although Mike's expertise was tinged with eccentricity.

One of the most serious design defects was with the governor which controlled the engine speed. Occasionally it would fail completely and allow the engine to increase to a speed which could damage the engine. The engine could then only be stopped by cutting off the engine's fuel supply. Mike Collis designed a new governor. This became a standard fitting and Mike received an award from the Herbert Lott Trust Fund which had been established to make awards for people who make exceptional contributions such as Mike's.

John Grove also received the same award. This was for his work on the Automatic Hydroplane Control Gear, 'George', which had been fitted in *Tabard* but rarely used because of its unreliability. John's solution was simple. The system required an input to tell 'George' the accurate depth of the submarine. This was achieved by measuring the outside water pressure. But the sea water pressure pipe was led horizontally from the control box through the pressure hull to the sea. Every time the submarine rolled in heavy seas 'George' would record this as a depth change. John Grove arranged for the sea water inlet to be moved to the keel where the submarine's rolling would have least effect. The problem was resolved.

We had another problem in the engine room. The older boats had much slower engine revolutions creating tolerable noise at a lower frequency. The ASR1s at high speed created high frequency noise making it almost impossible to hear anyone speak and therefore pass information or orders to others in the compartment. John Grove talked to the Naval Constructors at Bath about the problem and discovered that aircraft carriers were now being fitted with magnetic loop circuits, noise cancelling microphones, and radio receivers fitted ear-muffs. With John's personality he easily enlisted 'a splendid fellow in Bath' who knew where the equipment was being produced. This chap put him in touch with someone who 'was a good chap to talk to'. The work was being done at a Naval laboratory (probably in West Drayton). The aircraft carriers' requirement was to enable good communications to be available on a noisy flight deck, which was identical to our problem. The contact in the laboratory was very helpful and willingly gave John a noise cancelling microphone, a receiver fitted ear-muff, and a short description of how to rig a simple magnetic loop circuit. His final words to John were: 'Try not to let the powers that be know what you are up to.' With Vickers' help, John set up a magnetic loop circuit with the microphone and ear-muff supplied and it worked very well. John believes that we could never have completed harbour and sea trials safely without the loop. The secret was kept by all who knew about it until our acceptance trials. FOSM had a representative on board who sent a very enthusiastic signal to his Lord and Master (FOSM) and copied the signal to the world and his wife! The net result was that John received a mild rebuke from FOSM and very nice private letter from him saying 'splendid work – Bravo Zulu'! We heard later that the unfortunate man who had given John the equipment was sacked. The loop system is now widely used in public halls and churches.

Mike's interests were far wider than engineering. He decided that *Porpoise* needed a motto. The previous *Porpoise*, having been a minelayer, had an unsuitable motto so Mike decided to start from scratch. Mike went to the library and found that '*ludo, ludere*' meant 'play, gamble or gambol'. He suggested that the motto should be '*ludo cum mortis*'. (I gamble/gambol with death'). This was rejected on the grounds it was too macabre. He then suggested '*ludo cum fortuna*' (I gamble/gambol with fortune). This suggestion went to FOSM for approval. There was a better Latin scholar than any of us on FOSM's staff who pointed out that it was grammatically incorrect, and it became '*Cum fortuna ludo*'. Submariners play a ferocious game of ludo at sea which they call 'uckers'. The crew changed the motto's translation to 'lucky at uckers' or 'come for a game of uckers'.

My job was to ensure safe stowage of all the confidential books and communication equipment as well as the charts and navigational apparatus. My responsibilities were clearly less demanding than John's or Mike's.

I bought my first car in Barrow. It was a Morris 'E' type which I bought from Tommy Entwhistle for £72. Tommy was a Vickers design draughtsman and being an engineer by profession, he kept the car in beautiful condition despite its age. I bought it to replace my motor cycle. On arriving at Barrow I had decided that I would spend as many of my weekends as possible touring the Lake District on my motor cycle, but every Saturday morning when I set off, I found I became drenched with heavy rain before I had gone more than a few miles, so I decided to invest in a car.

Although Tommy had designed a number of things in the Porpoise Class submarine, we always knew him as the designer of the interlock system of the garbage ejector. One of the problems when on patrol in a submarine was how to get rid of all the rubbish, known as 'gash'. During the war submarines had to surface at night to charge the batteries and whilst doing so the gash would be thrown over the side. But this was potentially dangerous because if the gash floated it might give away the submarine's position to the enemy. We were now able to charge our batteries whilst dived by means of the snort system. Gash ditching experiments had been made by placing the gash in a large bag and firing it from the torpedo tubes. But the disadvantage was that a torpedo had to be withdrawn from a torpedo tube to make space for the bag. It was obvious that a separate tube was required for the ejection of gash.

The garbage ejector which evolved was a small tube about a foot in diameter which pointed downwards. It had an inner and an outer door. It was necessary to have fool-proof interlocks to prevent both doors being opened at once. The gash was ejected by pumping water into the top of the tube thus forcing the gash out. No air would float to the surface and give the submarine's position away and if properly weighted there would be no tell-tale signs of garbage on the surface. It was Tommy Entwhistle's interlocking system which made it impossible to open both doors at the same time so that the equipment was perfectly safe.

The car that I bought off Tommy had been tended with the equal care and attention that Tommy utilised when designing the garbage ejector interlocking system – with one exception. The steering system on the car was of the rack and pinion type. At some time, Tommy had obviously stripped this down and when he put it back together he had got the teeth slightly off centre. As a result the car had different turning circles depending on whether the car was turning left or right. To the left, the diameter of the turning circle was about fifteen feet, but to the right it was about sixty feet. This made it very difficult negotiating roundabouts. As I had to negotiate a busy roundabout on my way back to my digs I was never able to leave work during the rush hour. Anyone observing me going home after the rush hour had subsided, would have seen an 'E' type Morris having great difficulty getting round the roundabout and going into reverse from time to time to get the car pointing in the right direction.

Living within a civilian environment made us more aware of activities outside our Naval circle. Sandy Woodward joined a local dramatic society and had already performed in one play before suggesting to me that I should join to broaden my experience. He suggested that it was a good opportunity to do something quite unconnected with the Navy.

The first play in which I had a part was called *Mountain Air*. I played opposite a very attractive young lady called Joan Holgate. The final scene called on me to give her a passionate kiss before the curtain fell. This was something which didn't normally happen to me, not even in my private life. Although the lady was extremely kissable, the trepidation with which I awaited the final scene probably affected my performance.

The local drama critic went under the name of 'Talisman'. We didn't get a good write up for our efforts. Talisman wrote: 'How can one be nice to the good folk who presented *Mountain Air* in Barrow this week for a church restoration fund, and still remain honest to one's readers? But personal feeling must be subordinated to duty and it is with regret that I record the fact that this play was far, far below what I know the players concerned are capable of doing.' But he did say: 'I liked the performance of newcomer Bryan Smalley as the young ex-RAF officer. Although he has a great deal to learn there was a naturalness and ease about his work (apart from one horrible "dry") that was quietly impressive.' He concluded: 'The producer will want to forget this play as soon as possible – and so shall I.'

We had other amusements at Barrow apart from our thespian activities. Every Saturday night there was a public dance in one of the local halls, which we often attended. On one occasion John Grove attended with his wife Betty. Betty worked part time in the main Barrow hospital as a physiotherapist. John and Betty were accompanied by Dr Brenda Morris who was a work colleague of Betty's. I was by myself and was introduced to Brenda. I asked her to dance, and we were soon shuffling round the floor. In true Naval style I tried to generate conversation and asked her whether she had a particular specialisation.

'I'm a paediatrician,' she replied to my question.

'In that case you must be a very good dancer,' I replied confidently, intending to introduce a light hearted tone.

'Why's that?' she responded with a puzzled look on her face.

'Because you're an expert on feet,' I said, unknowingly getting myself into deep water.

'Actually a paediatrician deals with the development of children,' she said, putting me firmly in my place.

We finished the dance which was the last one I had with her. She went off looking for a partner who was less intellectually challenged.

James Pardoe was a keen fly fisherman. One day we were presented with a challenge from a local landowner. He had a river flowing through his estate across which a tree had fallen, partially blocking the river and spoiling the fishing. The owner had requested the local Territorial Army unit for assistance but they reported that they didn't have any heavy equipment so the owner turned to the Navy. This was an opportunity to get one up on the Army. After tossing several ideas around, John Grove came up with the answer. We would go into the river in our bathing costumes and saw the tree into logs. We started early one winter's morning in icy water. We finished by sunset blue with cold but the honour of the RN had been upheld.

Whilst the officers of *Porpoise* were keen to complete the building programme, so were the officers of *Excalibur,* the second of the HTP driven submarines with Lt. Cdr. Phil Wadman in command. The Admiralty had decided that *Excalibur* should have priority over *Porpoise* so she commissioned at the beginning of October '57 and consequently came out of the builder's yard before us.

After *Excalibur* left Barrow we soon had sufficient systems working in *Porpoise* to enable the submarine to dive for the first time and so a 'basin dive' was scheduled for a Sunday morning when the rest of the shipyard was reasonably quiet. A basin dive is carried out in an enclosed dock. The submarine is positioned by means of wires in the middle of the basin and then dives. There is no propulsion and the boat remains secured to the dockside. Although a first dive may sound as though it is something of a gamble, that isn't the case. Before the submarine dives, a vacuum test is carried out. All the hatches and outlets are shut and, with a low pressure pump called 'the blower', the air is pumped out of the submarine into the ballast tanks outside the pressure hull. When the vacuum is drawn and the pump stopped an internal pressure gauge is monitored. If the vacuum holds, it confirms that the submarine is watertight. Although there is some concern before the first basin dive, ours went off without any serious problems.

My next dramatic part was very small. I played one of the butlers in *The Importance of being Earnest* which was staged in November. I had only a few lines to utter and a few cucumber sandwiches to hand out to the principal players. This time 'Talisman' was rather kinder in his review. He praised all the leading characters and then added: 'The two butlers, Bob Pullen and Bryan Smalley, were more than adequate for what was demanded of them. How nice it was to see small parts well cast and impeccably played.'

Having completed the basin trial we continued towards the next stage which was to take the submarine to sea. I double checked to see that I had all my equipment necessary for sea and believed that I was well prepared until, about twenty four hours before we were due to leave harbour, I realised that I didn't have any Rev/Speed Tables. These tables would indicate how many revolutions were necessary for a given speed in knots. They were also useful when the captain ordered 'Slow Ahead together'. The motor room operator would need to know how many revolutions to put on when receiving such an order and conversely the captain would wish to know what speed the submarine would make through the water. I rushed up to the drawing office at Vickers and phoned the Constructor Branch at Bath and found that I appeared to be the first person to have thought of this. Fortunately I managed to get an estimate before we sailed and found, once we got to sea, that the given figures were more or less accurate.

Our first trip to sea didn't require us to dive, but we were able to test the propulsion and the steering in a variety of modes. We also tested the anchor and the capstan. We were naturally doubly careful to make sure that everything was right and that there were no accidents. We found that the capstan was grossly under powered. It worked on telemotor pressure. We had to keep the telemotor pumps running continuously in order to weigh anchor.

Until the submarine has been accepted by the Navy it cannot be commissioned or fly the white ensign. Instead it flies the red ensign indicating that it is a merchant ship. As Vickers were the employers of the captain of this merchant ship they had an obligation to pay him. This was only a nominal sum, I think a shilling a day, but as there was consideration on both sides it meant that there was a contract between the captain and the company. If there had been an accident it would have taken quite a bit of unravelling, involving arguments over whether the captain should be court martialled or dealt with by the mercantile marine authorities. Fortunately no accidents occurred. We returned to harbour that evening.

We then had to prepare for another short trial in the Irish Sea. Nobby Clarke was expecting to retire early under the scheme which had been introduced to slim down the Navy so Brian Hutchings was appointed to relieve Nobby Clarke in due course.

When the submarine is on the surface it is necessary to have good communications between the OOW on the bridge and the helmsman in the submarine below. Submarines were beginning to have an electronic communication system between the two, but past experience showed that this often failed owing to flooding of the system, or the sound emanating from it resembled a bubbling noise making it difficult to interpret the orders. To make sure that no order was misinterpreted it was the drill that all orders were repeated. For example the order from the bridge might be given 'Half Ahead together', to which the reply is 'Half Ahead together, Sir', and after the telegraphs had been set to the right position, the helmsman would report 'Both telegraphs showing half ahead together, Sir.' Even with this rigid procedure mistakes still happened. There was the story of the OOW on the bridge on a stormy night who was miserably wet and hoping for the hour to come when he would be relieved. He called down the voice pipe: 'What's the time?' The helmsman couldn't hear properly so he replied: 'Say again, Sir.' The OOW repeated the request which the helmsman still couldn't hear so he asked again for a repetition. Thoroughly irked by this inability to communicate and still praying for his watch to end, the OOW shouted down the voice-pipe as loudly as possible: ' TIME, TIME, TIME.' To which the helmsman replied: 'DIVE, DIVE, DIVE,' and promptly sounded the klaxon and opened all the main vents, causing the OOW to scramble down into the submarine with all haste and shutting the conning tower hatch behind him before a disaster occurred.

There's another story where communication between the OOW and the helmsman wasn't going too well when the OOW called down the voice-pipe: 'There's a fool at the end of this voice-pipe,' to which the prompt response came: 'Which end, Sir?'

On this occasion our problem was slightly different. The designers had decided to leave the old fashioned voice-pipe in the system. It had two valves which had to be shut on diving. The upper voice-pipe cock was on the bridge. Shutting it was the last thing that the officer on the bridge did before coming below. At the same time the helmsman would shut the lower voice-pipe cock. When we dived for the first time Nobby Clarke unfortunately forgot to shut the upper voice-pipe. When we surfaced the coxswain, who was on the helm, opened the lower voice-pipe cock and was deluged by the icy cold contents of the voice-pipe.

Although Nobby Clarke was in command, Brian Hutchings also came to sea with us as he had to learn the ship handling characteristics as quickly as possible.

Having made this short trip to sea we were now in a position to put the finishing touches to the submarine and complete all the furnishings, and as *Excalibur* had left Barrow, the submarine section at Vickers was able to devote more time to *Porpoise* and the other two submarines *Rorqual* and *Narwhal* which were following behind. But before we left Barrow, Sandy and I had been invited to take part in what was to be our last play. We were both asked to join the Furness Drama Association. This organisation was run by Ronald Metcalf, a draughtsman at Vickers' Yard, and his wife Betty. Local thespians thought it a great honour to belong to the FDA because membership was by invitation only.

We soon discovered that actors come in two groupings: those who take the major roles and those who take 'the juvenile leads'. Sandy and I were 'juveniles' on the grounds that there was no one younger than us in the company. We rehearsed in the Station Hotel which we found convenient because we could have a few quiet pints as the evening progressed.

I don't recall any auditioning. We were just invited to join and told which parts we would play. The scheduled play was *All for Mary* which was set in a Swiss alpine ski resort. I had the part of a young divorcée, 'the juvenile lead'. Sandy played the part of 'mine host' of the guest house where the action took place. I'm not sure where this put him in the pecking order but this didn't matter as neither of us cared. The lead was played by the producer's wife and the male lead by an effeminate bank clerk There was a bank manager's wife who played my ex-nanny who had somehow found herself in the same resort.

The nub of the plot was that I had booked in for a skiing holiday with my new wife, and my ex-wife had booked in with her new husband. Inevitably there were some bedroom scenes.

I didn't think it strange when I was told that I had been allocated a 'dresser'. She was several years older than me. I assumed that now we were in the big-time this was a normal procedure. My dresser paid me great attention and I have to admit that I found it flattering. As I was supposed to have a broken foot resulting from a skiing accident, I had a preformed bandage which I could slip on like a boot. It had been constructed by my dresser. It had a petite blue bow on it. I remarked to someone, probably Sandy, that I thought that this was going rather over the top. Whoever it was that I mentioned it to said: 'For goodness sake, Smalley, haven't you realised yet? She's a raving nympho-maniac. Her intention is not to dress you. It's quite the opposite.' Apparently the bow was a token of her affection for me. Her husband wasn't meeting her needs and I had been recruited to make good the shortfall. Being forewarned, I was then able to proceed with caution. I still feel guilty for letting the Navy down by not meeting her needs.

Eventually the opening day for the play arrived and I was still intact. There were several errors during the performance but no one seemed to notice. But the final performance could have ended in disaster. It was probably a good thing that Sandy and I were able to think quickly. As the play progressed, the plot required a certain amount of leaping about on the two beds which had been very crudely constructed. At a vital moment one of the beds collapsed. The audience, thinking this was all part of the plot, roared their heads off. Then, a minute or so afterwards, the second bed collapsed. By now, the audience was beside itself. Most of the cast were left speechless, but Sandy quickly grabbed a beer crate, which luckily we had emptied by this time, and went on stage with it. 'You notta worry, Señor. I feex!' he ad libbed, in a misplaced Spanish accent. No one seemed to notice that we had been transported to Spain. I took a beer crate on stage as well, thanking my lucky stars that I was getting a few moments respite from my undresser. After we had managed to lift up the beds and jam the beer crates underneath, we were able to make our exit to loud applause. The audience had no idea that we had completely lost the plot.

Talisman's headline read: '*All for Mary* is highly praised.' He wrote: 'I felt like an adjudicator colleague who, after a most inspiring festival production some years ago, appealed to a crowded house with the words "Ladies and Gentleman, what can I say?"' Later on he wrote: 'Bryan Smalley as Humphrey Miller, gave a fascinating performance. He never stepped out of character or convention and so delicately portrayed the stuffed shirt without conveying the pomposity which a less talented player would have brought to the character. He will make his mark in the amateur theatre.' About Sandy he wrote: 'The minor part of Alfonse was capably filled by John Woodward. He has a good stage presence and will do justice to more meaty parts.' Little did he know that we weren't taking it at all seriously and we were soon to sail away without any future thespian ambitions.

Porpoise soon progressed to the stage where we were able to take the submarine to sea on her last trial before acceptance. We were to go up to the Clyde for about a week. Brian Hutchings had taken over command from 'Nobby' Clarke. Each officer checked, and double checked, those things for which he was responsible until we felt confident to report to the Captain that we were ready for sea. Then we went ashore to our digs as arranged to allow the contract caterers on board to store for a week's trials. The caterers were from Glasgow and were quite used to taking larger ships down the Clyde on acceptance trials, but submarines, with their limited space, were a different matter altogether. We were to take over a hundred people on board, and the caterers had calculated, using a simple formula of a hundred people (times) four meals a day (plus) two pints of beer (times) seven days, plus an extra twenty five per cent for error, and so on. When we got down to the boat next morning we could hardly get on board. I went to my radar office where the Decca control panel was sited and I couldn't reach it because the compartment was full of beer crates. I managed to switch it on by using a broom handle which I poked between the beer crates. When Brian Hutchings came on board expecting the usual string of reports from his heads of departments that all was ready for sea, he received instead a litany of reasons why the submarine wasn't ready for sea. Captains aren't used to this. In addition to the beer and the food stacked in every conceivable compartment there was also a large amount of dirt and detritus in the bilges. If we had gone to sea in this state and there had been a leak, the water would have collected in the bilges and would soon have blocked the strainers to the pump suction pipes preventing us from pumping the bilges dry. Brian Hutchings refused to take the submarine to sea which caused a furore at the top levels of Vickers' management. But they knew that the Captain was right, and by the next morning's tide we had the bilges clean and the victualling stores reduced to a sensible level and we were off on our acceptance trials.

The reason we had so many of Vickers' men on board was that sea trials had become a trade unionists' bonanza. The men were paid for all the time on board, whether working or not, and this led to massive amounts of overtime. In addition there was an allowance for danger money, and by the time you added allowances for separation and living in cramped conditions and any other allowance the unions could think of, this was an opportunity not to be missed. Most of them didn't do a stroke of work. In the days when submarine hulls were rivetted together it was necessary to take a couple of caulkers along in case any of the joints leaked. *Porpoise* had an all welded hull and there was nothing for the caulkers to do, but they came along nevertheless.

On the way north to the Clyde through the Irish Sea it was a bit choppy and I realised that I had lost my sea legs and I was going to be sick. I told one of our sailors to find a bucket and take it back aft as fast as possible. I then made my way aft from the control room and was violently sick into the bucket. I was damned if I was going to let any dockyard worker see me being seasick.

Our first dive under our own power and without being attached to the shore by any means was in Loch Finnart. Although this is a very deep loch, at least if we had become stuck on the bottom our position would be known.

After we had completed the trials we returned to Barrow to complete the final touches. Lt. Norman Brookhouse joined us at the end of March to act for the time being as fifth hand. The Navy accepted *Porpoise* on 16 April and we held our commissioning ceremony the next day.

CHAPTER 13

Porpoise's first commission 1958-59

AFTER THE commissioning ceremony we sailed for Faslane to join the 3rd Submarine Squadron. By this time the 3rd Squadron had moved from Rothesay because of the inconvenience of not being on the mainland.

The new *Porpoise* incorporated all the experience gained from wartime operations; trials with surrendered U-boats, and the British 'T' conversions. *Porpoise's* two batteries were linked in series to give 880 volts for short bursts of high speed. Her range on the surface was 9,000 miles. The armament was Mark 8 and Mark 20 torpedoes. The most innovative piece of equipment was probably the 186 sonar. Low frequency sound travels much greater distances through the water than high frequency sound, but to detect low frequency sound it is necessary to have a much larger transducer to receive it. This problem was overcome by having a series of small transducers spread along the length of the hull. These were connected together electronically thus forming one transducer tens of feet in length. Its disadvantage was that the submarine had to go round in half a circle to sweep round the whole compass radius, but it was a major step forward in detecting targets at long ranges.

Faslane was an old wartime emergency port, which had been constructed in case Glasgow was so badly damaged by bombs that shipping could not get into the port. The jetty at Faslane was long and suited our purposes. A private company, Metal Industries Ltd., used the northern end of the jetty for breaking up old ships. When the film *A Night to Remember* was made telling the story of the sinking of the *Titanic*, some of the shots were taken on board a ship which was scheduled to be broken up at Faslane. The sailors from the submarine squadron were recruited as extras to dress up as passengers and jump over the side whilst the sinking sequences were being shot. They were paid a pound each time they made a jump. As soon as they got out of the water, they dried themselves off and queued up again in the hope of earning another pound.

The Captain S/M was about to change over. Captain John Adams MVO had been named as the new incumbent. The Commander S/M was Iwan Raikes. As we were a new class of submarine, every man and his dog wanted to have a look round, and when possible come to sea with us. We took a well known submariner, Commander J.C.Y. 'Randy' Roxburgh, to sea for the day and

Brian Hutchings was sounding off about how badly the control room had been designed. At the time 'Randy' Roxburgh was based at the MoD. As he left the boat he thanked Brian Hutchings for a most interesting day and then revealed that he had designed the control room layout. However there was some truth in Brian Hutchings' comments and a number of modifications were made to the submarines which followed us out of the builder's yard. On the other hand, to be fair to the designers and the builders there was not much wrong with the design of the submarine. After we had built eight of the Porpoise Class we went on to build another fourteen which became known as the 'O' Class, and a number of foreign powers soon became interested in buying the design from us. At the time of writing this book, most of the history of the Submarine Service refers to the success of the 'O' Class without acknowledging the groundwork which preceded it in the Porpoise Class.

At sea there was now no 'hot bunking'. Each man was issued with a nylon sleeping bag. When sharing a bunk it wasn't necessary to share the bedding as well.

Our first task was to 'work up' the submarine's crew so that it was an efficient team, and then try out all the pieces of equipment to test for defects and also to devise the best practice in their operation.

Once we had 'worked up' and passed our inspection we started a series of 'first of class' trials to establish the submarine's capabilities.

Shortly after the work-up Basil Whitecross was appointed back to *Dolphin* to do his 'perisher'. Sandy moved up from third hand to first lieutenant and I moved up to become third hand with responsibilities for the torpedoes and casing. Norman Brookhouse relieved me as the navigator. Andy Buchanan then joined us as the fifth hand.

We had to spend some time in *Porpoise* doing speed and stability trials. First we had to confirm the submarine's ability to recover from a steep angled dive. We started by putting on, say, ten degrees of bow down angle at five knots, and as we were plunging downwards ever deeper we would either go full astern to see how long it took to take the way off the boat, or we would put the hydroplanes to rise to see how much deeper we went before levelling off and eventually coming back towards the surface. If we wanted to encourage the bow to rise more quickly we could blow air into the forward main ballast tanks. Naturally there were combinations to these manoeuvres and we would increase the bow down angle and the speeds at which we did them in addition to doing them whilst turning so that there would be a corkscrew motion as we plummeted towards the sea bottom. As we grew in confidence we were diving at a 30 degree bow down angle. A motor cyclist leans inwards when turning but we soon discovered that the pressure of water on the submarine's fin pushes it outwards. It is eerie when experienced for the first time. Our Chief Stoker who had been through the war in submarines was clearly unhappy and on several occasions threatened to request to go back to General Service. But he stuck it out. After the speed trials we moved to Loch Fyne for less exciting noise trials and were able to renew our acquaintanceship with the Clark family at The George at Inveraray.

We then sailed for the Pool of London which a submarine usually visits once a year for good-will purposes, but this visit was on a higher official plane.

On our trip up Channel and into the Thames Estuary we experienced a serious problem with our main motors but we were able to continue to London. We crept up the Thames and secured between two buoys between Tower Bridge and London Bridge. The Customs and Excise authorities kindly provided a boat service.

We had a very full programme of official visits which started each day at 9.00 a.m. A boatload of visitors would arrive. We would show them through the submarine by taking them down the fore-hatch and re-appearing through the after hatch exactly half an hour later just as the boat was coming back alongside with the next batch of visitors, which having put them on board would take the earlier visitors ashore. There were quite a number of MPs and Members of the House of Lords as well as civil servants. The First Sea Lord, Admiral Mountbatten, was one of the visitors.

The visiting procedure continued until about 5.30 p.m. when we were given about an hour to get the boat and ourselves tidy before guests would appear on board for a cocktail party.

We had no control over who attended the daytime visits nor the cocktail party as this was all determined by the Admiralty. One of the things that became apparent during our stay was that every retired submariner for miles around also wanted to come on board. We tried to fit in the legitimate guests but there were a number with doubtful qualifications. As well as jamming the control room to its maximum capacity we also used the CPOs' and ERAs' messes. Basil Whitecross had both his wife and his mistress (a member of the Cavendish family) on board to the same party. At another of our parties there was a very noisy guest who soon showed evidence of having drunk too much and eventually became a thorough nuisance. I didn't attempt to control him as I thought he was the Captain's guest and in any case he was years senior and older than me. Sandy Woodward thought the same. The next morning the Captain showed that he was not best pleased with the activities of the night before. He said to Sandy: 'You are never to bring your friend on board this submarine again

Porpoise *in the Pool of London.*
Photograph courtesy of the Royal Navy Submarine Museum.

without permission,' to which Sandy replied, 'But we thought he was your friend, Sir.' Whoever he was, he had a very good party at our expense.

We finished that week in the Pool of London far more tired than after any week at sea. We then made our way down river to Chatham Dockyard to repair our ailing motors. As we didn't know how long it would take to cure the problem it was decided that we should stay there at least a month and we would take our seasonal leave from there. Sandy took his leave first and I deputised for him. As Sandy didn't know any one in London when we arrived in Chatham, he had asked his chum Chris Yelloly, a Supply Officer based in Chatham, for some contact addresses. After trying a number of contacts Chris tried Charlotte McMurtrie, a girl whom he knew from Carlisle, his home-town, who was working in London. She agreed to meet Sandy.

When I returned from my leave, I heard about this event and of the parties which had taken place in the flat at No. 7 Gledhow Gardens in the Old Brompton Road.

One of my ancillary jobs in the boat was wardroom wine caterer. We were allowed to purchase alcohol at Duty Free prices and to do this we used specialised wine merchants, Saccone & Speed. They naturally had a branch in Chatham. The wine caterer's job was tedious, with a plethora of forms to be completed and a need for tight security regarding the stock. One of the difficulties which added to my task was that Mike Collis only drank sherry or Merrydown cider. In those days Merrydown cost about 3s.6d. a bottle, but Mike insisted that I obtain it for him at duty-free prices. This meant that every time I ordered the Merrydown from the supplier I had to fill in a batch of special forms provided by Customs and Excise in order to get the cider three pence cheaper than the duty paid price.

John Grove and Sandy became concerned that I didn't have a particular girl friend and had decided that they were going to match me with a particularly attractive girl who worked for Saccone & Speed. On one run ashore they were trying to persuade me to date this young lady but I wasn't taking the bait. Eventually John said to me: 'Bryan, we're going to get you off with this young lady even if we have to lower you on to her with a crane!'

We were back in working order by 9 September and returned to our base on the Clyde.

John Grove left *Porpoise* on 24 September to go to the Imperial College of Science for nuclear engineering training. Spam Hammersley, a mechanical engineer, went on the same course. John was relieved by Mike Hosking

Porpoise's next commitment was to carry out trials at Arrochar on our torpedo firing equipment. It was approaching autumn which is a time of particular significance in retired submariners' calendars. On the first Friday in October, the officers' submarine reunion was held at Fort Blockhouse in Gosport, followed the next day by the Submarine Old Comrades Association annual get-together. The Association is abbreviated to SOCA. which is pronounced 'soaker' which is rather appropriate at their reunions. Most of SOCA's members at this time were men who had seen war service together, and they were particularly keen to learn about the new class of submarine.

To submariners the Jolly Roger has great historical significance. In 1900 the Controller of the Navy, Rear Admiral Arthur Wilson VC, declared that being in a submarine was 'no occupation for a gentlemen'. He added that 'submarines are underhand, unfair and damned un-English.' He despised them and regarded them as pirate vessels and said that any crews which were captured would be hanged as pirates. This feeling which prevailed amongst the senior officers of the Navy meant that the British were the last maritime nation to adopt submarines, but a flotilla had been established by the time the First World War broke out. On 13 September 1914, Lt. Max Horton torpedoed and sank the German light cruiser *Hela*. On return to harbour the submarine 'cocked a snoot' at Admiral Wilson by flying a Jolly Roger from the submarine as it returned to harbour.

During the 39-45 war each submarine had its own 'Jolly Roger', which as well as having a white skull and crossbones on a black background also had a number of other emblems indicating the submarine's achievements. It was possible to determine from the symbols on the Jolly Roger, the amount of tonnage sunk, the number of gun actions, and the clandestine operations undertaken.

One of the Chatham members of SOCA had made a replica of the previous *Porpoise's* Jolly Roger and had asked to present it to the new *Porpoise* at the SOCA's annual reunion. As we were programmed to do our trials in Loch Long at this time, the Captain was unable to go to Gosport to receive this gift, nor could the First Lieutenant be spared, so I was nominated to be the ship's representative and to say a few 'appropriate words'.

I collected the Jolly Roger which was beautifully mounted and framed. I don't think it mattered too much what I said to the assembled crowd. They were full of bonhomie and they needed no encouragement to applaud. I said briefly that we were pleased to have received it and that I was sure we would find somewhere to put it. This last remark was misinterpreted which led to guffaws and ribald comments.

Sandy's Sunbeam Talbot was in Portsmouth so I was asked to collect it and drive it back to Faslane. Sandy also asked me to call in at the flat in London where the four newly acquainted girls lived and to make an impression there for Sandy's benefit. The morning after the presentation I collected the Sunbeam Talbot and went round to call on 'the girls' taking care to arrive at coffee time. I took the Jolly Roger into the house with me as I knew it would make a good talking point and help me to 'market' Sandy's image. The girls were very attentive and asked a number of questions about life in a submarine but then I explained that I had a long journey to make and took my leave.

I was feeling pretty good. The hand over of the Jolly Roger had been successful and I felt sure that the visit to Gledhow Gardens had made the right impression, and here was I spinning along in a Sunbeam Talbot with a number of people looking on enviously as I swept past.

I got as far as St. John's Wood before I realised that I had left the Jolly Roger behind. I had to retrace my route, conscious of the reception that would have awaited me from Brian Hutchings if I had arrived without it. As I hadn't a particular girl-friend at the time I resolved that the four girls were all so nice that I would mark the flat down as a place to call next time I was in London.

Bryan showing the first Porpoise's Jolly Roger *after presentation at* Dolphin.

It was at about this time that I decided to upgrade my car. I bought a Standard Vanguard off Mike Ortmans for £400. When Brian Hutchings heard of this, he offered his usual unsolicited and unambiguous advice: 'You bloody fool, Smalley! That car is much too big and expensive for you. What you need is something like a Morris Minor.'

As soon as I returned to the submarine, all thoughts of nights out in London had to be set aside. The torpedo firing trials had begun. As the torpedo officer I had much of the responsibility for implementing them with the experts from HMS *Vernon*. In addition to ensuring that the torpedo tubes and firing gear worked correctly, we also had to devise a drill for embarking the torpedoes and loading them into the tubes.

Our routine was to load our torpedoes in the evening whilst lying alongside at Arrochar. We would slip the next morning at first light and spend most of the day firing torpedoes and making adjustments. When all our torpedoes had been expended we would come alongside and start the reloading cycle again. The senior rating in the fore-ends crew was Chief TASI (Torpedo and Anti Submarine Instructor) Mick Couch, an Irishman with a wonderful sense of humour.

On my 27th birthday, I told the fore-ends crew that if we completed loading in time to get to the Arrochar Hotel before it closed I would buy them all a drink. We worked as quickly as possible but without compromising the safety of the routine and walked to the pub, a distance of about three miles. We reached the pub just as 'last orders' was being called. We had one drink and then retraced our steps to our welcoming bunks.

The next morning I ensured that the casing was secured for sea and went to the top of the fin to report to the Captain. A worried looking Mick Couch was on the fin and asked me quietly how many torpedoes we had loaded the night before. I answered confidently that we had loaded eighteen. 'Well, Sir, there's only twelve there now,' he explained. I told him to look inside the torpedo tubes where he would undoubtedly find the other six. He assured me that he'd checked the tubes. By now the submarine was proceeding down the loch so I had to take the plunge and report to the Captain that we had mislaid six torpedoes. Brian Hutchings blew his top and blamed the loss on my Bacchanalian activities of the night before and my neglect of duty. Although grossly unjustified, this was no time to argue with the Captain. I was ordered to render my report on the loss in writing.

As we were now several tons lighter than expected, the trim had to be adjusted before diving. This gave me time to investigate further. In due course I discovered the facts from Mike Hosking who had been on duty the previous night. The trials team led by Lt. (OE) Geoff Veasey had made some adjustments to the firing gear which they then wanted to test. Mike gave them permission to fire water shots and instead of checking the tubes first they had fired the torpedoes out of the submarine. Even so the responsibility was mine. We should have placed a 'TUBE LOADED' tally on the rear doors. I reported my findings to the Captain who told me that if I could find the torpedoes and recover them within twenty four hours with no damage nothing further would be said.

Fortunately things were in my favour. When a torpedo is stowed in a tube with no immediate intention of firing it, a clamp is left on the propellers preventing the engine from starting. We had no difficulty finding the torpedoes embedded in the mud just forward of our berth.

We always took Brian Hutchings' explosive outbursts with a smile because we knew that he would never hold any of our mistakes against us for long. In fact we had an extremely happy relationship with him.

If a submarine captain has nothing to do, he will think up something, however trivial. We made a point of finding Brian Hutchings something to do 'to keep him out of mischief' as we were wont to describe it. But we must have been off our guard at one time which gave him time to ruminate. He suddenly declared that he considered all his officers 'unfit'. We were to 'take up an active sport' he told us in spite of the fact that he was probably the least fit of the entire wardroom. Andy Buchanan came up with the solution. He requested permission to keep a polo pony in the fore-ends. We waited with baited breath for any reaction. It never came and the fitness campaign went off the agenda.

After our trials in Loch Long we were due for another visit to Portsmouth and Sandy was still pursuing Charlotte. He devised a plan with the intention of raising his image even higher in her estimation. The plan was to bring all four girls from the London flat to Gosport, and to invite them on board the submarine for a drink, then to take them for a meal at an expensive restaurant in Portsmouth and to take them back to London afterwards in the Sunbeam Talbot which had moved south again. As Brian Hutchings liked to participate in everything that took place, he made sure that he was in the wardroom when the girls came on board to cast his eye over the 'talent' and offer his free advice.

The four girls came on board and we showed them round the submarine and did everything we could to impress them. By this time I was attempting to date one of the girls who did occasionally agree that I should take her out.

The next morning, which was a Sunday, Brian Hutchings came on board at lunchtime when he knew we would be on board having a pre-lunch drink.

'Well, Smalley,' said the Captain. 'I understand that the girl you were sitting next to last night is your current girl friend.'

'Yes, Sir,' was all I could muster in reply.

'Well, Smalley, you're a bloody fool.' He usually spoke to me in those endearing terms.

'Why's that, Sir?' I asked.

'She's not your type at all,' he advised. 'You ought to marry the little fat girl that was sitting in the corner.'

I let the conversation drop. There was no point in arguing with B. Hutchings when his mind was made up. But there must have been some good reasoning supporting his statement because, as things turned out, I married the 'little fat girl in the corner' five years later in spite of the unkind and totally inaccurate description.

A party in 'the Flat', 7 Gledhow Gardens – Sandy (extreme right),
Bryan (centre foreground).

We returned to Faslane for the 1958 Christmas and New Year period but Sandy and I took every opportunity to go down to London.

After the leave period we went back to the First of Class trials. One of the tests was to run the engines over an extended period at the maximum permitted normal power (95% of full power) whilst snorting. This was a severe test and after a period of time the CERA reported a very small rise in bearing oil temperature on the port generator. Then sparks began to fly as the shaft rubbed the generator casing. We had to surface and limp back to harbour on one generator.

Investigations showed that the problem was too serious to be fixed in Faslane and we had to make our way round to Rosyth. We managed to pass through the Pentland Firth and were making our way southward when our starboard supercharger disintegrated. This left us with a serviceable generator on one side with no engine to drive it, and a good engine on the other side with a useless generator attached. We were left with battery power only but with no means of charging them. We sent a signal asking for assistance. We were lucky that the weather was good with calm seas and we were able to propel using minimum power. In due course a tug was dispatched from Rosyth to take us in tow. In the meantime we conserved all the power we could to save the battery. We turned off all the galley stoves and means of heating water, and reduced the lighting to a minimum and relied on sandwiches and cold drinks. It was still January.

When the tug arrived it was my responsibility to connect up the tow to the tug. The submarine's towing wire was fitted so that it could be connected at the top of the fin. The wire runs down a recess in the fin and then forward where it is secured to a stouter chain cable. The recessed wire is cemented over to streamline it against water flow. When we were connecting up the wire I turned to the Second Cox'n and said: 'I suppose this is the first time you've done this for real.'

'No!' he replied. 'This is the sixth time I've been under tow. The last time was when we ran aground going into Blyth during the war.'

After that I kept my mouth shut.

We were feeling much less depressed now that we had some motive power to get us through the water but our mood of confidence was soon shattered. The tug's skipper radioed that he was running a hot bearing on his propeller shaft and he had to slow down and carefully nurse the tug back to Rosyth. In case the tug also lost all its power, a more robust 'Bar' boat was sent out from Rosyth to assist if necessary.

We had now been several days at sea without a hot meal and the battery was very low. After some discussion it was decided that we would have a 'brew-up' of hot soup, but to save the small amount of power still in the battery, we would heat it by means of a blow lamp. The Chief Stoker was asked to arrange this. The poor old Chief was shaken to the core. He had come through the war and he had nervously been through our commissioning trials when we had put unaccustomed angles on the boat whilst going at unheard of speeds, but his age and length of service were beginning to affect his fortitude. Now he was being asked to make soup in Britain's most modern submarine by means of a blow lamp. It was all too much. He 'slapped in' to be allowed to return to General Service.

Fortunately nothing further went wrong and we eventually made Rosyth safely. After the Chief Stoker cooled down he 'slapped in' again, but this time it was to withdraw his earlier request. We had travelled 120 miles on the battery and had been towed into harbour undetected by the media who would undoubtedly have blown the event up into a front page story.

The dockyard soon had our problems sorted out and we were ready to sail back to Faslane. Before leaving we were secured on the arm of a jetty whilst making our final preparations to sail. As we were leaving, an eddy caught our stern and swung our port after hydroplane against the dockyard wall with a nasty bump. We weren't sure whether we had done any damage but we continued on our way. When going aft later doing night rounds I heard a most horrible groaning noise emanating from somewhere just outside the pressure hull. I reported this to the Captain and at daylight the next morning we hove to and I went on to the casing with a couple of hands to see if there were any visible signs of damage. We couldn't see what the problem was so we continued on to Faslane. On arrival, a diver went down and reported that we had torn some of the fairing, or streamlining, leaving a large hole. This meant a docking in the floating dock which was now based at Faslane.

As we came out of the water we could see that we had completely dislodged the bearing which housed the after hydroplanes. The planes were hanging precariously. Hurried arrangements were made to get workers over from Scott's shipyard at Greenock to cut out the twisted metal and re-align the bearing and replace all the fairing plates. The job was an unusual and interesting one and we all worked round the clock to complete it as quickly as possible as we had another commitment which we didn't want to miss.

By now the RN nuclear submarine programme was getting under way. Spam Hammersley and John Grove were at the Imperial College of Science. Although plans for a nuclear submarine had been discussed as early as the end of the war, a Government directive to the Admiralty to wait until the land based nuclear power stations were ready, meant that nothing could be done until the mid-1950s. Delays with the British Dounreay reactor threatened to delay the submarine programme even further, and so in 1958 the US Navy was asked to supply a Westinghouse S5W reactor of the same type as in the Skipjack class. It was entirely due to Mountbatten's perseverance and charm that the Americans agreed to this proposal.

Mountbatten introduced a competition to select the most suitable name for this new submarine. A prize was to be awarded. There was considerable bar-room gossip in an effort to choose an appropriate name, but few suggestions appear to have been submitted. Captain Hugo Newton had recently been Captain S/M2 and was now the Naval Attaché in Moscow. Some wit suggested that the submarine should be called *Hugo Neutron* which wasn't received with wide support. Eventually Mountbatten himself chose the name *Dreadnought*. It isn't recorded whether he gave himself the prize.

Whilst on their course in London, John Grove and Spam Hammersley frequently relaxed by participating in Scottish country dancing in 'the flat'. At one point I called at the flat to call on the girls. The girl that I was pursuing was out. Gilly Paton was the only one in, and she was washing her hair. Her mother answered the door. She had come to London to fly out to Gibraltar the next day with Gilly for a holiday. She had brought a bottle of Old Grouse whisky for Gilly but had given her instructions that she should only share it with special friends as it was expensive. As Gilly wasn't available, Mrs P. felt that it was her duty to entertain me and offered me a drink. Seeing the whisky on the sideboard I suggested that I would enjoy a glass. Mrs P. didn't show any signs of reluctance as she poured the precious nectar. Goodness knows what Gilly was doing. She seemed to be taking an interminable time to wash her hair and so another whisky was offered, and then another and so on. In due course Gilly appeared and she explained that they both had an early start the next day and so I took the tip and left, leaving a considerable deficit in the precious whisky bottle. Not a very good impression to leave with someone who would eventually become one's mother-in-law.

On 9 June the US Navy launched the *George Washington*, the first nuclear submarine to be equipped with Polaris missiles. Three days later, *Dreadnought*, the first British nuclear powered submarine, was laid down at Vickers-Armstrongs Yard.

Porpoise visited Gibraltar in the same month. Gilly was in Gibraltar at the time. She had gone out to attend her brother Ley's wedding. He was an Army doctor serving in the Gibraltar Garrison and was to marry a fellow Army officer's daughter Alison.

Gilly's presence made our visit one of the most pleasant that I had yet made to Gibraltar. When not at sea on our day-running exercises Sandy and I enjoyed many happy hours swimming with Gilly in Rosia Bay. *Grampus* was also in harbour. The First Lieutenant, Bill Swinley, and the other officers including the Army were vying for Gilly's attention. We had one memorable day in Spain. Our Naval ID Cards could get us across the border, but Gilly had no visa so she borrowed a pass from an Army wife. Gilly had only a passing resemblance to the photograph but it got her into Spain. The party comprised Gilly, Sandy, Tony Bailey and me. We crossed the border without incident and with great relief. The first port of call in Spain was always a sherry bar in La Linea which enticed us with its *tapas*. We discovered that there was a *féria* being held in the village of San Roque at the top of a hill about eight miles north of La Linea. We engaged a dilapidated Mercedes Benz to take us there. The once luxurious car coughed and spluttered along the road and as the incline of the road increased the car slowed down to a stop. Anxious to establish our credentials as gentlemen, Sandy, Tony and I got out of the car and pushed it up the hill with Gilly sitting imperiously in the back but it wasn't long before Gilly found herself amongst the pushers. By the time we arrived we were ready for a drink. After relaxing in a bar we joined in the festivities. We each bought a hat which had writing round the rim which we assumed read something like 'Kiss me Quick'. After enjoying the *féria* we embarked in the Mercedes for the return journey. We only hoped that the braking system was in better nick than the engine.

On arrival back in Gibraltar we made our way to the Panama Club, the only night club in Gibraltar. Inevitably it was full of *Porpoise*'s ship's company and acquaintances from visiting ships. Our arrival gave rise to a raucous cheer, presumably because of our 'Kiss me Quick' hats. But one lady on a package holiday shouted in a loud Yorkshire accent: 'Shoot oop lads – and give t' cabaret a chance.' Our hats had given us an entirely different identity.

Promotions for Lieutenant Commanders and above were announced twice yearly by signal, at the end of June and December. We were still in Gibraltar at the end of June when the signal arrived announcing Brian Hutchings' promotion. It would take effect from 31 December. We were all naturally pleased and a number of parties were hurriedly organised.

After our pleasant sojourn in Gibraltar we returned to Faslane to prepare for Exercise Fishplay, a major exercise scheduled to take place off Bermuda. We had now completed most of the trials necessary on the new equipment and were taking fewer passengers to sea. We were very pleased to hear that we could now get on with something more akin to standard submarining. On completion of the exercise we would then visit the United States Navy's submarine base at New London, Connecticut.

Gilly's brother's wedding had gone off smoothly and Gilly had returned to 'the flat'. She and Charlotte then embarked on a holiday. They were taking Valerie, a visiting South African girl, on a tour round the west coast of Scotland. On 9 September they were making their way home and were only a few miles from London when they had a collision. It was caused by a young man in a sports car. He had become frustrated by a lorry which was overtaking another, and in an attempt to pass them both, he pulled out to his extreme right hand side and collided head on. Charlotte was driving and although badly injured was saved to some extent by the steering wheel, whereas Gilly, in the front passenger seat, went head first through the windscreen. Gilly spent about a week in Barnet General Hospital and was then moved to Northwood General Hospital for surgery after which she was discharged and returned to live with her mother in Perth.

We sailed for Exercise Fishplay IV on 16 September.

The navigational plan paid dividends until the day before the exercise was due to start. We were already dived after the long surface passage and were

Porpoise. *Photograph courtesy of Royal Navy Submarine Museum.*

giving the crew a chance to settle into the exercise routine and to make the submarine as quiet as possible. Just before the exercise was due to start we were all told to surface and remain there until further orders as there was a hurricane warning. We were grateful that the hurricane passed by well to the north, and had very little effect on us. We were then able to dive and get on with the exercise.

Keeping a periscope watch, although tiring, is always interesting. I shall remember this exercise particularly for one very fascinating although brief experience. We were at periscope depth in a fairly rough sea with a long swell. In this state it is difficult to keep depth and occasionally the top of the periscope dips below the surface. When this happens in the beautiful clear blue water such as that off Bermuda, it allows visibility through the periscope for several yards. We were ditching gash at the time through the gash ejector which Tommy Entwhistle had designed. Each bag should have been weighed down so that it sank to avoid giving our position away. One bag had not been properly weighted and floated slowly towards the surface. As it appeared in view of the periscope, an enormous shark appeared and tore the bag apart, apparently about two feet in front of my face. Then it was gone. I quickly turned the periscope to look aft but by that time the shark and his booty had disappeared.

Another incident during this exercise, although not so dramatic, is also well remembered. Submarines were now beginning to be fitted with Under Water Telephones. These are not like a normal telephone but transmit the sound through the water. Submarines could therefore talk to each other at close range. Sound can be transmitted in an all round mode or alternatively transmitted through a directional transducer providing limited security to prevent unauthorised listeners, but more importantly to prevent us from giving away our presence. During an exercise the telephone can be used to simulate certain actions. The code for firing a torpedo at an exercise enemy is 'Oscar, Oscar, Oscar'. During this exercise we were waiting for our quarry as quietly as possible believing that we were not making any noise which would give us away, when I heard 'Oscar, Oscar, Oscar'. It was so loud that the submarine was obviously only a few hundred yards from us. This didn't constitute a threat as we knew that the exercise enemy would be at a different depth to us. Nevertheless it came as a surprise as we were miles out in the ocean believing ourselves to be alone. But the irony of this incident was that the voice was obviously recognisable as British. It was none other than Tubby Squires who was to be the first lieutenant of *Dreadnought* on her commissioning. He was gaining nuclear experience in the USS *Skate*. He had delighted in helping the Americans detect and track a British submarine and to get within attacking range. Having exchanged identities and range, bearing and depths with him, we told him what we would do with him when we met him ashore in New London. He then disappeared noiselessly into the depths and once again we had the ocean to ourselves.

When we arrived in New London we had been at sea for six weeks and had plenty of excess energy to expend. This was my first visit to the United States and we found the hospitality which we received from the Americans as bountiful as had been reported by previous Royal Navy visitors.

After about a week of relaxation and a debriefing of the exercise we sailed for home and had an uneventful trip back across the Atlantic.

Our next trip was a courtesy visit to Copenhagen.

By this time *Porpoise* had been in commission for nearly two years and her Safety Certificate would shortly expire. A full refit would be undertaken before a new Safety Certificate could be issued and the second commission begin. At this time there were some murmurings of discontent amongst serving submariners. Allegations were made that an unofficial '*Porpoise*' club had been formed which was developing into an élitist group. This was because whenever an officer in a Porpoise Class submarine left the ship to take up another appointment (and by now there were about four in commission), the tendency was for all the officers below to move up one notch, rather than bring in another officer who only had experience of an older class of submarine. This was upsetting those who wished to serve in a modern submarine. The situation was exemplified in *Porpoise*. Sandy had moved from third hand to first lieutenant when Basil Whitecross left the ship to do his 'perisher' and I had moved up into Sandy's place. The appointers were looking for a first lieutenant to take *Porpoise* into refit and to stand by her while it took place. They were conscious that if I was chosen, there would be more grumbles from those who felt they had a better claim. As a result I was removed from *Porpoise* and appointed as first lieutenant of *Seraph* in order to break my continuity of service. But the plan was to move me back into *Porpoise* for the refit as the first lieutenant.

I left *Porpoise* on 6 November 1959 and joined *Seraph* the next day in the Clyde and relieved David Aylmer.

CHAPTER 14

Seraph 1959-60

GOING TO *Seraph* was not unlike going back to my days in *Scotsman*. *Seraph* was the submarine made famous during the war by Norman Jewell whom I had already served under on two occasions. Since her wartime days she had changed beyond all recognition. She was now a 'padded' target against which torpedoes were fired. Fortunately they didn't have an explosive warhead, but if the torpedo was working correctly it would home in on the noise made by our propeller and strike it with an enormous crunch. Quite frequently they would do such damage that we would have to go into dry dock to fit new propellers. We didn't fit the best propellers though we did keep their damaged edges well filed down so that they weren't too noisy and didn't create too much cavitation. That helped to make it more difficult to hit us.

Our Captain was Lemmy Strang. He had spent a considerable time in 'X' craft (midget submarines). I soon learnt that *Seraph* was a very wet boat caused mainly by her very low bridge. We seldom made a passage through the Irish sea without having the 'elephant's trunk' and 'bird bath' rigged. Lemmy put on his 'X' craft diving suit when we went to sea and kept it on until we returned to harbour.

Serving in the wardroom we had Lt. Brian Ellis RCN, Sub Lt. Peter Irwin RN and Special Duties Engineer Sub Lieutenant David Gutteridge.

When not required as a torpedo target we became a 'Mickey Mouse' target for ships improving their sonar skills. We operated from Portland and Faslane.

Among the ship's company we had some Israeli ratings who would eventually man the submarines which we were selling to their government.

We spent Christmas 1959 in Faslane, and after our Christmas and New Year leave we sailed south again for Portland. This was the roughest passage that I experienced in *Seraph*. Although *Seraph* was perfectly safe at sea it was always an unpleasant experience being on the surface in such conditions. In rough weather the waves often washed right over the bridge and one soon learnt to secure oneself to the bridge with the safety belt provided. Many officers of the watch have been washed over the side of the bridge to be left hanging by the safety harness.

We had an electrical artificer who had been unwillingly conscripted into the

Submarine Service. The wind was about force seven and the bird bath was filling so rapidly with water pouring down the conning tower that we had to keep a pump running on it almost continuously. Lemmy decided that we had done everything possible to make sure we were safe and had decided to get in his bunk in the hope that he could get some sleep in spite of the violent seas. As is the normal practice he wrote his 'night orders' for the information of the officers and petty officers of the watch. In conclusion he wrote: 'Shake me if the weather gets worse.' When the electrical artificer came into the control room to keep his watch he was quite convinced that we were going to sink at any minute and when he read the captain's night orders he decided that he would get out of submarines one way or another and as quickly as possible. We arrived safely at Portland and after we had been in harbour for a few days, the electrical artificer realised that his inexperience had led him to over-react and he decided to stick it out in submarines.

After the rather boring day-running at Portland we returned to the Clyde areas. Our next commitment was to take a Dutch Admiral to sea. The Dutch were contemplating buying our new homing torpedoes and required a demonstration to see how they worked.

HMS *Exmouth* was the ship firing the torpedoes and we worked off the coast of Arran spending our evenings anchored at Lamlash. Although it was important that the Dutch Admiral should be well treated whilst on board, it was more important that the torpedoes which were being fired at us should hit. Fortunately most of them did. He must have been impressed when one torpedo struck us on the propeller with a loud crunch causing the submarine to shake. That forced us to surface and return to Faslane.

Although my time in *Seraph* was short-lived, I had plenty to do. I joined in time to prepare the ship's company for the annual Captain S/M's inspection. Because of the nature of their work the ship's company tended to be a very hard drinking team of pirates and it took some effort to get them back into the practice of doing things in accordance with the regulations before the inspecting officers arrived on board. Many evolutions that the submarine might be expected to undertake had been neglected. The attitude was that if they didn't affect the immediate safety of the submarine then they weren't worth bothering with. I made myself rather unpopular by insisting that we undertook one major evolution each day. One task that we might be called on to undertake was to act as a decompression chamber in the event of a major diving accident. The fore ends could be used as a re-compression chamber to bring rescued divers slowly back to surface atmospheric pressure. This necessitated moving a considerable mount of equipment out of the fore-ends.

I decided to do this on the Saturday before the inspection and said that weekend leave could start once the evolution was completed. There was a considerable amount of 'sucking of teeth' but we completed the evolution successfully and what was more important, when the inspection was over, we had a good report from the inspecting officers.

I left *Seraph* on 1 March. *Porpoise* had 'paid off' and I joined her in Portsmouth Dockyard to relieve Sandy Woodward as the first lieutenant.

CHAPTER 15

Refitting *Porpoise* in Portsmouth 1960-61

THERE WERE several submarines in the Refitting Group each with a first lieutenant and engineer and some ratings overseeing the work. In overall command was Lt. Cdr. W.G. (Sluggy) Edwards known as CO Submarine Refitting Group.

The planning of a submarine refit is so complex that it is impossible for one man to know everything that is taking place at any one time. Consequently there were frequent meetings to monitor progress. Most of the minor machinery was removed and the pressure hull had to be made accessible so that signs of corrosion could be searched out. In *Porpoise,* we took out the lathe which was situated in a pokey compartment in the extreme after ends of the submarine. We discovered that a number of metal turnings had fallen into the bilges and had corroded some parts of the hull to about two thirds of its original thickness.

Although the officers still have a responsibility for the safety of the submarine it is possible to be more relaxed bearing in mind the submarine is not afloat. I took the opportunity to take part in recreational sailing. Whilst in *Seraph* I had seen a notice on the depot ship wardroom notice board which read that a retired lieutenant commander of the Royal Canadian Navy Volunteer Reserves was looking for a crew for his boat which was lying in the Solent area. I responded to the advertisement and established contact with the owner of *Rapparee*, Harold Rapp, a London ship broker. He agreed that when the sailing season started later on in the year I could crew for him, but before that occurred I had an important wedding to attend. Sandy and Charlotte's wedding had been arranged for April, and Sandy asked me to be his best man. Charlotte asked her three flat-mates, Morna Webb, Joan Richmond and of course Gilly, to be her bridesmaids. A rehearsal was arranged on the evening before. I was still driving my unreliable Standard Vanguard. I was asked to take three girls north with me to Wetheral just outside Carlisle which was Charlotte's home. Unfortunately the car let me down several times and we arrived late for the rehearsal which didn't leave Sandy in his best mood. Sandy was also terrified regarding the speech which I would make at the reception, but as neither of us had done anything about which we might be ashamed, I had no qualms. But to satisfy Sandy, I decided to tell an apocryphal story rather than relate some of our past experiences. I got the idea from when I had seen a shark through the periscope whilst off Bermuda. The story went like this: A sardine was swimming alongside its mother when a submarine glided past. 'What's that?' enquired the baby sardine. 'Don't worry about that, dear,' replied the mother. 'That's just a lot of men packed together in a tin.' The story suited the occasion and Sandy could breathe a sigh of relief.

After the wedding I returned to Portsmouth. The sailing season was just beginning and I made my first visit to *Rapparee*, an exceptionally well equipped 14 tons Thames measurement yawl which was based at Bucklers Hard on the Hamble. *Rapparee* had many fittings which were extremely innovative for the period. It had a shower and a charcoal burning heater, but probably the most enjoyable facet which added to our comfort was the food. The owner flew in frozen food from Switzerland. Each meal was packaged individually and only required to be boiled in the plastic bag before opening to reveal a gourmet meal. Whilst our competitors would be making do with meat and two veg (if they were lucky) we would be tucking into such delicacies as curried prawns. When in harbour we enjoyed eating at the Master Builder, the well appointed local hostelry. Life was a vast contrast to living in a submarine or on a ratings' messdeck.

During the week-ends when *Rapparee* wasn't participating in a race, we sailed in *Cyclops* which was the *Dolphin* yacht. Peter Paffard was usually the skipper. He was great fun to sail with. His sister Rosemary and her university friend Cynthia Pilkington often sailed with us.

My third experience of sailing at this time was aboard the twelve metre yachts which were preparing for the next British challenge for the Americas cup. I occasionally went out in them to make up a crew shortfall. They were in the process of choosing the crew which comprised mainly rugby players who were selected for their sheer strength rather than sailing skill. I wasn't selected and never expected to be.

It was towards the end of the refit that I received a telephone call to say that Captain SM in *Dolphin* wished to see me urgently and: 'make sure that you are well presented because the Flag Officer Submarines may also have a word to say.' My first reaction was to worry about what I had done wrong so I presented myself with some misgivings.

When I arrived I was soon put at ease. When the Navy made an instructional film it expected it to portray realism. All such films were vetted by an acceptance committee at the Admiralty. The Navy had just spent a considerable amount of money on a submarine training film which had been rejected by the committee. My orders were to go to the film studio and advise the editor how to improve the film to an acceptable standard.

The film was being made at the Merton Film Studios just outside Wimbledon which was only about five miles from home. At this time I had no steady girl friend and I had visions of taking starlets out to lunch and of rubbing shoulders with famous film stars. But nothing could have been further from the truth. When I arrived at the studios I discovered that they were nothing more than editing studios with a number of cubicles, each about twelve feet square. The main activity in these cubicles was to run film through the editing machine and to cut and insert pieces to get the picture into an acceptable condition. When the editor was satisfied with the visual components he then attached the sound.

I soon became friends with the editor and his assistant and we went through the film with a critical eye. I hadn't been involved in the shooting of the film and until I had been sent to Merton had no idea of its existence, but inevitably the principal 'actors' in it were all old submarine friends, in particular Andy Buchanan. It became apparent to me that there wasn't much wrong with the film itself but the sound track was unrealistic. There were long sequences where quite noisy evolutions were being carried out where there was no background noise whatsoever. The studio had a large library of sound effects. It was fascinating choosing appropriate background noises for all the activities in the film. I put my final imprint on the film by choosing the background music for the credits and then my mission was over. The film was still being shown to submarine trainees under the title *Submarine on Patrol* more than twenty years after it had been produced. Most of those who played the 'star' parts went on to greater glory, but not in the film industry. I had to return to Portsmouth where life was dull by comparison.

As the refit drew to a close the number of post refit trials increased and one by one, additional officers were appointed and we began to build our team for the next commission. We held our commissioning ceremony in *Porpoise* on 29 July. The officers were Lt. Cdr. Peter Herbert – CO; myself – first lieutenant; Lt. Neville Reid – engineer; Electrical Lt. Dennis Probee – electrical officer; Lt. Peter Francis – navigator; Lt. Peter Paffard – torpedo officer, and Sub Lt. Ray Hunter – fifth hand). Although we started our sea trials to test the various items of equipment we still had a number of defects. Eventually the submarine was accepted on 29 August, the Safety Certificate was signed and we were ready for our next commission. The next day we left the dockyard and crossed the harbour and secured alongside *Dolphin*, the base of the First Submarine Squadron to which we would belong. But before we joined the squadron we had to move up to Faslane for our work-up.

CHAPTER 16

Porpoise's Second Commission 1961-62

CAPTAIN S/M3 was now John (Randy) Roxburgh and the Commander S/M James Pardoe.

The work up followed the usual pattern of exercising all the emergencies that might occur and then practising our attacking skills. For me it was a pleasant return to my happy hunting ground making acquaintances with all the families that I had met during my previous time in the area. After exercising in the deep water off Arran we would often spend the night at anchor off Rothesay rather than go back all the way up the Clyde to Faslane.

We had the pleasure of visiting Inveraray whilst we were checking out our torpedo tubes in Loch Fyne and enjoyed the conviviality of the George Hotel with the Clark family.

In addition to our work up we also undertook some noise trials in Loch Goil. We were suspended between two buoys with all machinery shut down. Having achieved a quiet state we then ran various pieces of equipment to ensure that they weren't transmitting any noise outside the hull. We then moved to Loch Long enabling us to go ashore at night and revisit Arrochar. But we would go back to Faslane for the week-ends to keep in touch with the squadron staff officers to report progress as well as replenishing stores.

It was during our spell in Rothesay that I became involved again with the Scottish police. *Rorqual* was commanded by Sam Tomlinson of the RCN with another Canadian, Gordon Shirley, as his first lieutenant. Amongst the ship's company were a number of French Canadian sailors one of whom had been summoned to court for having a mild collision with another car. He felt that his grasp of English wasn't adequate and he asked for an officer to go to court with him. I was nominated.

The sailor's story was that he had been driving from Faslane to Helensburgh and on coming round a bend he collided with a Rolls Royce parked near the middle of the road. He did some superficial damage to a rear wing. The lady driver was arranging flowers in the nearby chapel. The sailor had another French Canadian as his passenger and he came along to court with us. Whilst waiting for the case to begin we noticed the lady arriving in the Rolls Royce with a police sergeant as her passenger. It was obvious from her dress and her demeanour that she was well connected in the county. She reminded me of Margaret Rutherford. The room was overheated and stuffy and we were uncomfortable in our uniforms. Our case was called and the charge read. It was obvious that the police sergeant was there to support 'Margaret Rutherford'. The cards were stacking up against us. He then called 'Margaret Rutherford' to the witness box. The bailie first asked her to confirm her name and age. She adamantly refused to state her age asserting that it had nothing to do with the case. The bailie capitulated.

By this time, the heat was getting the better of me and I started to doze off. After a few initial enquiries the police sergeant asked the lady if she could identify the car driver in court. She confirmed this and pointed directly at me. I came to life with a start! Regardless of this inaccuracy the case continued. The sailor was then called as a witness and stated that he had been driving at a reasonable speed but that the Rolls had been badly parked. He was wasting his time. Everyone from the bailie downwards found the opposition too intimidating. The sailor was found guilty, fined and ordered to drive more carefully in future.

I didn't think I'd done a very good job so I bought them a few beers on the way back to the base.

Porpoise was soon ready for inspection which I remember for two particular reasons.

First, whenever a simulated crisis occurred I naturally went along to take charge, that was my job. James Pardoe would be at the scene of the simulated crisis and on every occasion he would say to me: 'You're dead for the next ten minutes. Go and sit in the wardroom and do nothing.' I spent nearly all day sitting in the wardroom straining like a dog on a leash and counting away the minutes so that I could get back into the action.

The second memory is that at the end of the dived inspection I was called into the control room and told to surface the submarine going astern. This meant first of all getting the submarine to move stern first through the water and maintaining depth with the hydroplanes. The action of the planesmen would be reversed and so it would have been easy to get into a mess with the submarine porpoising wildly. We didn't fail on that count, and when I surfaced the submarine I blew main ballast tanks in reverse order starting with number '7' first. I thought this was the natural thing to do but for some inexplicable reason it greatly impressed the Captain S/M who remarked on it later to Peter Herbert. We passed our inspection with no serious criticisms although my only contribution was to provide a diversion for the Captain S/M for the last five or ten minutes of the day.

As soon as we had disembarked the inspection team, we sailed for Portsmouth arriving on the 26th and after a few days alongside at *Dolphin* we sailed for our first commitment. We passed down the Channel to exercise in the Falmouth areas. The RNAS at Culdrose was training helicopters in 'dunking' sonar techniques. They used us as a target and, when working in small teams of three or four helicopters, they could track a submarine by jumping ahead of its track. Our job was to try and break contact and make their task more difficult. We had the unfortunate experience of one helicopter 'ditching' and sinking before the crew could make their escape. We searched all night but were unable to find any survivors.

After a week in the Falmouth areas we returned briefly to Gosport before sailing for exercises in the 'Derry Areas. We spent three weeks in the 'Derry Areas and went up the Foyle on two occasions to renew our acquaintance with this fun loving city. We then returned to Gosport for an early Christmas leave period.

We were back at sea again on 3 January for exercises in the approaches to the English Channel, remaining at sea until we entered Portland Harbour on 14 January. We spent the rest of the month day-running from Portland for the benefit of surface ships working up until we returned to Portsmouth on 24 January to enter dry dock to repair a defect.

After putting right the defect, we returned to the rather boring and undemanding day running at Portland. One amusing story about Portland concerns the Navy's habit of quoting the Bible when transmitting messages. Portland was a particularly unpleasant place for submarines when making their surface passage out to the exercise areas. Portland Bill can create a very rough sea in bad weather when the wind is in conflict with the tide race round the southern point of the Bill. At these times the surface is churned up into a boiling cauldron. In the older submarines those on the bridge would get a good soaking. On one occasion a submarine captain sent a signal to base which merely read: '*Hebrews 13-8.*' The staff officers rushed for their Bibles only to find that the captain was saying: 'Jesus Christ. The same yesterday, and today, and for ever.'

We returned to *Dolphin* on 16 February to prepare for another passage up the Irish Sea for operations in the 'Derry Areas which would then be followed by 'Perisher running'. We sailed from *Dolphin* on 1 March and spent a week off the 'Derry Areas before going up the Clyde to Faslane.

We arrived at Faslane to take on board those officers who had been selected to undergo training for submarine command. The course is called the 'perisher', a derivation of 'Periscope Course'. This latter term had long fallen out of use and the course was now officially called the Commanding Officers' Qualifying Course, shortened to COCQ. The officer in charge was customarily a commander with the inevitable title of Commanding Officer of the Commanding Officers' Qualifying Course or COCOQC, pronounced 'coecock' for short, but more frequently referred to as 'the perisher teacher'.

Cdr. Martin Wemyss, the current teacher, expected very high standards from the submarine employed on perisher running which we were naturally quite prepared to meet. The 'perisher' really has a conflict of interests. As an aggressive submarine captain one would be expected to be good at attacking targets and to press home the attack. On the other hand there is an overriding responsibility for safety. One of the aims of the 'perisher' was to see if the expectant commanding officer had the balance right.

A submarine officer's progress would follow roughly the same pattern. He would work his way up as a fifth, fourth or third hand during his first three years' submarine service. Then he would expect to serve as a first lieutenant for about three years before being recommended to take the 'perisher'. During these six years his potential to rise to submarine command would be assessed. A most important qualification is an officer's attacking ability, often referred to as 'periscope eye'. This is the ability to translate what they see during a quick look through the periscope to what is actually happening on the surface. An inability to develop this proficiency is known as 'getting lost in the box'. It is the unpleasant duty of the 'perisher' teacher to make the final decision whether his students pass or fail. It is naturally shattering for an officer at the 'perisher' stage to be told that his submarine career has come to an end.

In a well run submarine it is a matter of great pride that the crew are particularly well 'worked up' when the 'perishers' are using that submarine. The planesmen and officer of the watch will make a special effort to ensure that the submarine is in good trim, that the planesmen and helmsman are experienced and attentive, and that everyone is doing his best for the 'perisher' pupil whose turn it is to make an attack. This is a very tiring and strenuous commitment for the submarine's crew. Everyone on board made a special effort.

As well as being a hard grind for the crew, the perisher became more of a strain for the students from week to week. During the first week there would probably be one ship approaching for the submarine to attack. The next week this would increase to two surface ships, and during the last week three or four ships escorting an oil tanker. As the course progressed the surface ships were allowed to become more aggressive if they detected the submarine.

It was in this exciting and interesting environment that we saw officers achieving their qualification to command their own submarine.

Towards the end of the course we were asked whether the perishers could hold a party in *Porpoise* one Saturday evening at Faslane. The invitations were the responsibility of the course members but I wished the party to go with a swing and made a few internal arrangements.

Submarine parties don't really need a theme. The valves and fittings provide enough atmosphere. Bright white lighting is not conducive to a party atmosphere so we would usually switch to 'red lighting'. I decided that I would give the party some colour by providing red and green ice.

By the evening everything was set for the party. As soon as we switched to 'red lighting' the red ice disappeared. Worse still for the green ice which turned black. After their first drink, most people indicated that they would prefer their next drink without ice: 'If you don't mind,' they said politely. I must say it is very distracting to have a drink which looks as if it has a piece of coal floating in it whilst you are talking to someone whose drink appears to have holes in it like Gruyère cheese.

The party brought to an end our commitment to the 'perisher' and we sailed to return to Gosport on 6 April. We then went back to a day running routine exercising off the Isle of Wight and out of Portland.

Peter Herbert had my interests in mind and made sure I prepared myself for command. At this time there were no qualifications required to command a submarine apart from the perisher but there were murmurings from general service officers who felt that they had to undertake a series of more onerous examinations in order to command a major war vessel other than a submarine. This was called collectively the Destroyer Command Exam. They felt that we should also be examined in the same way. The examination comprised a number of modules such as navigation, gunnery, TAS, communications, damage control and so on. There was a possibility that submariners would soon be expected to take at least the examination in navigation and Peter Herbert encouraged me to do this. I swotted for the exam and registered to take it at HMS *Dryad,* the navigation school. It was obvious that at least one of the questions would be the ability to work out and plot the results of observations of the stars. After making the calculations for each sight it was necessary to plot them as position lines. Hopefully the position lines would cross, but if they didn't it would be necessary to interpolate and estimate the ship's position. This is quite a difficult paper to mark. The examination was set by a qualified navigator (a 'dagger N'). To ensure that he hadn't made a mistake his paper had to be worked through by another 'dagger N'.

Porpoise had gone to sea for the day, but I was given permission by the Captain to stay behind and take the examination. I recollect that there were four questions in the paper and I wasn't surprised to see that the first one necessitated calculating and plotting a series of star sights. I had become inured to examinations by this time and so I calmly looked at each question and checked to see how many marks were awarded to each. In this way I could calculate how I would allocate my time. I worked out the star sights and then attempted to plot them. The plot didn't make sense and so I redid the calculations and came to the same result. By this time, I was a few minutes over the time allocated to the question and so I left it and answered the other three without difficulty. Being under strict examination scrutiny there was, of course, no talking until the allocated time passed and we had handed in our papers. Then all hell broke loose. Most of those being examined didn't get any further than the first question. They had been reluctant to move on until they got an acceptable answer. I learnt later that the officer who should have worked through the paper hadn't bothered as he had complete confidence in his colleague who had set the paper. I don't know what happened to the other examinees but I heard in due course that I had passed.

We continued the rather dull daily running throughout May but were looking forward to some relaxation as we prepared for an official visit to Gothenburg. On 1 June I had achieved six years seniority as a lieutenant and my basic pay rose to £2.18s.0d. a day (£1,022 p.a.)

We made the passage through the Dover Straits and arrived at Gothenburg on 6 June. Next to Stockholm, Gothenburg is the most important city in Sweden and is the principal Swedish port. Most of the inhabitants spoke excellent English and everyone enjoyed the visit immensely. As is so often the case we departed leaving many tearful young ladies on the jetty.

We were now scheduled to take part in Exercise 'Fairwind 7' off the north of Scotland. Part way through the exercise we were stood down and we made a quick dash into Loch Ewe to collect mail which we had pre-arranged. Then it was back to sea for the second phase of the exercise. and then to Invergordon, for the 'wash-up'. Then by some quirk of the planning organisation we were scheduled for another foreign visit to Bergen. After our visit to Bergen we sailed across the North Sea to visit Dundee. It seemed that the planners hadn't got any operational duties for us but we didn't mind cruising Scandinavia and Scotland.

We arrived in Dundee the next day. I had been looking forward to this visit for one particular reason. Dundee is only twenty miles from Perth where Gilly Paton had returned from 'the flat' after her car accident. I had decided that she was the girl for me. I had sent a letter on ahead of me to give the dates of our visit, and half expected her to be waiting on the jetty as we arrived alongside.

There was no sign of her and so I waited until all the necessary matters had been dealt with regarding our arrival and then went to the public phone box on the jetty to give her a call. The phone rang for some time and eventually Ella, the housekeeper, answered and in response to my enquiry I discovered that Gilly had gone for a holiday in France with her mother. Although we had an enjoyable time in Dundee it wasn't such fun as I had hoped. We then returned to Gosport for leave.

After our leave period we sailed for exercises in early August in the Plymouth areas. On arrival in the area Peter Herbert, with my training for command in mind, made me the CO for the day with all reports being made to me and giving me the responsibility to act on them. Things were going well and I was enjoying the exercise when we experienced a major problem in the engine room. We had to make our way to Devonport for repairs. My short period in command didn't last long.

It was while we were in Devonport that we feared that war was about to break out. The Russians were installing guided missiles in Cuba which threatened America. By standing firm against the Russians President Kennedy managed to bring more stable relations between the Warsaw Pact countries and the western world.

By 23 October *Porpoise*'s starboard crankshaft had been replaced and we put to sea for trials. After we had determined that the repairs were satisfactory we sailed for Gosport.

I left *Porpoise* on 12 November 1962 and was relieved by 'Nogs' Hoggarth with whom I had served in the Sea Scouts before joining the Navy. It was a great wrench leaving *Porpoise*. I had served in her for a total of four years and four months. She was always a happy ship and she remained in the submarine fleet some time after her younger sisters had gone to the scrap heap.

CHAPTER 17

Officers' Training Officer
and 'Perisher' 1962-63

M Y NEXT appointment was to *Dolphin* where I was to take over the job as Officers' Training Officer. This was a boost to my confidence as it meant that I had already obtained sufficient recommendations to take the 'perisher' and I need no longer remain at sea. Assuming I did the job as OTO satisfactorily I could look forward to the 'perisher' in due course.

I relieved Ken Forbes Robertson and had just settled into the job and taken a number of class sessions when I was summoned to see a staff officer. I had no idea why. Fortunately I hadn't committed a misdemeanour. I was told that one of the COs had lost his nerve and as a result I was to join the 'perisher' which was about to start.

I was appointed to the Perisher Number 51 on 18 December. The 'perisher' would start as soon as we had returned from our Christmas leave.

We started the 'perisher' in the new year at the attack teacher at *Dolphin*. Cdr. Martin Wemyss still held the post as 'perisher' teacher. Those on the course with me were Lts. Ken Forbes Robertson, Tom Green, Tony 'Red' Miller, Terry Thompson, and Hans Ort of the Royal Netherlands Navy.

The 'perisher' is one of the oldest courses in the Navy, having been implemented in 1917. Foreign students had been included since 1920. The course is steeped in tradition and mystique and is held in awe by other branches of the Navy. It has been described as the most comprehensive form of command training in the armed services and by necessity has its elements of ruthlessness. As already explained, a student can be failed at any time during the course which will mean the end of his submarine career.

The Submarine Attack Teacher was a very basic device. The building had two levels. The upper level had a flat surface with a periscope protruding through its centre from below. There were a couple of retired CPOs and a number of Wrens operating the teacher. On the flat surface could be placed a number of model ships which were able to move as though they were under way. On the floor below were the 'perishers' who took it in turn to make an attack whilst the rest acted as the attack team. It was all rather primitive and I was glad when that part of the course was completed and we were able to move up to the Clyde to a more realistic environment. Apart from the tension of the course it was also physically tiring.

In the Clyde we were accommodated at the Victoria Hotel in Rothesay during the week. We had an early start and were taken out to the submarine by boat. Then followed the run down the outer reaches of the Clyde on the surface before diving and starting the long grind. In the early stages we worked until darkness prevented us seeing the target through the periscope, but as the course progressed we also spent nights at sea. Initially we returned each night to the Victoria Hotel.

It was whilst we were in this phase that I became involved in the Positive Vetting system. On giving over some of their atomic secrets to the British, the Americans expressed concern about our security arrangements. Although we may have had some shortcomings, it has to be said that the Americans had experienced equally embarrassing episodes of security lapses. Nevertheless they insisted that the British should introduce a vetting system to ensure that the secrets that they had given us were safe. Sandy Woodward had put me down as one of his referees.

The interview was in my hotel room. Two officers had come to interrogate me. We went through a series of questions about how long Sandy and I had known each other and what did we have in common? Like most interviews of this nature I felt that I was just as much under investigation as the principal party. After some time I was asked what Sandy's father did for a living and I replied that he was a bank manager. At this the interviewers became extremely excited.

'How do you know he's a bank manager?' they asked.

'Well I'm not sure. I suppose Sandy must have told me.'

'When did he tell you?' they persisted.

'Well, I'm not sure he did, I believe Sandy said that he worked in a bank in Cornwall and I got the impression that he was the manager.'

'Which bank was it?' they went on, determined to pursue their enquiries.

'I'm not sure. Sandy was born in Mousehole, or it may be Marazion, and I think his parents still live there.'

I was becoming totally confused by this time. I had answered the questions to the best of my ability and I got the impression that I was about to be charged with impeding the course of justice, or worse still, perjury. In due course I was relieved to discover that Sandy had been positively 'PVd'.

During our last week on the perisher we had everything thrown at us. Not only did we have 'enemy' ships seeking us out, but we also had to plan and implement a number of tasks which a submarine might be ordered to undertake. I was given the task of planning a night landing. First of all I had to manoeuvre the submarine to its correct position and then, changing roles, I had go on the casing and paddle a canoe ashore to achieve my objective. I was told to go ashore and blow up Lochranza pier, which I knew well from my days in *Scotsman*. To prove that I had succeeded in my task I had to bring back the number of the telephone on the end of the pier. The canoe had space for two people so I elected to take Tony 'Red' Miller ashore with me. Fortunately the sea was quite calm and there was no moon. We went ashore carefully, knowing that the 'perisher' teacher might have arranged some opposition to greet us when we landed, but we managed to land unopposed. We obtained the telephone number from the kiosk at the pier head but couldn't resist the temptations of the hostelry nearby. The innkeeper and his few clients looked up in surprise when two dishevelled and unknown customers entered the bar. They were even more surprised when we ordered two pints of beer and a bottle of champagne. We returned on board without incident and handed over the bottle of champagne to 'Teacher' together with the slip of paper on which was written the telephone number which he took without comment.

That was the last night of our 'perisher'. On the way back up the Clyde, 'Teacher' sent a message to Captain S/M saying 'All is well', which we took to mean that he hadn't failed anybody in the last week. After our arrival in harbour we were all interviewed individually and I was told that I had been appointed to command *Aurochs*.

CHAPTER 18

In Command of *Aurochs* and on to Canada 1963-64

I JOINED *Aurochs* in Portsmouth dockyard on 10 April. Like *Acheron*, *Aurochs* had been built with the intention of operating in the Far East. She was laid down in June '44; launched in July '45, and commissioned in December '46 after hostilities had ceased. She was fitted with a 4-inch Mark 23 gun. By the time I took command some of the 'A' boats had been streamlined and with the exception of *Aurochs* all the guns had been removed. I therefore had the privilege of commanding the last British submarine with a gun. But the record didn't last long. As a number of conflicts arose, particularly in the Far East, it was deemed prudent to replace the gun in submarines in order to defend themselves whilst operating inshore on the surface.

When I joined, the First Lieutenant, Lt. Mike Highwood, and Engineer, Sub Lt. Ian Rogers, were already appointed having stood by the submarine in refit.

As soon as I settled in at the dockyard I took the Easter leave which was due to me. I determined to propose to Gilly during this leave and asked her to stay at my mother's house for a week-end. I was deeply disappointed when she said she would think about my proposal, but a day or two after I returned to *Dolphin* I was summoned to the porter's lodge to take a long distance phone call. It was Gilly who said: 'You know the proposition you made to me in your house... I've decided to say yes!' My first thought was to say, 'What proposition?' I didn't think that this was the way a proposal was normally handled. Thank goodness I restrained myself and sat on my pride. I told her that I would go back to my cabin and write to her. I hope my letter was more encouraging than my reaction on the telephone. In my letter I said that we would make arrangements when I was on my next leave and that we would be married during the leave after that. I received a prompt reply saying that my plan had been rejected. Gilly would make the arrangements and we would get married on my next leave. Well, I couldn't complain about that. Having had initial doubts about marrying me, it seemed that Gilly had really made up her mind. It was also rather a relief that I didn't have to bother about the organisation. All I had to do was to send Gilly a list of my intended guests and turn up on the day in best bib and tucker with sword.

I was able to concentrate my time in getting *Aurochs* ready for her commissioning which was to take place within a few weeks of our engagement. Lt. David Prince RCN joined *Aurochs* as torpedo officer, and Lt. Peter Cope as navigator.

Particularly because I was about to get married I thought it wise to buy a new car. The Standard Vanguard had become very unreliable. Gilly had already declared that she believed she had push-started it in every street in Edinburgh. One Saturday morning I went in search of a new car and found just what I wanted in Fareham. It was a fairly new Morris Minor. As I drove it back to *Dolphin* I suddenly realised that three years previously that was what Brian Hutchings advised me to buy.

Auroch's commissioning went reasonably smoothly with no major hold ups and we sailed for the Clyde for the work up which followed the usual programme. The Captain S/M3 was Capt. 'Tony' Troup. I knew all the submarine's systems well but I had never served in a submarine with a gun. The drill was easy enough to pick up as it was similar to that used in my Boy Seaman training. Our inspection went well and I suspect that Tony Troup wanted a bit of fun to finish as he kept the gun action till last. The action was going well although we hadn't yet hit the target when Tony Troup ordered an alteration of course. We had been firing over the port bow but on the new course we would be firing over the starboard bow. There would therefore be a danger of shooting away our jumping wire which stretched from the top of the periscope standards to a point on our bow. Just before the jumping wire came within the line of fire I ordered 'Check, Check, Check,' to stop the gun's crew from firing. This made Tony Troup quite cross. He told me that in war time you carried on firing and risked shooting the jumping wire to pieces. I didn't argue with him. He knew what he was talking about having taken command of his first submarine when he was only twenty one. Apart from that minor difference of opinion, we passed our inspection and left Faslane to return to Gosport from where we would be operating.

Working up in the Clyde had also been beneficial to my marriage plans. Gilly had come over from Perth on a number of occasions to discuss wedding details. At this stage I hadn't had an opportunity to get her an engagement ring as I still didn't know her finger size. Fortunately she had initiative, but I was rather surprised during one visit when she opened a box containing about a dozen rings. Cairncross, the main jewellers in Perth, had allowed her to bring them over so that we might choose one together.

After joining the Squadron in Gosport it soon became obvious to me that as the 'junior boy' I was going to get all the jobs which more senior submarine

Aurochs *leaving Portsmouth Harbour with Bryan in command. (Royal Naval Museum)*

captains didn't want, so we spent most of our time acting as a 'clockwork mouse', that is, a target for surface ships working up at Portland. This should have given me enough time to find somewhere for us to live after our wedding but a week before we were due to wed I still hadn't found anywhere suitable. In desperation I went to look at a small cottage in the grounds of Grenville Hall, Droxford, owned by a Mrs Macpherson. She had renovated the cottage in the expectation that her grandchildren would come to stay but it appeared that they rarely came and so she had decided to let it out. It was in pristine condition and a place which I assumed that Gilly would be very happy to have as her first married home.

To me, this was one of the main responsibilities which I had to undertake and I felt very relieved to have found a home and what appeared to be a very nice landlady. Of course, the other thing I had to do was to arrange the honeymoon. Gilly had left the arrangements to me although I had consulted her on where we should go. We chose Westport in County Mayo, western Ireland. I was a member of the RAC at the time and left them to arrange the ferry bookings. We decided to go in Gilly's car, an open topped Morris Minor.

I flew to Edinburgh with my mother the day before the wedding and arrived in time for a sherry reception on the evening before the wedding attended by most of Gilly's relations and also my best man, Donald Armstrong, a term-mate. Donald appeared at the drinks party in a very loud tweed suit with large checks. Gilly's Uncle George was not known for his sense of humour but he worked his way over to Donald to ask him: 'Who won the 3.30 at Wincanton?', pretending that he thought Donald was a bookmaker.

Donald and I stayed the night with Mrs Young, a friend of Gilly's mother. We woke to a wet and grey day, or as they would say in Scotland 'dreich'. It was August Bank Holiday Monday. Gilly had tried to book the wedding for the Saturday but it wasn't possible. As she had vowed that we would get married during this summer leave she had settled for the Monday. By now Uncle George was back to his normal self. Whilst the guests were in the church waiting for the bride to arrive, he was heard to say in a voice which could be heard by everyone: 'Monday's a very funny day to get married, isn't it?'

I was extremely nervous and had to calm myself with two gin and tonics before making my way to St. John's Kirk. Gilly was as cool as could be. She walked up the aisle on the arms of her uncle David who always looked like an ambassador. As she came level with me she turned and said: 'Nine stone!' I hadn't been aware, but that, apparently, had been her target.

As soon as I was married I was entitled to marriage allowance of 26 shillings a day. Together with my Lieutenant's pay (with over 6 years seniority) of £3.2s. a day, and my other allowances, my annual salary was now £1,605. Although this wasn't on my mind at the time, Gilly certainly didn't marry me for my money.

Wedding custom at that time was for the bride and groom to depart not long after the speeches were made. Robin Young, the husband of Gilly's school friend Fiona, insisted that it was a Scottish custom that the bride and groom should be carried down the stairs in a blanket. Fortunately the blanket took the weight of us both and no accident occurred. We were soon off on our honeymoon. We were heading for Ayr for our first night and felt very deprived as we drove past the Gleneagles Hotel where the evening's party was to take place.

The next day we had a gentle crossing from Stranraer to Larne and after a further night in Enniskillen we arrived at the Central Hotel, Westport. I had written to the hotel detailing my requirements very carefully but I was too embarrassed to say that I was on my honeymoon. I was rather surprised to find that we had a bedroom on the ground floor. This didn't spoil our stay, but as I was paying the bill before leaving I did mention that I thought it was odd that I had been accommodated on the ground floor. 'Well you see,' replied the receptionist, 'we read your letter carefully, and came to the conclusion that you were disabled.'

Bryan and Gilly's wedding – St. John's Kirk, Perth.

After a pleasant and relaxing honeymoon we made our way over to Dublin where we were to spend a night before catching the following night's ferry to Liverpool. We hadn't booked a hotel and had some difficulty finding one. Eventually we were offered a family room in a temperance hotel. The room was a garret in the roof and had about ten beds. Typically Irish, I thought. We went out for an evening meal and a cinema show and returned to find all the beds had been turned down by the maid. Little did she know that we had been married less than a fortnight.

We arrived at the ferry in plenty of time. There were no Ro-Ro ferries sailing out of Dublin at that time. We had to watch Gilly's car (SWS 594) being lifted up by sling to be deposited into a ship's hold, and we then boarded another ferry. Unfortunately I hadn't made my requirements clear to the RAC and I found that no cabin had been booked. We spent the night sharing a wooden armchair in the lounge while Gilly fretted that the ship carrying her precious car would sink before it arrived at Liverpool.

We eventually arrived at Grenville Hall and I was relieved to see that Gilly liked her new home. There were a number of houses on the estate including one occupied by a retired submariner, Captain Jackie Slaughter.

The honeymoon was over and it was back to work. Rear Admiral Horace Law, who had been the Commander in *Triumph*, had become FOSM.

Aurochs' programme for the rest of August was 'day running' with the occasional nights at Portland, but when in Gosport I was able to get home.

In September we were scheduled to visit Bilbao. We were to join up with *Adamant*, the Depot Ship from the 2nd Submarine Squadron. I had asked Gilly to fly over and stay in a hotel while we were there. My torpedo officer David Prince's wife, Barbara, went as well. They flew directly with a small airline called BKS Airways reputed to have been established by Messrs Brown, King and Smith who had pooled their Army gratuities. Gilly made a few enquiries about the trip and was told that it would be in a Dakota. She was told that the flight would be direct provided a head-wind didn't force them to refuel in France. Gilly arrived several hours before the submarine and settled in to our hotel. She hadn't been there long before she received a telephone call from the British Consul's wife who explained that the wife of the Captain of the depot ship was flying into Biarritz with the more up-market British European Airways, but the aircraft had been delayed. The Consul's wife instructed Gilly to be ready to come to a lunch party if the Captain's wife hadn't arrived. Gilly is always exceedingly polite, but she explained to the Consul's wife that she wasn't used to being ordered about, nor was she accustomed to being used as a stand-in guest at lunch parties. She told the Consul's wife to look elsewhere. I was horrified on hearing this story, but on reflection I sided with Gilly. After all she'd married me, not the Navy.

There were two other memorable incidents whilst we were in Bilbao. When a British ship visits a foreign port it always attracts great excitement from the expatriates. Many attend the Sunday church service which is usually followed by coffee in the wardroom. Some families even wait for a Naval visit in order to have their children baptised on board. We therefore looked forward to this special service. I realised that arrangements weren't going as well as I had hoped when there was no sign of the padre with only about five minutes to go before the service. At the last moment the padre arrived and hastily threw a dirty white ensign over a table as an altar and the service began. It didn't take long to realise that he was under the influence of drink. As soon as the service was over he was off ashore again. The next morning I went to see the Commander S/M, 'Spike' Park, to tell him that I thought this was a poor way to behave. I didn't know Spike but knew that he had a well developed sense of humour. He laughed at me and said that he quite agreed with my point of view, 'But you see, Bryan, I'm a left footer.' A left-footer is the Naval term for a Roman Catholic. He wasn't too concerned whether the Anglican service had been a success or not.

The second incident was during our departure. We were obliged to take a pilot and I assumed that the harbour authorities would send one of their best. We slipped satisfactorily but had to turn round to face the harbour entrance. In turning us round, the pilot took the submarine over a mud bank and I thought we were going to run aground. I started giving the orders regardless of the pilot. It was quite obvious that he had no idea of our draught and like many observers was fooled by the small amount of the hull (freeboard) which shows above the surface in a submarine. In extricating myself from the predicament I used a considerable amount of power and stirred up large swirls of muddy water. I was conscious that all the officers in the depot ship and a large crowd on the jetty were watching with apprehension. As I sailed out of the harbour, I sent a signal to the depot ship which comprised only one word: 'Phew!'

After we had settled in at Stable Cottage, Gilly's mother decided to pay us a visit. It gave us an opportunity to do some entertaining, and others within our small community repaid the hospitality. My mother-in-law had lived a very sheltered life as the wife of a doctor in general practice but she became well acquainted with Naval language after attending Jackie Slaughter's cocktail party. There are countless stories about his coarse language and swearing. He never moderated his language regardless of the situation. But he had served gallantly throughout the war and was in command of *Sunfish*, the first submarine to sink an enemy ship in the war.

Foolishly, I had no feelings of apprehension as we walked across to his house for his party. I presumed that in retirement and in the company of older ladies he would restrain himself. On being offered a drink, my mother-in-law asked for a sherry whilst I chose a gin and tonic. On arrival, my drink tasted as though it was ninety per cent gin. I sipped it slowly but Jackie Slaughter was soon back asking me whether I would like to have my glass refreshed, which I declined. He then asked me whether I liked the gin and I assured him that I did.

After some time he came back again and noticed that I still had more than half a glass remaining.

'Smalley,' he asked, 'is there anything wrong with that gin?'

'No Sir,' I replied.

'Are you quite sure?' he persisted.

'Yes Sir,' I assured him.

'In that case f***** well drink it!'

I took my mother-in-law back home as soon as possible before she fainted.

After a period of day running we were scheduled to make a visit to Manchester. We were to go with *Truncheon* which was commanded by Graham Rogers who was senior to me and therefore in charge. I expressed surprise to my superiors that we should go up the canal when we could easily have visited Liverpool, but I was told that if one drew a circle of about thirty five miles round Manchester you would have enclosed about half the population of England. The purpose of our visit was to encourage as many people as possible to come on board and hopefully attract a few recruits.

On the morning of 10 October we arrived off Liverpool ready to take passage up the Manchester ship canal. We took a pilot on board who manoeuvred us easily from the open water of Liverpool harbour into the canal's entrance. We proceeded satisfactorily and eventually came to the first lock. Whilst waiting for the water level to change the pilot asked if he could go below for a look round. When we were ready to proceed I had to call the pilot back on to the bridge. Each time we came to a lock the pilot went below for a further 'look-round'. The canal is only 125 feet at its widest part. Although it was possible to pass oncoming ships, it was nevertheless quite an anxious moment as each ship squeezed past. One difficult moment was at the sharp right hand bend at Runcorn which nearly ended in disaster. I let the pilot con the ship; after all, that was what he was being paid to do. We were about a third of the way round the bend when he turned to me and said: 'Well, skipper, I don't think we're going to make it!' I immediately took over and ordered the

Aurochs *in Latchford Loch, Manchester Ship Canal.*

starboard engine to go astern in order to pull the submarine round into a tighter turn. My faith in the pilot was beginning to wane. At the next lock he was down below again for another look round. As we progressed it became obvious to me that he was becoming progressively drunk. When I went below after securing alongside I discovered that the bar was open. Mike Highwood explained that when the pilot went below he asked for a drink. Mike felt it was impolite to refuse. It transpired that the pilot had never gone further than the wardroom bar.

We were secured alongside Old Trafford Wharf which was outside the jurisdiction of the City of Manchester but within the Borough of Stretford.

Graham Rogers and I found ourselves coping with two local authorities' hospitality. I made arrangements to call on the Managing Director of the Manchester Shipping Canal Company Ltd. but I wasn't sufficiently important and was passed on to the Company Secretary. I took the opportunity to tell him what I thought of his drunken and incompetent pilot. He explained that pilots were administered by their union and were allocated jobs strictly in order of rotation. I also told him that I was disappointed that his company was letting the canal fall into an unacceptable state of repair. I think he was rather shaken by a mere lieutenant talking to him in this way.

Gilly had driven up from Droxford to be with me and we stayed with my cousin Jack Earnshaw and his wife Ruth and daughter Catherine.

After the visit we went back to the mundane day-running out of Gosport and Portland.

We sailed from Gosport on 7 November for passage to the 'Derry Areas to take part in a JTC (Joint Tactical Course). By now we had exchanged engineers and David Wixon had taken over. It was his first submarine. It was a rather unfortunate appointment for him because *Aurochs'* engines were beginning to show signs of their age and needed more than the usual care.

We went up harbour to Londonderry on 21 November to 'wash-up' the exercise. It was during our stay in 'Derry that President Kennedy was assassinated. We spent the next week at sea in the 'Derry Areas in a very sombre mood.

Towards the end of the week we developed an engine defect. We made an abortive attempt to make repairs in 'Derry but eventually returned to Gosport. We arrived at Gosport on 1 December.

I had several foreign officers under training whilst in command of *Aurochs*. One of them was Indigit Singh from the Indian Navy. We were hoping to sell them our submarines but having trained them they then bought four Soviet 'Whisky' class submarines.

We had arrived in Gosport to repair our broken engine earlier than expected. Gilly was in the Nuffield Club playing bridge with Sandy when she saw an Indian arrive at the club. She thought it was Indigit but couldn't be sure. Eventually she plucked up courage to ask him and on discovering that *Aurochs* was in harbour she hurried home before her reputation was tarnished.

It took us a week to repair the engine defect. For me it was a less pleasant time. One of the keys to the safe for our confidential books had been lost. Although it was extremely unlikely that the safe's contents had been compromised it was nevertheless a serious matter. To confuse the issue, it wasn't exactly clear which books were in the safe at the time. The contents list was locked in the safe. As a result I had to appear before a court martial on 9 December. Although ably defended by Cdr. John Moore I decided to plead guilty rather than go into the unpleasant details which might have incriminated one of my officers. But after the court had deliberated on the evidence and decided that I was guilty both the prosecuting officer, Captain Ernie Turner, and John Moore spoke out on my behalf before the court decided on a sentence. Captain Turner said: 'I have always found the accused to be a loyal, hardworking officer, and he showed great keenness in taking over his command of a submarine. He has shown great promise and until now has always been most correct in all matters connected with his duties. I am certain that he will never make the same mistake again, and I am prepared to continue to have him as a commanding officer in my squadron.' John Moore added: 'At no time have I known him to be anything but an honest, hard working, and zealous officer. He gives a great deal of thought to the running of the submarine and to the tactical applications of problems which confront us today. At Portland, where he has been on several occasions, I have heard reports of him as one of the more successful submarine captains in the exercises taking place there.'

It was very humbling to have my senior officers talking about me in that way. I was given a severe reprimand. After the court concluded its business Capt. Turner told the press that: 'Lieut. Smalley stays in command of *Aurochs*. He sails in half an hour on exercises.'

All this took place immediately before I was to sail for Exercise Lime Jug. I was asked by John Moore whether the court martial had affected me sufficiently to prevent me from sailing. After assuring him that I was OK, I took the submarine to sea that afternoon. Although we didn't have much excitement during the exercise I had one satisfying experience.

I knew that HMS *Hampshire* was taking part in the exercise. She was a brand new ship about which I knew little, and as her sister ship *London* was in harbour I had earlier asked permission during my time in harbour to go on board and have a look round to learn of her capabilities.

We sailed for the exercise and made our way to our patrol area in moderately rough seas. We patrolled our area quietly waiting to detect the noise of approaching ships, but nothing came. Nor did we see anything as a result of our tiring periscope watch. We had been on patrol for a number of days with no activity when we detected a ship moving at moderate speed. As the ship drew closer we identified it as *Hampshire* and I realised that there were no other ships in the vicinity. I managed to manoeuvre *Aurochs* into a position where I could fire a salvo at her from an ideal position just forward of her starboard beam. Of course I didn't fire the torpedoes but instead took a periscope photograph to prove what I had done. I also fired a green grenade which indicated a simulated torpedo firing, but *Hampshire's* lookouts failed to see it. I concluded that she had been detached from the main body to undertake some task and had foolishly relaxed sonar and visual vigilance. It would have been fatal in wartime. My photo appeared in the exercise report but I omitted to keep a copy for myself. I had a quiet chuckle about the claim that the new County class had 'considerable capacity to operate independently'.

1964 began with the appointment of a new first lieutenant, Tony Norris, known as 'Schonk'. Our year's programme began with day running out of Portland with week-ends back in Gosport but during the latter part of January we were given something less boring to do. We took part in Operation Phoenix which, although a minor exercise, gave us two weeks at sea with an opportunity to work for a decent length of time together as a team without shoreside distractions.

As well as training the Indian Naval Service we also had a German officer on board. Unlike Indigit who was respectful and polite I found him too deferential which annoyed me. Whenever I gave him an order he would acknowledge it and also click his heels. In spite of the extreme irritation which I felt, I hadn't the courage to ask him to desist.

By now I had got to know Tony Norris. He was an extremely opinionated officer who preferred to plough his own furrow. When one made a comment he seemed to delight in disagreeing publicly with it. But I found the greatest impediment to good relations was the fact that he lived next door to the local Member of Parliament, Dr Reginald Bennett, with whom he discussed the way I ran the submarine. His uncomplimentary observations unfortunately occasionally reached the newspapers.

In March we were programmed to take part in Exercise Magic Lantern followed by a visit to Gibraltar.

We arrived in Gibraltar on 12 March and were programmed for day running to test some new equipment. We were allowed to sleep ashore in a local hotel. It wasn't long before I wrote to Gilly asking her to come out and join me as soon as possible. I posted the letter in the late afternoon and thought no more about it. Gilly was four months pregnant at the time.

The next day I was invited to a cocktail party given by Commander John Cole and his wife. John Cole had been the Commander (Supply) in the Third Submarine Squadron and had always done everything possible to help the submariners. He was about to leave Gibraltar on his retirement from the Navy. I was looking forward to his party.

I'm not sure how it happened but I was invited on board the minelayer *Plover* for a drink before going along to the Coles' house. The Captain of *Plover* was Lt. Cdr. John Messervy GM MBE whom I had never met. Like me he had joined the Navy as a Boy Seaman. He became a diver and developed a reputation for fearless courage. He received his MBE after removing live mines from the wreck of the ex-Port Line ship *Port Napier* in Loch Alsh. He was awarded the George Medal in 1959 for removing six live torpedoes from the hull of a sunken Japanese submarine off Singapore. John Messervy also had a reputation for wild escapades.

I arrived on board a few minutes after the invitation stated. The Quartermaster explained that the Captain was in the bath and I was told to make myself at home. He then went off to find the wardroom steward. As time passed, other guests arrived including a number of Wren officers. In due course John Messervy arrived. I became uneasy because the time for us to go to John Cole's party was well past and no one was making any move. When it was decided to leave, I had rather a shock, because I had been assigned to a Third Officer Wren called Mary.

On arrival at the Coles' house I was met by David Morrell. He explained that he had been frantically searching for me because Gilly had arrived and was waiting for me in the hotel. I bade a polite goodbye to my new found lady friend. I rushed back to the hotel and explained the situation which Gilly kindly understood. I had posted my letter the previous evening and it had been delivered the next morning. Gilly drove directly to Heathrow to catch a flight. She was with me in less than twenty four hours after I posted the letter. Although Gilly forgave me, my allocated paramour, Mary, never spoke to me again so I was never able to apologise for spoiling her evening even though I had no intention of fulfilling her expectations.

We arrived in Gosport on 14 April and commenced a leave period. During my leave Gilly and I made early preparations for the arrival of our baby. Gilly had intended to have the baby at home but our GP advised against this. We found a maternity hospital which seemed suitable and the information we received about it said that prospective parents were welcome to look round on Wednesday afternoons. I went along with Gilly to the hospital at the appointed hour. The hospital was an old converted mansion set in an overgrown garden. At 3 o'clock precisely the front door was flung open and a huge matron appeared. If she hadn't been in uniform I would have assumed that she was an all-in wrestler. Her eyes immediately fell on me and a look of horror overcame her.

'What are you doing here?' she demanded.

I held the letter in front of her so that she could see it and replied, 'It says here that prospective parents may look over the hospital.'

'That means expectant mothers,' she bawled. 'Go and wait amongst the rhododendrons until your wife comes out.'

Here was I – instead of giving orders, I was being bossed about like a miscreant schoolboy.

Whilst in Gosport I took the opportunity to call on FOSM's staff to enquire about my next appointment. I was told that I was earmarked to go to the Boys' Training Establishment, HMS *Ganges*, at Shotley to be a Divisional Officer. I rather baulked at this. I explained that I'd spent a lot of time running out of Scotland and more recently from Gosport and as I was fairly recently married I wanted a job abroad. There was some delay before I heard the outcome, but was eventually told that the Canadians had been asked if they would accept me on an exchange appointment so that I could become the lecturer in submarine warfare at the Canadian Forces Maritime Warfare School in Halifax, Nova Scotia. I would relieve Dick Heaslip. The idea pleased Gilly and me immensely.

Whilst in harbour we were also preparing *Aurochs* for an annual inspection on 14 May. It was a fairly routine affair which we passed with little difficulty.

I was promoted to Lieutenant Commander on 1 June and my pay, with marriage allowance added, now came to £1,800 a year.

We continued to be employed running out of Portland during the week as a 'mickey mouse' for the working-up surface ships.

We returned to Gosport for the week-ends but I had to return to Portland each Saturday by car to discuss the surface ships' progress during the previous week, but *Aurochs* was programmed to stay in Portland over the bank holiday weekend at the beginning of August to open the boat to the public for Navy Days. I was therefore isolated from Gilly for most of the time as the date for the arrival of the baby approached. The expected arrival date of the baby was 21 July but the day running continued beyond that. By the time the baby was ten days overdue the doctor decided that a maternity hospital wasn't the right place for the delivery and he arranged for Gilly to be admitted to St. Mary's Hospital in Portsmouth. On the bank holiday weekend I went home, leaving the first lieutenant to handle the Open Days. I visited the hospital but found we didn't have much to talk about, so on my next visit I took a chess set in to the hospital and Gilly and I played chess during visiting times, leaving the chess board with its pieces in place under the bed until my next visit. The nurses and the other patients thought we were quite odd.

Still the baby didn't arrive and the doctors decided that they would induce it. By this time it was fourteen days overdue. But on the Monday night I had to go back to Portland as we were off to sea early the next morning. The day at sea on Tuesday 4 August was uneventful and we surfaced at about 5 o'clock in the evening. The first thing that normally happened after surfacing at the end of the day was to send the 'surfacing signal'. This must always only contain one word, 'Surfaced', and to ensure that it gets to the right people quickly it goes under the priority heading of 'Operational Immediate'. It is customary to write out the signal before surfacing, then having surfaced the captain orders the Radio Supervisor to send it. My Radio Supervisor was Petty Officer Butcher. On surfacing I ordered him to send the signal and shortly afterwards he called me on the intercom in a distressed voice telling me that the operator ashore had told him to wait. I reassured him that there must be a more important signal that the shore operator was dealing with. In my mind I realised that just by calling the shore operator he would know that we were safe. A short time later he reported that he had received a signal saying that 'the Captain's wife has had a baby son and that both are doing well'. The shore operator then told him to send his Operational Immediate signal.

We continued day running until the Friday and then returned to Portsmouth. I rushed to the hospital where I was able to see my four day old son for the first time. I learnt that after a prolonged labour the doctors had decided to perform a caesarean.

We had been discussing names for some time and had agreed that a girl would be called Fiona Mary, but we hadn't decided on a boy's name. So our son had a tag on his tiny wrist which said 'The Smalley Baby'. We felt we had let him down badly but still couldn't agree on a name so we each wrote down three boys' names in preferential order giving three points to the preferred name and two to the second and so on. Thus we decided on David whose name came out with five points. The nurses and patients were now completely convinced that we were an extremely odd couple.

Gilly's mother was very concerned about her daughter's confinement. Although she already had two grand-daughters and a grandson from her son Ley's wife, Alison, this would be the first from her only daughter. To make the situation easier for Gilly she paid for a nurse to come and live with us for the first two weeks after Gilly had been discharged from hospital.

It was ten days before Gilly was discharged from hospital. I collected her by car. In the hospital the babies wore small hospital nappies. When I collected Gilly and David, he was wearing a large terry towelling nappy for the first time. As we walked to the car the nappy fell off into the wet and grime of the car park. We realised we had a lot to learn about bringing up babies.

We already had our supply of terry towelling nappies and Sister Ayrton, our nursing support, told us that it was now possible to buy disposable nappies. She didn't entirely approve, but said that if we had some we could cut them up and use them as nappy liners. She instructed me to go to the nearest chemist and bring back a box. I went to the chemist in Droxford and explained my mission. The chemist asked me what size box I wanted. I had no idea, so he gave me a box measuring about 2ft by 2ft by 3ft. On arrival home I was given a rocket by the sister who told me that I had too many. I was sent back post haste with clearer instructions and had to explain the situation to the chemist with some embarrassment.

The day after Gilly was discharged from hospital, Neil Warneford, a term mate of mine, relieved me of my command of *Aurochs*.

I was able to have a few days at home with the family. At about six each evening I would have a 'horse's neck'. Normally Gilly would have had one occasionally, but as she was feeding David she stuck to fruit juice. Naturally anyone else in the house would be offered a drink of their choice. Sister Ayrton explained that she rarely drank – 'perhaps a glass of sherry occasionally'. I persuaded her to try a horse's neck. She found it agreeable and after taking her time over the first one agreed to a second. A similar situation occurred on the following day. Eventually the baby's feeding and changing routine changed, and by six o'clock 'Sister' would be ensconced in her chair waiting for 'the bar to open'. We discovered that she had a fund of amusing stories about her nursing experiences.

In due course I received confirmation that the Canadians had accepted me as a relief for Dick Heaslip. I was instructed to prepare myself in a number of ways. First, I had to undertake the Joint Tactical Course at the Joint Maritime Warfare School in Londonderry. I also had to go to the Naval Intelligence Division in the Ministry of Defence for a briefing on the latest Warsaw Pact capabilities and particularly its submarines. Then I was appointed to HMS *Rhyll* to take part in an exercise which was being held in the North Atlantic to give me surface ship experience. It meant a lot of time away from home.

At this time the MoD was changing its policy regarding travel to appointments abroad. Travel by sea had become too expensive and time consuming. The new policy was to send kit on ahead by sea and then follow it by air. I was told to follow this procedure and so all my belongings apart from essential items had already been despatched by sea. Whilst I was at sea in *Rhyll*, Gilly received a telephone call from the MoD asking her if we would rather go by sea. She naturally agreed, and when I arrived home I supported her decision.

Gilly also had to make many other preparations. She asked about any medical requirements. She was seen by a female Naval doctor who had qualified with her brother at St. Andrew's University. The doctor promptly pumped Gilly full of a number of injections. Gilly then asked her whether these would affect the breast feeding of her baby. 'Don't feed the baby for a fortnight,' replied the doctor. She was clearly not a paediatrician, about whom I had some experience.

Before departing for Canada we bade Mrs Macpherson a fond goodbye and sadly left our first home where we had been so happy. We spent a few nights in Perth with Gilly's mother and then made our way to Southampton to board the Cunard liner *Carmania*.

Gilly is not a good sailor and our passage was moderately rough. She didn't feel able to participate in many of the entertainments on board. In spite of the medical advice she was still breast feeding the baby and felt that she shouldn't take any medication for sea sickness. I was reluctant to leave her alone with David in our cabin and so I didn't participate to any great extent in the social activities. What was worse was that my dinner jacket had gone on ahead and a grey suit was the best I could muster. I suppose we were about halfway across when the Captain (who was also a Captain in the RNR) sent for me and gave me a dressing down for not behaving as he would expect from a Naval officer. He expected me to participate more fully in the ship's social activities. The irony was that another Lieutenant Commander on board was bedding every willing young female he could find. It appeared that that was more in line with what was expected.

We ate in the first class dining room which had a serious flaw. The ship had recently been renovated and Lady Cunard had advised on the decor. The forward bulkhead was completely covered by a mirror which I assumed was intended to make the dining room appear larger. If you looked into the mirror in rough seas you could see yourself and other diners apparently being lifted into the air and then dropped from a great height to the depths below. The sight accentuated any difficulty one might be having in retaining one's meal.

Cunard were very keen to demonstrate the quality of their catering arrangements. During the trip they arranged to show us through the kitchens, an offer which Gilly declined. Also during the voyage, which lasted six days, the chief steward would go to a number of tables at breakfast-time each day and ask the diners to choose their special menu for dinner that evening. The chief steward came to us at breakfast on about the fourth day and asked us to choose. There was still a roll on the ship which wasn't helped by the jerking motion induced by the ship's stabilisers. Gilly looked at the steward with a grey face and said: 'I think I'll have a bit of boiled fish.' The steward then looked at me. I was dying to have lobster thermidor or something equally exotic, but in sympathy with Gilly I said: 'I'll have a bit of boiled fish too.' The steward turned away in disgust.

Although our final destination was Halifax, *Carmania* was sailing for Montreal. The sea calmed as we entered the mouth of the St. Lawrence River and the rest of the passage was uneventful. We stopped in Québec just long enough to disembark a few passengers and then moved on to Montreal. Montreal was suffering from some discontent with the Québecois who were seeking independence so we were apprehensive about the reception we might receive, but as soon as we stepped ashore we were approached by a native who asked: '*Parlez-vous le ding-dong?*' He had been sent by the Naval Attaché to meet us and was obviously on our side, mocking the language spoken by the French Canadians. The immigration official wrote in my passport 'Duration of Present Status' in an almost illegible hand. I assumed that was a standard phrase.

CHAPTER 19

The Maritime Warfare School, Halifax, Nova Scotia 1965-66

HAVING CLEARED immigration and customs we were taken to the railway station where we awaited the overnight train to take us back eastwards to Halifax, a distance of about 700 miles. The train was comfortable and we had a compartment to ourselves.

We were very lucky with our accommodation in Halifax because John Aspin, one of the Canadians being trained in the UK for the Canadian Submarine Service, had a vacant house which we rented. The entrance to Halifax harbour is comparatively narrow with Halifax on the south west shore. Dartmouth is on the north east shore and the two are connected by a road bridge. Further inland the harbour opens up into a large basin and our house was on Dakin Drive in Birch Cove overlooking the basin. We were delighted with it as soon as we saw it. Dick Heaslip whom I was to relieve had already left for home and we were rather lost for people to approach for advice, particularly regarding the purchase of a car. Fortunately Alan Kennedy spent an hour or two ferrying us round the car showrooms until we found an old Austin which we could afford. Alan was now the CO of *Acheron* which was on loan to the RCN. We only had a sterling bank account and had no means of paying for the car, but we were quickly taught something about the Canadian economy. We had never heard of a 'credit rating' but were told that the first thing we had to do was to borrow money. Then as quickly as possible we should pay it back. This would give us a high credit rating so that we could borrow more easily in the future. I managed to transfer some money from home within twenty four hours and from then on my credit was good.

The day after my arrival I presented myself for duty at the Maritime Warfare School. It was staffed by a mixture of Canadian Air Force and Naval Officers plus an American submariner and an RN TAS officer plus myself. Command was held jointly by Commander Bob Falls and Wing Commander Bob Hook. One of the Canadians, Lt. Cdr. Al Gorseline, had spent time on exchange with the RN and was a staunch Anglophile and became an invaluable friend and adviser to us during our time in Halifax. We were further helped by our neighbours, David Ramsay, one of the RN submariners on loan to the RCN, and his wife Jane, and Joan and Eddy Endacott, an RN submarine engineer.

Rear Admiral W.M. Landymore became FO Canadian Forces East Coast on 16 November and on 15 December Canada dispensed with the Union Flag and adopted the Maple Leaf as its national flag. Many of those serving in the Canadian Forces objected to the abandonment of the White Ensign and Admiral Landymore resigned.

I had been briefed on the Royal Canadian Navy before I left home and of course I had known and even trained officers and men who were to form the embryo RCN Submarine Service. The Canadians experienced sensitivity about their international standing because of their proximity to the all-powerful USA and because of Britain's position as head of the Commonwealth, regardless of the fact that by the end of the '39-'45 war the Canadian Navy was the most sophisticated of all the British Commonwealth Navies. After the war the Canadian Navy concentrated on anti-submarine warfare. It was enhanced by the aircraft carrier *Bonaventure* which during my time in Canada operated Tracker anti-submarine planes and Sea King helicopters. The post war period led to the building of a series of very successful escort vessels. The first was the St. Laurent class which was followed by seven Restigouche class destroyers. Four repeat Restigouche class destroyers were then ordered which became the Mackenzie class. The final ships of the original St. Laurent class were the *Annapolis* and *Nipigon*.

By the time my arrival, the seven earliest St. Laurent class destroyer escorts had been well proven. The whole class had started a conversion programme in 1961 when variable depth sonar (VDS) was fitted. This comprised a sonar set which was lowered by electronic cable from the stern and which was capable of being used below the temperature layers. It gave a greatly enhanced performance over hull mounted sonars. At the same time a helicopter platform was added at the ship's stern and the funnel was replaced by twin uptakes to make way for a helicopter hangar which housed a *Sea King* helicopter.

To overcome the difficulty of landing helicopters on a small deck in rough seas the Canadians had invented an extremely ingenious gadget known as the 'Bear Trap' recovery system. The helicopter lowered a wire into a gridded device (the Bear Trap) which clamped the wire firmly. The helicopter then winched itself onto the deck where it was safely secured.

It can be seen that the RCN was in a very healthy state when I arrived and it was a challenge for me to get acquainted with a number of new techniques.

Gilly also had much to learn. I was told that although I was not in a NATO appointment I was entitled to a NATO driving licence. This could be obtained merely by filling in a form. But Gilly's British licence only allowed her to drive for a month by which time she must obtain a Canadian licence. The Canadian system comprised a written examination followed by a practical test. There were many differences between driving in Canada compared to driving at home and there were rules which one disregarded at one's peril. Most of the houses are of a wooden construction and fire is a real danger. The law forbade parking within a certain distance of a fire hydrant. I examined Gilly on the rules until we felt she was able to take the test. The written test went well as did the practical test until the end. The car had turned into a road which had very few cars parked in it. The examiner told Gilly to park in a convenient space. She parked in a clear space feeling pleased that all had gone so well until it was pointed out that she was alongside a fire hydrant. Fortunately she passed.

Another advantage of being under the assumed NATO umbrella was that I was entitled to buy 12 bottles of tax free spirits each month. This meant that I bought them at about one third the normal retail price. I was to discover later that this was an easy means of acquiring popularity. But the privilege helped me discover the difference between the British and Canadian attitudes to alcohol. Drinking was heavily frowned upon in many quarters and spirits were not available in general stores. They had to be bought in 'liquor' stores which were Government controlled. From the attitude of the sales staff, there was considerable disapproval of this man who it was assumed would be drinking 144 bottles a year, or more than a third of a bottle a day. I dismissed any implied criticism on the grounds that they were jealous. The fear of the perils of alcohol were also illustrated in the law which prohibited the opening of liquor stores on days when an election was being held.

Although we arrived in the winter months we realised that the Canadians were far more ready to deal with cold weather than we were at home. As soon as snow was forecast, the local authority would call in its work-force and make preparations for snow clearance. We were particularly lucky because the foreman lived in our road which was an unmade track. In the winter months he drove a jeep with a small snow plough attached. Our road was always swept clear of snow at the first opportunity. On the main highway the snow wasn't always cleared by snow plough; there were massive snow blowers which would suck up the snow and blow it well clear to the side. Any car in the way of a snow clearing vehicle would be bulldozed out of the way. Once you got used to the inflexibility of the rules it was an easy environment in which to live.

Shortly into the new year, on 24 January, Winston Churchill died. It marked the end of an era. There is no doubt that his death was felt just as deeply in Canada as it was at home.

We soon discovered that the medical system was entirely different in Canada. We learnt that Canadian doctors didn't make home calls, nor did they necessarily treat their patients. If there was a medical problem you called the surgery on the phone, and the first person you spoke to was a secretary. She would enquire about the symptoms and would decide if the doctor needed to be consulted. Or she might pass you on to a nurse who would deal with minor problems. At first we rather disagreed with this reluctance to grant an appointment to see a doctor but we soon learned that it made sense and resulted in a very efficient system. We also discovered that young babies are allocated to a paediatrician. Dr Crosby who looked after David provided a standard of care that we were quite unused to.

I soon learnt the routine at the Maritime Warfare School which was based within HMS *Stadacona,* the principal Naval establishment in Halifax. Our starting time was officially 0900, but we started the day with a half hour coffee break. This may give the appearance of being over-relaxed but it was an invaluable idea. With such a diverse team, there were many ideas to be discussed including the merits of the different ways that each Service operated.

We ran several courses ranging from a few days in length to a longer course of two weeks. We also conducted a number of experiments in the trainer to develop tactics. Our most interesting and demanding course started in Halifax and ran for two weeks. Those attending comprised ships' attack teams; maritime air-crew; and a number of other interested parties. After discussing the capabilities of our own detection devices and weapons, we also briefed on those of our possible enemies, and explained the tactics available to counter any threat they might pose. After the introductory course, we then moved down to Bermuda with our ships and aircraft where we put these ideas into practice. We had about two of these exercises each year. I usually flew down to Bermuda in the Canadian Yukon passenger aircraft but on one occasion I took a lift in a Neptune Maritime patrol aircraft.

As well as flying the American built Neptune aircraft, the Canadians had also designed and built their own maritime patrol aircraft, the Argus, which had started life as the Bristol Britannia. It had a sophisticated assembly of detection and attacking equipment including: Magnetic Anomaly Detection (MAD) for detecting a submarine's magnetic field; Air Navigation and Tactical Control (ANTAC); Sonobuoys; radar; and depth charges.

In Bermuda we were accommodated in, and ran our exercises from, the Kindley Air-Force Base, one of the bases leased to the Americans during the war in exchange for a number of American ships transferred to the RN, an arrangement that had been negotiated by Winston Churchill.

Bermuda had a Marks and Spencer store including a food section. The way to make oneself popular was to take back as many English sausages as one could carry. They weren't available in Halifax.

We did our best to befriend all the people we met in Halifax and gave occasional parties but we found that initially we weren't invited to any Canadian home. This didn't worry us unduly but we wanted to participate and get to know people. We found that we had a lot in common with the Americans. We thought this affinity might be because we were all away from our homes. We played cards with one American couple. They were from the deep south and had accents to match. The wife's father was a judge. They had accents exactly like the deep brogues that are heard in the films of the deep south. It was difficult to believe that when someone uttered a simple phrase such as 'Two no trumps', we would have to ask for a repetition several times before understanding what had been said.

On one occasion I disgraced myself by criticising Gilly unfairly after a hand. I was so ashamed that the next day I phoned a florist and asked them to deliver some flowers to Gilly. On arrival Gilly refused them. She wasn't accustomed to anyone sending her flowers. She took a lot of convincing that they were for her.

As well as the longer exercises away from home, we occasionally went away for shorter periods. Sometimes these would be meetings in various military bases in the States but we also made periodic trips to lecture at the Royal Canadian Military Academy at Kingston, Ontario and at the Royal Canadian Air Force Staff College in Toronto.

After a while I came to the conclusion that Canadians tend to be extremely competent fliers although they have occasional lapses. Once we had got to height we would get out the cards and settle down to a game of bridge. If we were a man short the pilot would sometimes come aft to make up the deficiency. I recall the occasion when one of the engines spluttered and died. The tank in use had run out of fuel and the pilot had to rush forward to change to another tank.

We frequently flew in extreme temperatures, often needing to douse the whole aircraft with antifreeze as part of the pre-flight preparations. On one of these occasions we were in Toronto where the air temperature was minus 20 degrees Centigrade. After a delay while we doused the aircraft in antifreeze we eventually got airborne but then discovered that a piece of electrical equipment which supplied the heater wasn't working. An enterprising crew member said that he could remove its counterpart from the starboard side and install it on the other side to restore heating power. Having removed the device he found that he couldn't fit it on the port side and when he tried to put it back on the starboard side it was so cold that it had lost its shape so that it couldn't be fitted in its original place. We flew from Toronto to Halifax with no heat, no light, and several of our navigational instruments inoperative. As we passed each possible landing site the pilot made an assessment whether he was able to make the next one. We proceeded in this way across Canada but eventually landed at Halifax with great relief.

Another feature of life in Canada was the system of fining people for traffic offences. Whereas at home all offences were dealt with by a Magistrate, in Canada most motoring offences and fines for committing them were clearly laid down. Offenders received a ticket which had to be paid within a specified time. Many Canadians paid little attention to these laws which they regarded as an irritant. They saved up their parking tickets until they had about ten and then would drive to the office where the fines had to be paid. The office was not unlike a present day supermarket check-out. All one had to do was to queue up and hand in the tickets which were then processed through a cash machine and you paid the fine. The street outside the office was a 'no parking' area. Canadians tended to park immediately outside the office knowing that when they came out they would have received another parking ticket which would start their collection of tickets for their next visit.

During my two years in Canada I only collected one parking ticket. That was when I discovered that the whole system was entirely undemocratic. When my turn came at the desk, the girl took my ticket and before I could say anything she turned to me and said:

'That'll be ten dollars.'

I wasn't going to accept this rough justice so I replied:

'I want to plead not guilty.'

She didn't turn a hair:

'That's OK, but it'll still cost you ten dollars.'

This was outrageous. She wasn't interested in anything I had to say. I came back quickly:

'In that case I'm pleading guilty but insane.'

'Listen, Bud,' she said, showing signs of impatience. 'You can plead what you like, but this ticket's going to cost you ten dollars.'

By this time the queue was getting restless. I paid up and beat a hasty retreat.

It was six months before we were invited into a Canadian home. The first invitation came for Gilly to have tea with one of the wives. Gilly was apprehensive. In the weekly paper there was always a column giving accounts of social occasions. It all seemed terribly old fashioned. The report would read that 'Mrs So-and-so gave a tea party, Mrs X poured the tea, and Mrs Y cut the cake.' It seemed that these activities gave one a certain social elevation. Gilly thought she would enquire about all the niceties and was advised to wear a silk dress and a hat. She didn't have a silk dress but went along in the best dress she had. She was relieved to discover that her tea party wasn't at the same social level as those reported in the paper.

Canadians were great outdoor people. Many of them had cabins out of town, mostly close to the sea or near a lake so that they could fish. During the summer months there was a statutory long weekend once a month and people would take off to the country for a weekend in their log cabins.

There was also great excitement as the hunting season approached. Nova Scotia allowed deer hunting and held a lottery at the beginning of the season to allow the lucky winners to shoot one deer. There was great rivalry to obtain these licences and successful hunters would return to town with their prize draped over the top of their vehicles and with horns blazing. On the day the hunting season began there would usually be one or two deaths. When the week-end was over my work colleagues would ask their friends whether they had 'bagged' anything. The reply was frequently: 'No, but I took a couple of sound shots.' A 'sound shot' was when a hunter fired towards an unsighted sound in the hope it was something worth shooting.

Gilly and I went river fishing on one occasion. There appeared to be no private riparian rights in Canada, as any individual has the right to fish along a river bank. We soon learnt about the black fly which attacks any accessible area of bare skin resulting in unbearable itching. We only went river fishing once.

As summer drew to a close we started to make preparations for one of our long exercises, but instead of being off Bermuda, this one was to take place on Canada's west coast. I had become conscious that I was enjoying myself seeing a lot of Canada and America, whilst Gilly remained in Halifax with our baby son David. Whilst she never complained, I thought it was rather unfair on her. I asked my boss if I could take my two weeks' summer leave immediately before the west coast exercise took place. My plan was to work our way across to the west coast and as the exercise was due to start I would send Gilly back and remain for the exercise.

We were lucky in that our friends, Taff and Fran Jones, offered to take David into their home while Gilly and I were away. Taff Jones, a Welshman, had started his seafaring career in the Merchant Navy, but had met his wife Fran, a Canadian, whilst visiting a Canadian port. After they married, Taff left the Merchant Navy and joined the RCN.

We took an Air Canada flight to Edmonton. At Edmonton we hired a car and drove south to Calgary. We had a particular reason for visiting Calgary. Gilly's mother's cousin, (Aunty) Bee Sidey, lived there. She and her brother and sister had left Scotland at the beginning of the century looking for a better life. They took an Aberdeen Angus bull with them. They travelled to Halifax by sea, and then moved westward by train until they settled just outside Calgary. They bred from the bull and became successful livestock farmers, but in due course oil was found under their land and they were made for life. The family had become quite numerous and we had arranged to meet them all for an evening's get-together in Calgary. One of the relations told me proudly that he had once seen the sea. He had flown to New York and whilst preparing to land he had flown over it. He was convinced that our mutual experiences of the sea established an everlasting affinity for each other.

We then moved on to Banff. After checking in to a motel in the evening it began to snow. The next morning we threw back the curtains to a clear blue sky but with a foot or two of snow lying on the ground. There was a deer only a few feet from the window and several others sheltering in the trees beyond. We went for breakfast and were told that the motel was isolated. The snow clearing facilities were clearly not as efficient as those in Halifax. We spent the next thirty six hours trapped in the motel. Although meals were provided there was no entertainment. To keep our spirits up we had a bottle of brandy, one bottle of ginger ale, and one book. We took it in turns to read the book. I drank the brandy until the ginger ale ran out.

Eventually the road was cleared of snow and we started our sight-seeing of the local area before heading westward stopping at the wonderful tourist attractions as we went. Eventually we arrived in Vancouver. After a few days there we took the ferry to Victoria on Vancouver Island. After seeing the sights in Victoria we moved northwards and stayed in a motel which advertised fishing boats for hire. Gilly and I hired a boat and tried our hands at fishing. I caught a salmon. It weighed about six pounds and as I pulled it over the side of the boat it looked to me to be a fearsome beast. I left Gilly to extract the hook. The motel owner kindly cleaned it and put it in his freezer overnight. The next day I went to the RCAF Base on the island with which we would be working during the exercise. I found someone who kindly agreed to keep the fish in deep freeze until I was able to get it back to Halifax.

By now it was time to start the exercise and I reluctantly took Gilly to the airport and put her back on a flight to Vancouver and then on to Halifax. We had enjoyed a wonderful holiday and seen a totally different aspect of Canada.

Our exercise went well. There was plenty of suitable water for exercising to the west of Vancouver Island and so we didn't have to move the thousand miles which were necessary for east coast exercises. I was able to ride the Canadian submarine *Grilse* during the sea-going phase of the exercise. *Grilse* was an American built Balao class submarine, formerly the *Burrfish*. She had been loaned to the RCN in 1961.

After the exercise, the staff of the Maritime Warfare School returned to Halifax. We flew in a Yukon which was very comfortable, but I hadn't managed to retrieve my salmon.

On arrival back in Halifax I discovered that John Aspin had written to say that he was on his way back to Halifax and would like possession of his house. Fortunately Commander John Hervey who was the CO of the submarine squadron was about to go home. His house in Cascade Drive was fully furnished and we took over the house and the furniture. It wasn't far from Dakin Drive. Once again we struck lucky because the house was ideal for our needs.

Most RN people who were appointed to Canada bought a duty free car to take home with them. There were a number of garages in Halifax which sold right-hand drive vehicles entirely for that purpose. You had to own the vehicle for a year before it could be exported. We bought a VW Variant Estate at about this time. In Halifax it wasn't that unusual, but if one went some distance out of town people would walk round the car unbelievingly when they saw the right hand drive.

Our most amusing experience was an occasion when we were on a fast road with a gentle curve. Gilly was in the left hand seat but had turned round to do something to David in the back. A Royal Canadian Mounted Police car came round the bend and I could see the look of horror on the driver's face when he saw Gilly's bottom sticking up where he reasonably expected to see a driver.

It was shortly after I returned to Halifax that the United States Navy invited the RCN to send a qualified submariner to help them run an exercise from their big Naval Base in Puerto Rico. As the Canadians didn't have anyone else to spare with the required qualifications I was told to prepare to take up the position in the new year. I would be away for six weeks.

Before the Christmas holiday period came we discovered that Gilly was expecting another baby.

Al Gorseline, whose cabin we occasionally visited at the weekends, was on good terms with the local fishermen. It was shortly before Christmas that he asked me whether I would like to go lobster fishing and I accepted with enthusiasm. I took a bottle of rum as a present. As soon as we boarded the small craft I handed over the rum which was immediately opened. As soon as we left harbour, water was brought to the boil on a small stove on which we started cooking lobsters. I learnt that the law forbade the landing of lobsters which were below a given size. However, it seemed that the fishermen kept a number of the smaller lobsters in a sack on board for their own consumption. The fisherman needed a special permit to take Al and me out fishing. Apparently, the fisherman had been returning to harbour shortly before our trip when he saw the fisheries inspector waiting for him on the jetty. In a panic he threw the sack containing the undersized lobsters overboard. When he arrived alongside, the inspector told him that he had come to deliver the licence that Al and I needed for the trip.

When my bottle of rum was empty another was produced. By the time we got ashore I had drunk as much as I could cope with. On arrival home I went straight to bed. Al went off to his church where he was rehearsing the part of Joseph for the nativity play.

We had a quiet Christmas and New Year with a number of parties. By this time I had retrieved my salmon from the west coast. It came across in the bomb bay of an Argus aircraft. Apart from the tail which was a bit floppy, the rest was still frozen. Once the tail was removed we assessed the fish to be edible and Gilly supplemented it with crab stuffing. It was the highlight of a memorable party.

The last party we went to before the New Year jollifications came to an end was the day before I was due to fly south to Puerto Rico. The party was in Dartmouth on the north side of the harbour. It was accessible via a toll bridge. It was a filthy night with an extremely cold wind and snow was falling. We were on the approach road to the bridge when my car packed up. There was no way to turn round even if I could restart the engine. Fortunately a police car was at hand, and as they are wont to do in Canada the driver just came up behind me, bumper to bumper, and pushed me over the bridge. It occurred to me that I might get over without paying, but he stopped at the toll, waited for me to pay and then pushed me into the side of the road off the main thoroughfare. We went the rest of the way to the party by taxi and returned home the same way. Normally Gilly would have driven me to the airport but as we had no car we hired a taxi the next morning. It was customary in Canada and the States to travel in uniform. As I left home I was wearing my snow overboots and my thick Naval overcoat. I was conscious that I'd left Gilly to recover the car.

It was early in the morning and the first flight of the day for that aircraft. The cold weather made it difficult to start the engine and we were late getting airborne making me miss my connection at Boston.

I had great trouble with immigration at Boston. It was probably caused by the different ways that servicemen move around in Britain and Canada compared with the States. In Britain you are told to go somewhere and you are then trusted to get there in the best time available. You probably have a form with which to reclaim your expenses. In the States whenever you move from one place to another you do so with written orders. These 'orders' are your bible. The immigration official eyed me suspiciously. I was wearing a uniform with which he was unfamiliar. He was a large man and was wearing a uniform which was a size too small. It emphasised his bulk.

'Where's your "orders", Bud?' he asked.

' I don't have orders, but I'm on my way to Puerto Rico,' I replied.

He rubbed his chin and thought for a while. 'Why are you going to Puerto Rico?'

'I'm being lent to the United States Navy.'

He couldn't think of an answer to that so he tried another tack. 'Where have you come from?'

'Well, originally I come from Britain, but today I've come from Halifax because the Royal Navy has loaned me to the Royal Canadian Navy.'

He stared at me for a long time. I think I'd got him confused. In the end he said: 'On your way, Bud. You're too difficult for me.' I breathed a sigh of relief.

I was impressed with the speed and efficiency with which I was transferred to another aircraft. My second destination was New York. Once again I missed my connection and had to wait several hours for an alternative flight. Eventually we were airborne and my final destination was in reach.

By the time we reached San Juan it was about 10.00 p.m. As soon as I stepped out of the aircraft I was hit by a wall of hot air of the highest humidity possible. It was difficult to breathe. After clearing immigration and customs I found the taxi rank which was a line of the most clapped-out vehicles one could imagine. I told the driver that I wanted the Naval Base. He made several comments in Spanish which I was unable to interpret. On arrival at the base there were the usual efficient guards in white Naval uniforms with belts and gaiters and armed with long truncheons which they swung menacingly.

I explained that I wanted the officers' quarters.

'Not in this taxi, Bud.'

I didn't know why everybody thought I had been christened 'Bud'.

'Why's that?' I asked.

'Because this taxi driver has committed a felony and is not allowed on the base.'

I later discovered that only a few taxis were allowed on base because most of the drivers had criminal records.

I was directed to the officers' quarters. I felt very sorry for myself as I trudged along under a darkened sky in unbearable heat with a suitcase and rubber snow shoes in my left hand, and a grip in my right hand with a heavy overcoat over my forearm. Fortunately there was someone on duty in the officers' mess who was able to find me a bed for the night.

In the morning I presented myself for work wearing the proper uniform for the day which was white shorts, open necked shirt and white socks. From the startled look on the American officers' faces I was something of an apparition. I discovered later that none of the rigs worn by the Americans included shorts. I obviously came from a very quaint navy.

Unfortunately I can't remember the names of any of the officers that I served with although I can remember a great deal about their characters. A submarine Depot Ship had come south from a United States east coast port. It was commanded by a Captain USN who was always referred to as the 'Commodore'. He had a Chief of Staff who was a man of imposing physique. He had been a player of American football of some standing and I learned later that he gained his university place as a result of his sporting accomplishments. Initially he was rather anti-me which I assumed was really anti-British. On one occasion we were in the town of San Juan when he pointed to the sign above a branch of the Chase Manhattan Bank.

'See that up there?' he said. 'That's the largest bank in the world.'

'I thought it must be pretty big,' I replied. 'It has a branch in London which has more banks than any other city in the world.' The conversation fell silent. I think he decided not to challenge me again in case I had another pat answer.

I worked with an American lieutenant commander with whom I shared a room. He was a fellow submariner and had just been passed over for promotion. After we established a working routine we would return from our work place in the evenings to rest before supper. We would lie on our beds whilst my counterpart related all his problems and explained how he was going to resolve them. I called these nightly monologues his 'State of the Union' address. I don't think he quite understood my humour.

We were employed in the Operations Room. To get the exercises started it was necessary to lay the charts out and to establish exercise areas. I kept volunteering to help but found myself on the sidelines. This went on for a couple of days until the Commodore came into the Ops Room and asked his Chief of Staff what duties and responsibilities I had been given. This rather surprised the CoS who spluttered an inadequate answer. The conversation dropped to a low tone so that I couldn't hear what was being said and the two senior officers went outside. On his return the CoS gave me a number of responsibilities and told me that I had to take my turn with the other officers in sharing the night duties. This was better; I could become part of the team. The exercise started with a series of short activities with each submarine working in an allocated area, usually in company with a surface ship. I learnt that the submarines would return to harbour each Friday night and we would have a wash-up on the Saturday morning and a briefing for the next week's exercises. Whether or not I did things in the normal American manner I don't know, but I soon had a weekly exercise schedule worked out using some of the RN nomenclature such as Serial Number for each individual exercise. I soon learnt some of the differing operating procedures. In the RN, once a submarine is on the surface it is free to cross another submarine's allocated area as it is then treated as a normal surface ship. The Americans always went round the edge of the exercise areas. It was a factor which one had to take into consideration when planning the movement of a submarine from one exercise area to another.

The first wash-up on the Saturday morning was amusing but rather worrying. If I made a comment about the way a submarine had operated in the previous week the COs would tend to turn to look at the Commodore with a puzzled look. Although they never posed the question verbally you could read the question in their eyes which asked: 'Who is this limey telling us how to run our Navy?' If the Commodore replied at all it would be to support me and we would be invited to move on. Any implied dissension didn't last long.

There could have been a problem for me with regard to signals, particularly when I was the only officer on duty at night. There are several agreements regarding the sharing of information between one navy and another. In the area where we were operating there were three principal restrictions. These were identified on signals and would read: 'US eyes only'; 'US/UK eyes only'; or 'US/UK/CAN eyes only'. I assumed that I would not be entitled to read 'US eyes only' signals. Occasionally one would come to me for action and I would return it to the Communication Centre saying: 'I don't think I'm supposed to see this.' It wasn't long before I was told to deal with all signals which were distributed to me.

I had been in San Juan about five weeks and I thought things were running quite smoothly and a routine had been established. I was therefore rather puzzled when the Commodore sent for me. I reported as ordered.

'Smalley,' he said, 'You've been working very hard and you haven't had much recreation. On Saturday I've scheduled a minesweeper to take you to St. Thomas for the day. I want you to have a day's rest. The sweeper's captain has been told that this trip is entirely for your convenience.'

I didn't know what to say. The island of St. Thomas was about fifty miles to the east of San Juan and was a well known holiday resort. It occurred to me that there must have been a lot of others on the base who would have enjoyed a day on this lovely island, but the ship was to be my private yacht for the day.

It was only a week or so after that happy experience that the Commodore told me that he was going to take a day off. He was going to call on a long-standing friend who lived on the island of St. Croix. 'It's about 120 miles to the south east, so I'll take an aeroplane,' he explained. 'I'm taking you with me and we'll have lunch together.' Then after a pause, he added: 'By the way, my friend's name is Victor Borge.' Our visit was a memorable experience.

By this time the exercise was drawing to a close and the time came for me to pack my bags and prepare for the homeward journey.

The flight home was uneventful until the last leg which was from Boston to Halifax on an Air Canada flight. The first stopover in Canada was at St John, New Brunswick when all the passengers had to disembark. The luggage was unloaded to clear customs and immigration. At some stage I noticed that I had been separated from the other passengers. I was taken into a small room and given a cup of coffee, and a female member of staff stayed with me and made polite conversation. In due course I was accompanied back to my seat with my hand luggage being carried for me by my female escort. Before she left me I couldn't resist asking why she had been so solicitous. 'Well, you see,' she said, 'we noticed that you hold Diplomatic Status.' The man who had written 'Duration of Present Status' in my passport in such a poor hand on our arrival in Montreal had done me a favour.

I spent the next few weeks in Halifax which was fortunate because Gilly was expecting our baby at the end of June. We were lucky in finding a gynaecologist who was highly recommended. We already knew that the medical services in Canada were of the highest standard. Gilly had discovered with considerable pain and inconvenience when David was born that the shape of her pelvis didn't allow her to have a normal delivery. The Canadian doctors measured the bone structure in the area and discovered the problem much sooner.

We booked a place in the Grace Maternity Hospital which was run by the Salvation Army. Gilly's mother was horrified on hearing this. She visualised a run down hospital, short of funds and scraping to make ends meet. Nothing could have been further from the truth. The hospital had all the modern facilities and would have put most British hospitals to shame. We even discovered that for a very small payment, patients could have their own telephone by their beds. At this time at home, the telephone service was operated by the government and it was often the case that prospective customers waited several years before they were allocated a phone.

As my time in Canada was coming to an end, I received a communication from the appointing officer at *Dolphin* that I would be joining the nuclear submarine *Valiant* on my return, but first I had to undertake the Nuclear General Course at the RN College, Greenwich.

It was at this time that our landlord wrote to say that he wanted to terminate our rental agreement. We were lucky because Bill Hurst, an RN navigator who had been teaching at the navigation school, was about to return home. Our third house was in Wedgewood Avenue. Once again not too far to move.

Our baby was due towards the end of June at a time when I had to be in Toronto with some of my colleagues to make a presentation at the RCAF Staff College. The gynaecologist was a keen golfer and he had an important golf tournament at the week-end, so he told Gilly that he would do the caesarean the following week. That fitted in nicely with my Toronto commitment as I would be back in time for the birth. It didn't matter too much about the house move because I could handle that by myself. We were to fly to Toronto by commercial airline. Gilly drove me out to the airport, and I disappeared for the next forty eight hours or so. The presentation at the Air Force College went well and we made our way to Toronto Airport to catch our return flight to be told that the aircraft was delayed owing to technical difficulties. In due course we got airborne but because of various other problems we found ourselves on a flight which apparently was going to land at every major airport between Toronto and Halifax. When we landed at Montreal I was able to leave the aircraft and phoned home to explain that we had been delayed. There was no one in the house to answer the phone but the wife of one of my colleagues who had also phoned his home told him that Gilly had gone into hospital to have the baby. The next time I was able to get off the aircraft was at St. John, New Brunswick, and my phone call revealed that a baby had been born. I then had to wait until we arrived at Halifax for my next phone call. I then discovered that I had another son and both son and mother were doing well. I was so relieved that I bought all my colleagues a cigar and then rushed off to the hospital to make sure all was well. I then heard the full story. After dropping me off at the airport Gilly was driving home and by the time she got to the Armdale Rotary (a well known roundabout in Halifax) she started contractions. She went home and phoned the gynaecologist who told her to come straight in to the hospital. As soon as she arrived he operated and produced our son. But apart from that, he had made sure that his golfing weekend hadn't been spoilt.

Having ensured that mother and son were safe, I had to move house the following day. As we didn't have to move far, I had hired a 'truck' to move everything we owned from the house we were leaving. The truck hiring agreement was on an hourly basis so I was keen to complete the move as fast as possible. I had asked some of my colleagues to come round to help me with the move. I had bought two or three crates of beer with which to reward my helpers. Unfortunately I offered them a beer before we started. The result was that they finished the beer before they turned to as furniture removers. The move didn't go as fast or as inexpensively as I had hoped.

We had no difficulty in deciding our second child's name and he was called Ian. Dr Crosby became Ian's paediatrician and after examining him carefully she told us that he was perfectly healthy but that he was likely to suffer from a hernia within the next year or two.

We were now preparing to return home. We had bought a considerable number of items whilst in Canada which would be difficult to transport home. Not only had we acquired a rocking chair which I had bought for Gilly's 29th birthday, but I had been helping Taff Jones in the running of a local Scout troop. At one of their camps they gave me a set of moose antlers which the Scouts had found. Packing them was going to be a problem, but I approached Eddie Endacott, an RN engineer with the submarine squadron. He had many contacts in the dockyard. He arranged for the manufacture of all the packing cases we needed. I asked him if I could contribute towards the cost. The answer was the standard price. A bottle of duty free rum.

My relief was Todd Slaughter, the son of Jackie Slaughter who had been our neighbour at Droxford. He was a chip off the old block.

Before leaving for home we had a party for all our friends. Towards the end, one of the Canadian guests came up to me and told me that the reason they hadn't welcomed us into their homes in the first few months was that they felt that they couldn't entertain us to the standard that we might expect. It occurred to me that the Canadians' standard of living was beyond our wildest dreams. Before coming home, Gilly and I discussed whether I should apply to join the Canadian Navy. There was only one thing which stopped us. Gilly's mother was still alive and a widow, and my mother was in the same circumstances. Gilly's mother was 72 at the time and mine was 69. We decided to return home.

We were booked to come home in the *Franconia,* the sister ship to the *Carmania* which had brought us over. We had to board the *Franconia* in Montreal but on this occasion we had a car, so I obtained permission to leave Halifax a few days early. As Gilly hadn't seen anything of the United States I wanted to drive south into the States and then drive westward and eventually re-enter Canada at Niagara. We would then visit my sister in Toronto for a few days before working our way back east to Montreal. We had to be in Montreal twenty four hours before the ship sailed on 11 October, for the purposes of loading the car on board.

What had been planned as an exciting journey cum holiday turned out to be one of the most unpleasant experiences of my life. As we left, David appeared to have something wrong with him. He wasn't feeding properly and wasn't sleeping. His constant crying told us there was a problem but he couldn't tell us what it was. We hoped it was something that would soon pass. We travelled through New Brunswick and down into Maine and then westward on the New York Thruway. The countryside was wonderful in the fall period but with David's sickness we didn't enjoy the scenery. David was sick at almost every meal. Fortunately people were always very understanding at our predicament. The New York Thruway should have been a fast road taking us to Buffalo and the Canadian border but as we approached Buffalo we encountered a fearful snowstorm. It took less than an hour for the snow to become about a foot deep. Everyone in the car except me was crying so I decided to leave the highway at the next junction and find a motel. We found a motel and I made sure that Gilly and Ian were comfortable. I then set off to find a hospital and a doctor to treat David. On arrival I thought my problem was over. But then I was asked who was going to pay for the treatment. Fortunately it was a Friday and we were able to contact the British Naval Mission in Ottawa who gave their assurance that the Naval Mission would pay the bill. Only then would the medical staff start their examination. The doctors diagnosed an ear infection and substantial dehydration. I was much happier now that I knew what was wrong and was in the possession of medication. I returned to Gilly and Ian in a happier frame of mind.

After a good night's rest, and with the roads completely swept of snow, we continued our journey directly towards Toronto giving the Niagara Falls a miss. On arrival at my sister Audrey and her husband Bob's house we learnt that their children Gary and Gillian had chickenpox.

After a short stay in Toronto we moved on to Montreal. We arrived in plenty of time to meet the deadline for loading the car. After checking in at a hotel we took the car to the docks and then had twenty four hours to occupy before reporting on board the ship. I wanted to take Gilly out for a meal in the evening as something of a 'thank you' for all the trouble she had been through on the journey. David was showing signs of recovery and we engaged a baby-sitter to look after both boys.

The political situation in Montreal hadn't changed since we arrived two years before. We were therefore very cautious about where we went and what we said. We chose to eat in a restaurant whose menu appeared appetising and

Bryan, David, Ian and Gilly – Christmas 1966.

affordable. It was down some steps in a cellar. In order not to alienate the staff we ordered in French but the waiter responded in English which allowed us to revert to English. We decided that by speaking in French we had broken the ice and we had been accepted. I was puzzled when everything we ordered was written on the paper tablecloth. At the end of the meal the waiter only had to tear off that part of the tablecloth and convert it to a bill. It was a memorable meal.

We sailed from Montreal in RMS *Franconia* at midday the next day, 11 November, Armistice Day.

Our circumstances were nearly the same as those coming out with a breast fed baby to look after. We were determined that we wouldn't earn the captain's displeasure and would enter every competition possible. This time I had a dinner jacket with me. We engaged a crew member as baby-sitter and Gilly took an injection against sea sickness which she was assured wouldn't do her or the baby any harm.

We had a pleasant voyage and won a good number of competitions. After a few days I quite expected the captain to send for me to tell me to be less competitive. On the sixth day we called at Cherbourg and then over to Southampton.

After our car had been landed we were able to set off for my mother's home in Hampton Hill and found great difficulty in driving on such narrow roads.

After a few days we moved on to Perth to stay with Gilly's mother and settled into a restful leave. After a while I hadn't received any notification of when my course at Greenwich was to start. I phoned FOSM's staff and caused something of a panic. My course started on the first Monday in January but they had forgotten to tell me.

CHAPTER 20

The Nuclear Course and *Valiant* 1967-68

THE NUCLEAR COURSE which I attended was the fifteenth to be run at Greenwich which meant that there were already a fair number of officers and senior ratings qualified to man our nuclear submarines. The course was almost completely theoretical although there was some opportunity to put the theory into practice because the Navy had installed a small reactor at the college. It was called Jason.

The explanation of nuclear reaction is relatively simple. Nuclear fission occurs when the nucleus of an atom of uranium is split. This releases a large amount of heat and fissile products such as gamma rays, and neutrons. These neutrons collide with other uranium atoms creating more heat and more neutrons. But without a means of control, an explosion would eventually result. The process is controlled by the use of rods of cadmium or boron to slow the moving neutrons. In the case of the British submarine reactor, cooling water is then run through the reactor. This heat is then transferred to a secondary circuit which takes steam to the steam turbine propulsion. Without proper screening, the highly radioactive gamma rays will cause the death of anyone in the reactor's proximity for any significant period of time.

Although the explanation is relatively simple, the calculations necessary to understand it were more demanding. Whilst I was coping with the course I spent my free time looking for accommodation for the family. I learned that *Valiant* would be going into Chatham dockyard once a year for a nine week maintenance period. Gilly and I decided to buy a house in the Chatham area. This would give me some guaranteed time at home. Towards the end of the house searching process Gilly came south with the boys. We were helped enormously by David Morrell and his wife Margaret and eventually bought a house on the same estate as them in Maidstone.

The course at Greenwich was successfully completed and I flew out to Singapore from Lyneham courtesy of the RAF to join *Valiant* and to relieve Sandy Woodward. I travelled in a Comet and arrived on 7 March. As expected the weather was hot and humid. *Valiant* was secured alongside HMS *Forth* on Number 9 Berth in the Naval Base.

When I arrived on board there were few officers there. They were ashore playing a game of rugby. The grounds there are rather like beige pumice stone. Mad dogs and Englishmen! Fortunately by keeping our hatches shut we were able to keep the boat remarkably cool because of our efficient air conditioning system.

The wardroom comprised Cdr. Peter Herbert (CO), and myself and the following officers in order of seniority: Lt. Cdr. John Jacobsen (Snr. Electrical Officer); Surg. Lt. Cdr Tom Fallowfield (MO and with responsibility for radiation monitoring); Lt. Cdr. Vic Buxton (Snr. Engineer); Lt. Cdr. Jim Marsh (Elect. Officer); Lt. Cdr. P.J.E. Cooper (Engineer); Lt. Cdr. Tim Lee (Navigating Officer); Lt. Cdr. Richard Killick (Elect. Officer); Lt. David Wixon who had been my Engineer in *Aurochs*; Lt. James Ashby (Engineer); Lt. Harry Brazier; Lt. Mike Boyce. The Navy List editors were still assuming that submarines were minor war vessels and they failed to record the names of officers who were serving in them apart from the captain and the engineer so I may have made a mistake in the above list.

Valiant had been completed in July the year before. Following the criterion that names of former battleships should be used, the original name chosen for her was *Inflexible*, but after consideration this was seen to be inappropriate for a submarine and the name was changed to *Valiant*.

After receiving a briefing from Sandy on a number of aspects I relieved him as the Executive Officer. On 10 March we went off to sea at 0600. It was immediately apparent that I had many things to learn about the way a nuclear submarine was handled. On the bridge Peter Herbert ordered 'lower the egg-beater'. This was new to me and I learnt that this was a small electric motor which could be lowered and used to manoeuvre the submarine, in particular to pull it away from the jetty. It was rather like a 'souped up' outboard motor. Once we were clear of the harbour we had to set the submarine in a state which optimized her ship handling characteristics. To do this we flooded number 6 main ballast and set the after planes to 5 degrees of rise. The purpose in doing this was to create the possibility of getting 'on the step'. In this condition, a sharp turn at full speed pulls the bow up on to its own bow-wave. The stern drops and the submarine is then planing. It was also customary to raise the snort induction 3 feet to draw fresh air into the submarine rather than through the conning tower hatch. The snort mast was necessary when propelling by secondary propulsion.

Having got into deep and less encumbered waters we dived and went through the full gamut of tests and exercises. We stayed at sea for five days, returning to Singapore on 15 March. Having had my first nuclear submarine

Valiant. *Photograph courtesy of Royal Navy Submarine Museum.*

experience we then prepared for the trip home. The intention was to do this dived throughout the whole trip.

At 2030 on 29 March we went to Harbour Stations. As soon as we were ready for sea we slipped and started our journey home.

It wasn't until 0805 on 31 March that we were both outside territorial waters and in water deep enough to dive. I quickly had to learn all the new states of readiness both of the reactor and propulsion equipment and the crew. On diving we were at 'Watch Tracking' and at the 'Full Power state'.

On our voyage home it was necessary to keep the crew in a state of alert. Consequently an evolution was carried out at least once a day. There were of course other problems which arose and kept us on our toes. One problem in particular was a puzzling reading of a small amount of nuclear radiation in the atmosphere. It was low enough not to be harmful but still caused us worry, particularly because we couldn't identify its source. To be on the safe side we slowed down from time to time and ventilated the submarine with fresh air. We later discovered that someone had brought a clock on board with a luminous dial without realising the consequences. Our systems were sufficiently sensitive to detect this. It pointed towards deficient management of the radiation monitoring system which was Tom Fallowfield's responsibility. It is essential that a background radiation reading is taken before a submarine proceeds to sea.

Not only did we exercise fighting a fire frequently but we often had real small fires in the secondary oxygen generators. The submarine was fitted with a desalinator which took salt water and purified it, giving a virtually unlimited supply of fresh water. Some of this fresh water could be split into a mixture of oxygen and hydrogen by means of an 'electrolyser'. The oxygen was then used to freshen the air supply whilst the hydrogen was pumped over the side. Both hydrogen and oxygen are dangerous gaseous elements, and the electrolyser wasn't entirely reliable. From time to time, we used the old fashioned oxygen generators to boost our supply. These were robust tubes into which a 'candle' comprising compressed chemicals was placed. A door at the base was then closed and an electrical element heated the candle until it burnt steadily producing oxygen. Occasionally, particularly after constant use, the seal at the base would fail and flames would appear. This wasn't a great problem provided it was dealt with quickly by someone who was well trained. I had several fore-endmen in whom I had complete confidence. One of them was Gabby Hayes with whom I had served in *Porpoise*.

After rounding the Cape of Good Hope we slowed down and made our way to an exercise area used by the South African Navy. We had been ordered to spend a day exercising with them. This had been arranged at the highest diplomatic level but we had been warned that this was to be kept secret. Before we made the rendezvous we had time to bring our attack team up to scratch, and we practised snorting which is something which normally we would only need to do if we lost nuclear power. We had two small diesel engines for this purpose. We rendezvoused with the South African Navy on 11 April and spent the day attacking them and they in turn attacked us. At the end of the day we bade each other goodbye and we were able to wind on the revs. and continue northwards.

We had been told to send our ETA at Faslane when we were at the same latitude as Gibraltar. Our signal reported that we would be arriving on Saturday 22 April. When we next read the submarine broadcast we received a signal telling us not to arrive until the Tuesday. It was explained that if we arrived at the weekend we would be unlikely to attract the press coverage that the MoD hoped for. Dutifully we slowed down and arrived alongside at Faslane at 1115 on Tuesday 25 April. It had taken us twenty six days to come home which was a record voyage.

FOSM was on the jetty to meet us at Faslane and was piped aboard. He addressed the ship's company at 1135. At 1150, thirty five minutes after securing alongside, our first leave party was on the jetty on their way home.

The rest of the day was spent with the press conducting interviews and being shown through the submarine.

After our short rest period we sailed for Gibraltar on 30 May, exercising with a number of ships whilst on passage, and arriving in Gib on 4 June. Israel's six day war started the following day creating worldwide tension. On the first day the Israelis attacked Egypt and destroyed 374 planes on the ground and invaded the Sinai peninsula. The Egyptians blamed the US and the British resulting in three Arab states cutting off oil supplies.

On the sixth day Israel observed the UN cease-fire and the fighting in the Middle East ended. The war left the western powers pondering over the Arab states' ability to use oil as a political weapon.

As we were due for our annual maintenance and docking we returned to Chatham. By this time *Valiant* had sufficient running experience to know how all the systems worked and it fell to me to re-write the ship's standing orders to incorporate all the lessons learnt. But there was another more urgent task. We had been programmed to go on a surveillance patrol or what we preferred to call 'a trip up north'. Our equipment was much more sophisticated than that which we had in *Tabard* and it was essential that all operators should be linked in to a communication system so that information could be shared. But each operator had different needs. I had to design a system which would give them the information that they needed without swamping them with information which was unnecessary. Having designed the system it was left to John Jacobsen's staff to install it.

We were undocked and back at sea on 21 September and making our way up to the Clyde areas. Our first task was to develop techniques which we might use on our surveillance trip. Conventional submarines were unable to maintain speed for any length of time and generally had to monitor the Soviet fleet from a distance. Their main sources of information would be from the interception of radio signals, although occasionally ships would pass overhead affording the opportunity to make sound recordings of their main propulsion and auxiliary machinery.

A nuclear submarine had the advantage of unlimited staying power. We could keep up with the Russian fleet or an individual ship for as long as we wished. We therefore spent some time exercising with a Royal Fleet Auxiliary (RFA) tanker. Initially we would get the RFA to steer a steady course and whilst we were at a depth where we couldn't foul our fin with the RFA's propeller we would approach it from astern. As we grew close we would adjust our speed to match the RFA and sit underneath the ship taking recordings of its machinery. In spite of several Warsaw Pact ships being built as a class, there were always a number of differences to each ship which would give it its own noise signature. Once we had captured this noise signature it became possible to identify a particular ship by means of the noise it was emitting. This was important particularly for use with the American SOSUS system which had been laid on the sea bed in a number of places and which was monitored from stations ashore.

Whilst we were underneath the unsuspecting ship we could also raise our periscope and take photographs of its underwater fittings. Photographs of the propeller were particularly important because cavitation from the propeller creates its own noise and we wanted to know how advanced the Soviets were in reducing cavitation.

As well as developing techniques for monitoring the Soviet Fleet's activities we also needed to develop ideas on how we could support our own forces. For some years there had been a disagreement over whether submarines should confine their activities to listening for an enemy (passive mode) or whether they should become active and transmit sound in order to obtain an echo from nearby targets. The two camps divided roughly into the Americans preferring to stay passive and the British going active. The enormous power available in a nuclear submarine meant that it was possible to transmit a very strong pulse from the sonar set. *Valiant* was equipped with the 2001 sonar which had its transducers wrapped round the bow. It was realised that if a nuclear submarine could keep station under a friendly surface ship it could get below a sound layer and use active sonar to detect enemy submarines approaching the surface force. The problem was how to develop a system whereby the friendly submarine could communicate with the surface ship and pass reports of its detections. We had an underwater telephone, the 185, but it was used for transmitting voice. Our electrical officers were able to modify the equipment so that information could be passed using a RATT (Radio Teletype) system.

Although we were preparing for our 'trip up north', we still had time to take part in Exercise Midsummer during November in the SW Approaches. (I never discovered why it was so inappropriately named.)

Before we sailed for the exercise, I received a letter from Gilly saying that Ian had developed the hernia which Dr Crosby had forecast and was awaiting a bed in Maidstone Hospital. Although I hated leaving her to sort out all the family problems there was nothing I could do. The exercise went well and we spent a considerable amount of time sitting underneath a County class destroyer acting as its variable depth sonar set. The improvised underwater communication system worked well which was particularly helpful to me. I was in the control room when a signal was passed down to us saying that the surface ship had received a telegram for me reporting that the operation for Ian's hernia had taken place and he was recovering well.

Cdr. Robin King had been appointed to relieve Peter Herbert in April the following year. He lived in a married quarter at Faslane. He intended spending Christmas at his wife's home in America, and he very kindly offered Gilly and me the use of his house whilst he was away. Gilly and the boys were able to come north for the leave period.

On 15 December a storm blew up whilst I was ashore in Robin King's house. It started to blow in the evening but we weren't expecting it to be particularly severe, but it gradually got worse and I was worried about the safety of the submarine. I decided to go back on board, but by this time there were so many trees blocking the road that I was unable to get to the submarine base. It was now blowing a hurricane and all electrical power had failed. When I did manage to get through in the early hours of the morning I learned how *Valiant* had suffered from lack of shore power which was necessary for the cooling of the reactor. The duty officer, Mike Boyce, had done all the right things to keep the nuclear reactor and the submarine safe. He had implemented the emergency cooling procedure ensuring that the reactor didn't overheat.

We learnt later that twenty people had died in Scotland during the storm.

We remained at Faslane until mid January and then made our final preparations for going north. Apart from the excitement of the hurricane we had a very happy family Christmas, but I was still worried about the burden that Gilly was bearing in bringing up our family. It was a tension between life in the Navy which I loved, and the responsibilities incumbent on me as a father. I decided to ask for early retirement even though I had no other occupation to fall back on. I submitted my letter to this effect. I had always been interested in politics and decided that when I retired I would endeavour to become a Conservative MP.

We continued our preparations for our surveillance trip. There were good and bad points. We had a small compartment in which we were able to install our additional radio and recording equipment. We found it worked extremely well. It was made by a small but growing company called Racal which until that time we had never heard of. On the other hand we were having our usual difficulties with lack of stores. This wasn't because our depot ship wasn't making every effort to support us but from our point of view certain items were so important that we couldn't sail without them. To the civilian depot ashore they were just another item of stores, and of course the excitement and tension in the preparations tended to magnify our problems.

No one in the ship wanted his department to let the side down with any shortcomings

Before sailing on our trip we had to make a series of dived runs at different speeds over a noise monitor. The purpose was to record our own noise signature so that this could be removed from the recordings which we would make of Soviet ships.

We sailed at the beginning of February and started to make our passage northwards. As soon as we dived we developed a defect. We were unable to see through the main periscope and we were forced to surface to identify the problem. We found that the glass at the upper end of the periscope had fractured. This glass had a heater to prevent condensation. The heater had been left on whilst we were on the surface. Normally this wouldn't matter, but not so when diving in extremely cold waters. The rapid change of temperature had caused the glass to fracture. We were reluctant to go back to Faslane, so made arrangements for new lenses to be flown out to Orkney. When the stores had arrived on the Island we closed in towards the mainland and took a lee between the mainland and Hoy and a helicopter delivered the replacement lenses. We wondered what any islander might think about the purpose of our visit and how many reported that an enemy submarine had been sighted so close to the shore. The new lenses were fitted as quickly as possible although this was an intricate task. The fittings had to be watertight right down to our maximum diving depth. We were apprehensive on diving but the ERAs had done a good job.

Having rounded North Cape we worked our way eastward and advanced our clocks accordingly. We always kept local time. We were moving towards the exercise areas off Murmansk. What I write now is purely from memory. I can usually refer to ships' logs which are deposited at the Public Records Office but during the period when we did anything exciting the logs are still retained at the MoD. The last log before the gap which covers our patrol has written on it in clear red letters 'Next Control Room Log "Secret".' The Confidential Pink List which detailed the ships' programmes reported that *Valiant* was 'Exercising in the NW Approaches'.

As soon as we arrived in the area we came across an exercise taking place, but these were mainly small coastal craft. Although we were interested in the radio communications which passed between them they weren't the type of ship that we wanted to get underneath. We were more interested in the ocean-going ships and submarines who would be likely to break through the Iceland-Faroes gap in times of tension.

We managed to obtain a vast amount of radio and underwater sound

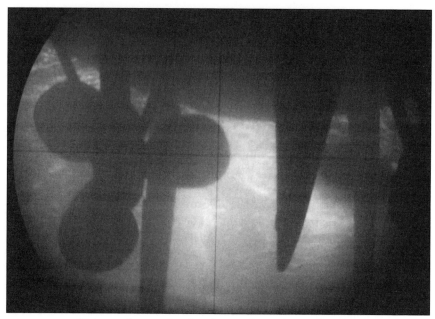

Periscope photograph taken from underneath a surface ship.
Photograph courtesy of Royal Navy Submarine Museum.

recordings but the most satisfying and exciting part of our patrol was when we came across a destroyer of the latest class. We were able to get behind her and creep slowly up until we were just aft of her. Choosing the depth carefully we raised the periscope and were dazzled by the sight of her propellers. Not only were we able to describe them but we also took photographs. In spite of the excitement all was calm. Very little noise could be heard in the control room but crew members were talking softly into their microphones passing information to plotters and those controlling the recording devices. I was relieved that the internal communication system which I had designed was doing all that it was meant to.

We withdrew from the Soviet exercise areas on 31 March and set course for home arriving at Faslane on 5 April. After disembarking all the valuable information which we had gathered we started a well earned Easter leave period.

During the leave period Robin King relieved Peter Herbert. When he took the submarine to sea we went through every evolution we could think of, exercising the attack team, torpedo firing and exercising fire in the galley, telemotor burst and air bursts in the compressed air systems. We spent some evenings at anchor off Rothesay giving us the opportunity of visiting our old haunts of the Victoria and Glenburn Hotels.

On 1 June I had four years seniority as a Lieutenant Commander and my pay rose to £5.12^{1}/$_{2}$ new pence a day. It was about this time that I was told that my next job would be as Assistant Flotilla Operations Officer (A/FOO) to FOSM.

We continued operating in the Clyde Areas until the middle of June and then had a few days in harbour preparing for a visit to Hamburg. This was to be our first official European visit. At this time a great deal of effort was being made to convince foreign powers that a nuclear submarine was safe. Although experts would understand this, it was difficult to persuade the population at large, and decisions whether to allow us entry into foreign ports were largely based on political criteria. After our visit to Hamburg a visit to Rotterdam was on the programme but the Dutch authorities refused to grant us permission.

We sailed from Portsmouth on 26 June and commenced the surface passage through the Straits of Dover and into the North Sea. This was always a worrying time with such heavy traffic particularly the cross-Channel ferries moving across the normal flow. Our navigation lights were still close together as they were in a conventional submarine giving other ships the impression that we were a small manoeuvrable fishing vessel. By now, the mines which had littered the North Sea after the war, forcing shipping to stay within the narrow swept channels, had been cleared. The voyage was uneventful. We entered the mouth of the Elbe in the middle of the night so that we could arrive alongside during the morning. After we secured alongside we were met by a host of curious visitors, not least a team of scientists who spent the whole visit sampling the water surrounding our hull to see if there was any seepage of irradiated water. We came away at the end of the visit with a clean bill of health.

Our visit was punctuated with a number of interesting events but two of them stand out amongst the others. One was a lunch given for us by the civic authorities in the Rathaus (Town Hall), a grand affair on a par with lunches given by the Lord Mayor of London. The second was a trip round the harbour in the harbour master's launch. We expected a working type launch to take us up and down the river, but what we boarded was more akin to a gin palace. The launch had a very wide beam and the after end had an immaculate teak deck with comfortable seats arranged for a party. A local wine merchant was on board and we had a wine tasting evening with the most expensive wines to sample. The savour of an Eiswein still lingers on the tongue.

We sailed from Hamburg on 3 July with many happy memories. As approval for our visit to Rotterdam hadn't materialised, we went back to Portsmouth for

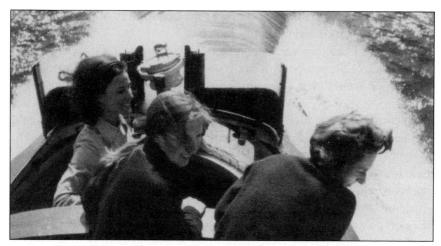

Poppet Wixon, Charmian Marsh and Gilly on the bridge of Valiant.

a few days. As planners didn't want us kicking our heels for too long we were soon programmed to do some day running from Portland. This wasn't too welcome. Submarines were becoming too large to operate dived in the confined and shallow waters of the English Channel. The main problem was caused by the VLCCs (Very Large Crude Carriers). If we met one whilst dived, there wasn't sufficient water between its keel and the sea bed for us to squeeze underneath. Nevertheless we took the opportunity for a little light relief. We invited all the ship's company's wives to come with us on the trip from Portsmouth to Portland. Probably because of the difficulty of finding baby sitters or the long distance that some wives might have to travel, only a few wives took up the invitation. From the officers' wives we had Jim Marsh's wife Charmian, David Wixon's wife Poppet, and Gilly. Charlotte Woodward was kind enough to look after our two boys.

We sailed on a calm sea and remained on the surface. At one stage when I had the watch we got all three girls on to the bridge. I arranged for them to be forward of the fin from the position where the ship was conned whilst I stood further aft. This produced an interesting photograph with the three girls chatting away and not giving the impression that they were paying attention to their duties as acting officers of the watch. As we approached the exercise area we ordered them below so that they could open up the submarine for diving, but we monitored their activities carefully to ensure that no valve was left in the wrong position. We only remained dived for a short time. On arrival in Portland the wives returned home by car.

After a short period in the Portland Areas it was time to make our way back to Chatham for our annual maintenance period.

We took it in turns for each half of the ship's company to take their summer leave. It was after I had returned from leave that we had the unfortunate incident of having two fires on board in one day. The first was a small fire which we quickly extinguished ourselves. Nevertheless it was necessary to report it by signal with full details to the Admiral Superintendent of the Dockyard.

The second fire was in the main machinery space close to the nuclear reactor. Our difficulty was that because the whole compartment was filled with smoke we weren't able to locate its source, so we naturally took the sensible precaution of asking for assistance from the Kent Fire Service. There was already a well drawn up plan detailing how to deal with a situation such as this and the Fire Service were well equipped and trained. The duty engineer, Paul Cooper, took charge down below and I established an operational base at the gangway. The specialist fire team from the Kent Brigade soon arrived at the dockside and I briefed them on the situation. I knew that reactor safety wasn't threatened but the situation was fraught for some time. Eventually the fire was extinguished. It had started in a filter to a ventilation fan. The filters contained carbon granules which absorbed impurities in the air such as airborne oil particles. The lesson learnt was that the carbon in the filters should be changed more frequently than the planned maintenance schedule allowed. After sorting ourselves out the standard signal was sent to the Admiral Superintendent.

In the middle of the next morning I was ordered to report immediately to the Admiral Superintendent. This didn't surprise me as I quite expected him to want more detailed information than that on the signal but I was surprised when I found that he wasn't interested in the details. He gave me a roasting for having two fires on board the submarine on the same day. He gave me a direct order that I wasn't to have any more fires on board during the rest of our stay in his dockyard. I was both dumbfounded and angry. Did he really think I could determine when a fire might break out, and did he think that all fires were automatically my fault? Fortunately we finished the maintenance period without any further incidents.

We left Chatham on 9 September and spent a short time exercising in the 'Derry Areas before returning to Faslane.

It was whilst we were in Faslane that it was decided to have what was intended to be a team building exercise. The plan was to have a number of activities during the day followed by a ship's company dance. Mike Boyce was appointed to arrange the day-time activities. Unfortunately he assumed that most of the ship's company were as fit as he was. He arranged for a lorry to take us out into the wilds of Scotland and drop us off with instructions to walk back to the base. I found myself in the same group as the second coxswain. The weather was mild and initially the walk was most invigorating but after a time we began to tire and took a rest. We started again but this time we tired more quickly and took a longer rest. Our feet were becoming sore. As the afternoon passed and the evening sun began to set we were virtually on our last legs. We were so relieved when a lorry appeared which had been sent to seek us out. We were thankful that we didn't have to walk the last few miles. Eventually the second coxswain admitted that he was entirely knackered but he hadn't been prepared to give up whilst I was still on my feet. I had to admit that was the reason why I had persevered.

At the dance which followed it was with great difficulty that we took to the dance floor. I braced myself to dance with the second coxswain's wife and spent the whole dance having my ear pounded. She told me in no uncertain terms that she hadn't come all this way to find that her husband was too tired to provide her with the pleasures that she had been looking forward to.

Our next exercise was Silver Tower a major NATO exercise to the north of Scotland.

Whilst at sea we had two fires on board, the first in the electrolyser space and the second in Number 1 telemotor pump. Both were potentially more dangerous than usual but were dealt with effectively without any admirals, who had no knowledge of nuclear submarines, telling us how to do it.

We remained at sea until 28 September when we arrived at Rosyth for the exercise wash-up. We departed from Rosyth on 2 October for Faslane. After a rest period we sailed for the Mediterranean on 21 October for Exercise Eden Apple.

Our Mediterranean exercise was uneventful and concluded on 16 November with a wash-up in Malta for all the participating ships and submarines except for *Valiant*. The Maltese authorities refused to allow us into Valletta harbour and we had to make for La Spezia instead. I had arranged for Gilly to come out to La Spezia during our week's stay there. She travelled out by train via Paris with Sue Ashby, the wife of James Ashby, one of *Valiant's* engineers. They took a compartment with couchettes and found themselves sharing it with two Italian men who thought they were on to a good thing. Their constant aggressive advances and propositions rather frightened the girls who concluded their journey by going to the loo together and making sure that neither girl was left in the compartment by herself. They eventually arrived tired but unscathed.

During our stay in La Spezia each half of the ship's company took three days' leave. Gilly and I took the opportunity to visit Pisa and Florence.

In Florence we went into what appeared to be rather an expensive restaurant. To keep our expenditure within budget we decided that we would only have one course. We were greeted with a flourish by a waiter with an attitude which we had never experienced at home. He obviously thoroughly enjoyed his job. We scanned the menu to find something not too expensive and eventually chose a main course item. In response to the waiter's request about our choice for a starter we told him that we didn't want anything to start with. He went away to place our order and came back with a couple of aperitifs explaining that they were 'with the compliments of the house'. He then explained that our main course would take some minutes to prepare and he recommended a starter which he suggested wasn't too expensive. As we had been given the free aperitif we didn't want to disappoint him so we accepted his advice and agreed to have the starter. As soon as he had placed the order he came back to the table and serenaded us in an attractive tenor voice with a couple of operatic arias. We began to enjoy ourselves so much that we thought we ought to have a bottle of wine. We worked our way through the main course. Whenever the waiter was free he attended our table with more choral renditions. By the time we had finished the main course we felt it would be ungrateful not to have a pudding. Having had a most enjoyable meal we were then served with a liqueur 'on the house'. Neither of us can remember how much the meal cost. By that time we were too well fed to care.

After our pleasant and restful visit to La Spezia we started the journey home calling in at Gibraltar for a short visit. Mike Ortmans, my relief, joined us and on the way back to Faslane I was able to hand over my duties to him. We arrived at Faslane on 11 December. Having bade farewell to my friends I made my way south to *Dolphin* to take up a post on FOSM's staff.

CHAPTER 21

FOSM's Staff 1969

M Y DUTY on the staff was as Assistant Fleet Operations Officer (A/FOO). Graham Rogers was my boss as FOO. This was to be my last job in the Navy but at the time I hadn't been told the date when I would be allowed to retire.

FOO's role was strategic planning. There were always more requests for submarine time than there were submarines available. Graham and I had the job of allocating submarines to the most important tasks. As well as ensuring that the Submarine Service played a significant part in NATO exercises there were also a large number of requests to test prototype equipment and to carry out a variety of experiments. It was rather like working out a complicated puzzle where there was no ideal solution. We were also continuing to promote the acceptability of the presence of nuclear powered submarines into foreign and British ports. John Grove was by now a captain and was Flotilla Electrical Officer. He had collected an OBE for his work in *Dreadnought*.

The family moved down to a rented house in Wickham. After I had found my feet in my new job I started to think about employment once the Navy had released me. This was given greater urgency when Julian Beauchamp, a fellow submariner who was working in the MoD, came to ask me if 31 December would be acceptable to me as a resignation date. I agreed and then started making contact with the Conservative Party on how I could pursue a career as an MP. I found that I was in good company with Chris Ringrose-Voase who was also on FOSM's staff and had the same aspirations. We were quite encouraged when one of us saw an advertisement advertising vacancies for research officers in the Party's Central Office. We both applied, but neither of us had the courtesy of a reply.

I thought I might find my way into the Party by becoming an agent. I discovered that the Party had an agent in each constituency, but these worked under a more senior agent who looked after a region. I arranged an appointment with the regional agent in Salisbury. He was an extremely nice person but told me that agents never moved on to becoming Members of Parliament. Obviously I had to try another tack, so I wrote to Conservative Head Office and asked if I could call on the appropriate person to discuss my ambitions. It was agreed that I should see the Chairman of the Party. He was extremely polite when he welcomed me to his office but he explained that the Conservative Party had recently decided on a new policy. The Party wouldn't be accepting any more ex-Servicemen. The Party's aim in the future was to encourage university graduates to work for the Party either in Central Office or as assistants to MPs. After they had gained a few years experience they would be adopted as prospective parliamentary candidates. I wasn't given the opportunity to explain the advantages of having MPs with different backgrounds whose wider knowledge and experience would be of great benefit to the Party. It became obvious that if I was to achieve my aspirations I would have to work hard to convince those who ran the Party that I had the right credentials.

I decided to leave this activity and turn my attentions to finding a job to keep the family going whilst I pursued my ambition.

I retired on the last day of December 1969. I was leaving a Navy which I loved and which had been responsible for shaping my character and developing me to a position which I hadn't dreamed of when I joined. I have in mind a quotation which is reported to have come from the American Admiral Nimitz when he submitted his final report to his President before retiring: 'The battleship can be regarded as the capital ship of the past, the aircraft carrier as the capital ship of today, and the submarine that of tomorrow.'

I was extremely proud to have played my small part in that transformation.

CHAPTER 22

Epilogue – People's progress

JPB (Paddy) O'Riordan, the midshipman RNVR whom we understudied whilst at sea in *Artemis* on our training class, was refused a permanent commission on completion of his National Service, but in a letter from Their Lordships he was informed 'that in view of his former officer service he may enter the Royal Navy as an Able rather than Ordinary Seaman.' This he did, and after going through the system became a proper officer. He re-joined submarines going on to command conventional and nuclear submarines as well as the Submarine Sea Training organisation. He retired from the Navy as Rear Admiral J.P.B. O'Riordan CBE (for activities in the Barents Sea while in command of HMS *Glasgow*) and is now a Deputy Lieutenant for Northamptonshire.

John Fieldhouse who was my captain in *Acheron* held the post of FOSM and was the First Sea Lord during the Falklands War. He was Chief of the Defence Staff from 1985 to 1988 and retired as Admiral of the Fleet the Lord Fieldhouse of Gosport GCB GBE, the highest ranking officer in the history of the Submarine Service.

Brian Hutchings, my captain in *Porpoise*, retired as a Post Captain. He became a Director of Waitrose and was responsible for the running of all the supermarkets. He later served as a Main Board Director of the John Lewis Partnership.

Sandy Woodward with whom I served in *Porpoise* was the Battle Group Commander in the Falklands War and retired as Admiral Sir John Woodward GBE KCB.

John Grove with whom I served in *Porpoise* held the post of Chief Strategic Systems Executive (formerly Chief Polaris Executive), and retired as Rear Admiral John Grove CB OBE.

Peter Herbert, my captain in *Porpoise* and *Valiant*, was FOSM during the Falklands War and retired as Admiral Sir Peter Herbert KCB OBE.

Mike Boyce with whom I served in *Valiant* held the posts of First Sea Lord and Chief of Defence Staff before retiring as Admiral the Lord Boyce GCB OBE KStJ DL and Commander, The Legion of Merit (US).

Bryan Smalley pursued his ambition to become a Conservative MP. He managed to obtain an interview with an MP who was a vice chairman of the Conservative Party. After a brief interview Bryan was told to come back after 'he had done something useful'. Bryan took this up with his MP, Sir Derek Walker Smith, who arranged a second interview. Although Bryan was put on the list of prospective Conservative parliamentary candidates he was earmarked as a maverick and was never called for an interview by a constituency association.

Index